WAGNER REMEMBERED

Stewart Spencer was born in Yorkshire and studied Modern Languages at Oxford. He taught Medieval German Literature at the University of London and has subsequently worked as a translator. He is the editor, with Barry Millington, of *Selected Letters of Richard Wagner* (1987), *Wagner in Performance* (1992) and *Wagner's Ring of the Nibelung: A Companion* (1993). He has translated books on Wagner, Liszt, Mozart and Bach and his translation of Hans Werner Henze's autobiography, *Bohemian Fifths*, was published by Faber in 1998.

WAGNER
REMEMBERED

Stewart Spencer

faber and faber

LONDON · NEW YORK

First published in 2000
by Faber and Faber Limited
3 Queen Square London WC1N 3AU
Published in the United States by Faber and Faber Inc.,
a division of Farrar, Straus and Giroux Inc., New York

Phototypeset by Intype London Ltd
Printed in England by Clays Ltd, St Ives plc

A CIP record for this book
is available from the British Library

ISBN 0-571-19653-5

2 4 6 8 10 9 7 5 3 1

CONTENTS

ILLUSTRATIONS

With the exception of items 17–18, copies of which have been supplied by the Bayerische Staatsbibliothek in Munich, all the illustrations are reproduced from non-copyright material in the author's collection.

The illustration on the front cover is a detail of a previously unpublished caricature of Wagner and his second wife, Cosima, by one of the leading German portrait painters of the second half of the nineteenth century, Franz von Lenbach (1836–1904). Lenbach produced a number of official portraits of the couple (the majority not from life), but this is his only known cartoon of them. It is dated 'Tegernsee, 5 November 1874' and was sketched on the back of a Patron's Certificate that the Wagners had sent to him in the hope that he would help to underwrite the cost of the first Bayreuth Festival. Far from completing the form and returning it with his 300 thalers (about £1,500 at today's prices), he used the back for the present less than deferential pen-and-ink drawing. Measuring 240 × 130 mm, this drawing is now in the private collection of Albi Rosenthal, whose generous permission to reproduce it is most gratefully acknowledged.

INTRODUCTION

The demonization of Wagner started even as the first calls for his canonization were being considered. It will always be a moot point whether it is Wagner or the Wagnerites who should be held responsible for this situation, but there is no doubt that it is one that has coloured virtually every reminiscence of him. While his subsequent critics painted him in ever blacker colours, his hagiographers busied themselves with the beatification process, invariably mentioning his kindness to animals and, where all else failed, drawing a distinction between the 'inner sanctum' of his art and a life that they dismissed as an irrelevance. For Wagner's contemporaries to dismiss that life as an irrelevance was not so easy, of course. Indeed, it is striking to find how often they regarded life and works as an indivisible whole, suggesting that the later dislocation between man and artist is something of which Wagner himself would not have approved. It may also help to explain why, with rare exceptions, Wagner did not hold forth in print or spoken word on the underlying meaning of his music dramas.[1] (If he had done so, that meaning would be infinitely circumscribed and the works themselves would arguably not have survived their author's death, for it is their ability to assume new meanings for later generations that has kept them in the repertory.)

Wagner's life was unusually eventful and would be worth retelling even if he had not been one of the nineteenth century's most controversial composers. As such, it seemed to me to justify a chronological, rather than a thematic, approach. At the same time, however, his life impinged on the lives of so many of his contemporaries, many of whom felt an evident need to record their impressions, that comprehensiveness is out of the question. In other

1. On more than one occasion, I found myself rejecting reminiscences precisely because the memoirist has Wagner larding his conversation with lengthy passages from his prose works; see, for example, Nordmann 1886 and Mason 1901.

words, I do not regard the present volume as a source book. Forced to be selective, I have tried not to be tendentious, but to allow as many different voices to speak as possible. The only voices that I have consciously excluded are those of three fellow composers – Berlioz, Brahms and Liszt – whose complex relations with Wagner cannot be adequately explored in a volume of this kind. The same is true – *a fortiori* – of Wagner's relations with Nietzsche. Rather than translate everything afresh, I have used existing nineteenth- and early twentieth-century translations, where available, for their period feel. (It will be clear from the bibliography which texts have been newly translated.) The annotation is more extensive than in other volumes in this series for three reasons: first, there are cultural and biographical references that require an explanation; secondly, Wagner studies continue to be bedevilled by countless myths and misconceptions and, in an attempt to dispel some of them, I felt the need to appeal to a higher authority; and, thirdly, readers may in this way be directed to other writings and reminiscences on the same subject.

In a discipline which, in recent years, has been increasingly riven by ideological divisions, it is a pleasure to record the selfless generosity with which friends, colleagues and total strangers have placed their expertise at my disposal. The members of the Richard Wagner-Gesamtausgabe in Munich – Klaus Döge, Christa Jost, Peter Jost and Egon Voss – have fielded a volley of questions of often Byzantine complexity with apparent disregard for their own more pressing researches. I am particularly grateful to Hannu Salmi for providing a copy of the Russian secret police report on Wagner and to Rosamund Bartlett for translating both this and Nikolay Kashkin's memoir of Wagner. Roland Matthews kindly allowed me to reuse his translation of Valentina Serova's memoir. For suggesting material for inclusion and for answering individual queries, I must thank Bernhard R. Appel, Mike Ashman, Oswald Georg Bauer, Paul Bentley, Otto Biba, Patrick Carnegy, Barry Cooper, Bill Cooper, Mary Criswick, John Deathridge, Jeremy Dibble, Rosemary Dooley, Günter Fischer, Francesca Franchi, Ingrid Fuchs, Ray Furness, Widmar Hader, Fiona Hardy, Sabine Henze-Döhring, Joachim Herz, Roger Hollinrake, Joseph Horowitz, Leslie Howard, Sir Charles Mackerras, Gerd Nauhaus, Katrin Reinhold, Frank Rubli, Mavis Sacher, Beat Schläpfer, Isabel Stierli, Isolde Vetter,

Hildburg Williams, Stella Wright and the staff at the British Library, the London Library, the Royal College of Music, the Royal Academy of Music, the School of Slavonic and East European Studies, the Bayerische Staatsbibliothek, the Bibliothek der Hansestadt Lübeck, the Dresden Stadtmuseum and the Beinecke Rare Book and Manuscript Library, Yale University. Eva Zöllner has, as always, proved a veritable pillar of strength in answering endless questions on German idioms and culture. My final debt of gratitude is to my editor at Faber and Faber, Belinda Matthews, whose exemplary encouragement, support and constructive comments have proved beyond doubt that reports of the death of the caring editor in English publishing houses are much exaggerated. To her and her colleagues – especially Ian Bahrami and Trish Stableford – I am no less indebted than Wagner was to *his* publishers.

The excerpt from Queen Victoria's journal is published by the gracious permission of Her Majesty the Queen. The passage from Frederick Gye's diary appears by courtesy of the Royal Opera House Archives. For permission to reproduce other copyright material, I should like to thank Hermann Böhlaus Nachfolger (Eduard Devrient), Musikverlag Schott Musik International (Ludwig Strecker) and Thames and Hudson (Auguste Renoir). The publishers would be pleased to hear from any copyright holders not acknowledged here.

I am especially grateful to Ralph Kaminsky for letting me reproduce Wagner's letter to Pauline Viardot and to Albi Rosenthal for generously allowing me to reproduce Lenbach's previously unpublished drawing of Wagner and Cosima.

STEWART SPENCER

A NOTE ON CURRENCIES

1 thaler = 3 marks
1 Austrian florin = 2 marks
1 louis d'or = 19.56 marks
1 franc = 0.80 marks
1 pound = 20 marks

Comparisons with present-day prices are not easy to draw, but it is generally reckoned that the purchasing power of the above currencies is now fifteen times less than it was in the 1850s. In other words, one of Wagner's thalers is now worth 45 marks.

1 (1813–42)

1813   *22 May* (Wilhelm) Richard Wagner born at the House of the Red and White Lion in the Brühl in Leipzig's Jewish quarter, the son of Johanna Rosine Wagner and (probably) the police actuary Carl Friedrich Wagner. He is the youngest of nine children. His father dies on 23 November

> *27 March* Russo-Prussian troops occupy Dresden. Napoleon defeats the Bohemian army at Dresden, 26–7 August, but is defeated in turn at the Battle of the Nations at Leipzig on 16–19 October
> Philharmonic Society founded in London
> Kierkegaard and Verdi born
> Rossini, *Tancredi* and *L'italiana in Algeri*
> Ernst Arndt, *Lieder für Teutsche*
> Jane Austen, *Pride and Prejudice*

1814   *28 August* Johanna remarries. Her second husband is the painter and actor Ludwig Geyer. The family moves to Dresden

> *30–1 March* Allies enter Paris. Napoleon is banished to Elba.
> Congress of Vienna opens
> George Stephenson constructs first steam locomotive
> Pope Pius VII restores the Inquisition and revives the Index and the Jesuits
> Bakunin born
> Fichte dies (51)
> Schubert, *Gretchen am Spinnrade*
> Byron, *The Corsair*

> 1815   *9 June* Congress of Vienna closes
> *18 June* Battle of Waterloo
> Bismarck born

> 1816   Carl August of Saxe-Weimar grants first German constitution

1817　German students meet at Wartburg Festival to celebrate
the Battle of Leipzig
Jane Austen dies (41)
Weber takes up his appointment as Royal Saxon Kapellmeister
in Dresden

1818　Hegel appointed professor of philosophy in Berlin
Karl Marx, Gounod and Turgenev born
Schopenhauer, *The World as Will and Representation*

1819　Metternich sanctions repressive Carlsbad Decrees
Queen Victoria, Prince Albert, Jacques Offenbach and Mary
Ann Evans born
Schubert, 'Trout' Quintet
Géricault, *The Raft of the 'Medusa'*
Byron, *Mazeppa*

1820　Spends some weeks at Christian Wetzel's crammer at
Possendorf, where he also receives piano lessons

Final Act of the Conference of Vienna under Metternich
authorizes the German Confederation to interfere in the
affairs of states unable to maintain public order

1821　*30 September* Geyer dies

Baudelaire, Dostoevsky and Flaubert born
Keats (25) and Napoleon (51) die
Weber, *Der Freischütz*
Constable, *The Hay Wain*
Goethe, *Wilhelm Meisters Wanderjahre*
Hegel, *Philosophy of Right*

1822　Enters Dresden Kreuzschule under name of Richard Geyer

Shelley (29) and Hoffmann (46) die
Schubert, 'Unfinished' Symphony

1823　Rossini, *Semiramide*
Spohr, *Jessonda*
Weber, *Euryanthe*

1824　Smetana and Bruckner born
7 May Beethoven's Ninth Symphony performed in Vienna

1825　Stockton and Darlington Railway opens

Hanslick born
Boieldieu, *La dame blanche*

1826   First literary endeavours; family moves to Prague, but
        Richard remains in Dresden

        Weber dies (39)

1827   Moves to Leipzig to rejoin family

        Beethoven dies (56)
        Schubert, *Winterreise*
        Bellini, *Il pirata*
        Heine, *Buch der Lieder*

1828   *21 January* Enters Nicolaischule in Leipzig under name of
        Richard Wagner. He is moved down a class
        Begins private harmony lessons with Christian Gottlieb
        Müller

        Ibsen and Tolstoy born
        Schubert dies (31)
        Auber, *La muette de Portici*
        Marschner, *Der Vampyr*
        Grimm, *Deutsche Rechtsalterthümer*

1829   Earliest compositions: two piano sonatas, a concert aria
        and a string quartet (all lost)

        Rossini, *Guillaume Tell*
        Marschner, *Der Templer und die Jüdin*
        Mendelssohn revives Bach's *St Matthew Passion*

1830   *16 June* Leaves Nicolaischule at Easter and enrols at
        Thomasschule. Briefly studies the violin. Prepares piano
        transcription of Beethoven's Ninth Symphony. Composes
        four overtures (all lost)
        'Drum-Beat Overture' performed in Leipzig on 25
        December

        July Revolution in Paris
        Revolution in Belgium
        Polish Uprising
        Bellini, *I Capuleti e i Montecchi*

Berlioz, *Symphonie fantastique*
Hugo, *Hernani*

1831   23 *February* Matriculates at Leipzig University to study
music. Fails to complete course. During autumn starts
lessons with Thomaskantor, Theodor Weinlig. They last
six months. Among the works from this period are *Sieben
Kompositionen zu Goethes 'Faust'*, a sonata for piano for
four hands (later instrumented), an Overture in D minor
(performed at the Leipzig Hoftheater on 25 December), a
Piano Sonata in B flat major op. 1 and a Fantasia in F sharp
minor

> Constitutions granted in Hesse-Cassel (January), Hanover
> (March) and Saxony (September)
> Hegel dies (61)
> Bellini, *La sonnambula*
> Hérold, *Zampa*
> Meyerbeer, *Robert le diable*
> Bellini, *Norma*

1832   Becomes friendly with Heinrich Laube. Continues to write
vocal, instrumental and orchestral works
His D minor Overture is revived and on 30 April his C
major Overture performed, also at a Gewandhaus concert
Visits Vienna and Prague
Starts work on opera *Die Hochzeit* (abandoned in March
1833)
C major Symphony performed at Prague Conservatory,
November
The leading German soprano Wilhelmine Schröder-
Devrient appears in Leipzig as Agathe (23 December) and
Leonore (27 December)

> Hambach Festival of South German Democrats advocates
> armed revolt: increased repression follows
> Mazzini founds 'Young Italy' movement
> Laube founds radical *Zeitung für die elegante Welt*
> Gregory XVI's encyclical condemns freedom of conscience and
> of the press
> Manet born
> Goethe (82) and Scott (61) die

Donizetti, *L'elisir d'amore*
Goethe, *Faust II*
Hugo, *Le roi s'amuse*

1833 Begins works on opera, *Die Feen*, based on Gozzi's *La donna serpente* (completed 6 January 1834)
17 January Takes up post as chorus master in Würzburg, an appointment engineered by his brother Albert and possibly designed to avoid military service. Rehearses operas by Auber, Beethoven, Boieldieu, Hérold, Marschner, Meyerbeer, Rossini, Weber and others

>   Brahms born
>   Hérold dies (41)
>   Auber, *Gustave III*
>   Marschner, *Hans Heiling*
>   Mendelssohn, 'Italian' Symphony

1834 *15 January* Leaves Würzburg and returns to Leipzig via Nuremberg. Suffers first recorded attack of erysipelas
March Schröder-Devrient returns to Leipzig as Bellini's Romeo, Beethoven's Leonore and Rossini's Desdemona
Reads Heinse's *Ardinghello* and Laube's *Das junge Europa*
Writes his first article, 'German Opera', for Laube's *Zeitung für die elegante Welt*, 10 June
Visits Bohemia and plans new opera, *Das Liebesverbot*, based on Shakespeare's *Measure for Measure*. In late July is appointed music director of Heinrich Bethmann's touring company and makes conducting début with Mozart's *Don Giovanni* in Bad Läuchstadt on 2 August. Becomes infatuated with the actress Wilhelmine ('Minna') Planer

>   Slavery abolished in British Empire
>   Laube banished from Saxony
>   Schumann's *Neue Zeitschrift für Musik* launched
>   Boieldieu dies (58)
>   Berlioz, *Harold en Italie*
>   Bulwer-Lytton, *The Last Days of Pompeii*

1835 *January* Writes overture and incidental music for *Columbus* by his friend Theodor Apel

Tours southern Germany in search of singers for
Bethmann's company
August Begins to make notes for future autobiography
November Minna leaves to take up engagement in Berlin
but returns in response to a stream of letters from Wagner

> Saint-Saëns born
> Bellini dies (33)
> Bellini, *I Puritani*
> Halévy, *La juive*
> Donizetti, *Lucia di Lammermoor*
> Jacob Grimm, *Teutonic Mythology*
> David Friedrich Strauß, *Life of Jesus*
> Büchner, *Dantons Tod*
> Bulwer-Lytton, *Rienzi*

1836   29 *March Das Liebesverbot* receives its disastrous first
performance under Wagner in Magdeburg. Bethmann's
company disbanded
Attempts to have *Das Liebesverbot* staged in Berlin
22 *June* Impressed by Spontini's *Fernand Cortez*
Follows Minna to Königsberg, where she has been offered
an engagement, but fails to find work at the theatre
Completes *Polonia* Overture and drafts scenario for *Die
hohe Braut*, which he sends to Scribe in Paris
24 *November* Marries Minna

> Meyerbeer, *Les Huguenots*
> Glinka, *A Life for the Tsar*

1837   15 *March* Completes *Rule Britannia* Overture
1 *April* Offered post of music director in Königsberg
31 *May* Minna leaves Wagner for a merchant called
Dietrich. Wagner pursues her to Blasewitz, where, in
response to Apel's suggestion, he reads Bulwer-Lytton's
Rienzi. Begins to sketch opera
Offered post of music director at Riga, which he takes up
on 1 September. Here he is secure from his creditors. Minna
has again left him but joins him in late October

> Queen Victoria succeeds William IV
> Ernest Augustus suppresses constitution in Hanover and in

December dismisses seven professors of Göttingen University,
including the Grimm brothers
Cosima Liszt born
Lortzing, *Zar und Zimmermann*
Berlioz, *Grande messe des morts*

1838   Writes libretto for comic opera *Männerlist größer als
        Frauenlist* but breaks off composition after only two
        numbers
        August Completes libretto of *Rienzi* and starts work on
        the music
        Between 15 November and 7 May 1839 conducts six
        symphony concerts in Riga, including works by
        Beethoven, Cherubini, Mendelssohn, Mozart, Weber and
        himself

        Bizet born
        Berlioz, *Benvenuto Cellini*

1839   Wagner's contract is not renewed in March. He and Minna
        flee Riga in order to escape from his creditors. They slip
        across the border between Russia and East Prussia on 10
        July and sail from the port of Pillau on the 19th. Stormy
        sea voyage to London, where they arrive on 12 August.
        On crossing to France, Wagner unexpectedly meets
        Meyerbeer in Boulogne and receives letters of
        recommendation
        Arrives in Paris on 17 September. Fails to gain a foothold
        on the French musical scene
        Writes *mélodies* and insertion aria for *Norma*. Attends
        performance of Berlioz's *Roméo et Juliette* (either 24
        November or 1 December) and drafts first movement of a
        '*Faust* Symphony'

        Fox Talbot and Daguerre pioneer photography
        Darwin, *Voyage of the 'Beagle'*
        Cézanne and Mussorgsky born
        Mendelssohn conducts first public performance of Schubert's
        'Great' C major Symphony in Leipzig
        Verdi, *Oberto*
        Turner, *The Fighting Téméraire*

1840 4 *February* Performance of *Columbus* Overture at
Conservatoire under Habeneck
Drafts scenario for *Der fliegende Holländer* and sends it
to Scribe in the hope that he may be commissioned to
write an opera for the Académie Royale de Musique
Begins series of articles for Maurice Schlesinger's *Revue et
Gazette musicale*
19 November Completes *Rienzi*
Works on arrangements of popular French operas for
Schlesinger

> Friedrich Wilhelm IV ascends Prussian throne
> Tchaikovsky and Zola born
> Paganini dies (57)
> Proudhon, *Qu'est-ce que la propriété?*
> Lortzing, *Hans Sachs*
> Donizetti, *La favorite*
> Schumann, *Dichterliebe*

1841 4 *February* Performance of *Columbus* Overture under
Schlesinger
Continues to write for French and German journals
May Moves to Meudon to work on *Der fliegende
Holländer*
Rienzi accepted by Dresden Court Theatre on Meyerbeer's
recommendation
30 October The Wagners move back to Paris
The full score of *Der fliegende Holländer* is completed on
19(?) November

> Dvořák, Chabrier and Renoir born
> Halévy, *Le guitarrero* and *La reine de Chypre*
> Schumann, Symphonies in B flat major and D minor
> Feuerbach, *The Essence of Christianity*
> The population of London in 1841 is 2,235,344, that of Paris
> 935,261 and that of Berlin approximately 300,000

1842 7 *April* Wagner and Minna leave Paris and reach Dresden
five days later

FERDINAND AVENARIUS (1856–1923)

Avenarius was the son of Wagner's (half-)sister Cäcilie Geyer (1815–93).[1] His account of Wagner's childhood was published within weeks of Wagner's death in 1883 and was based, he claims, on authenticated anecdotes passed on to him by his mother.

Following Geyer's death the family continued to live in one of the tall old houses on the Jüdenhof. The eldest children soon had decent incomes, Geyer's surviving paintings had risen considerably in value, and there also appears to have been a royal pension, as my grandfather's refined manners had made him a popular visitor not only to the Saxon Court but also to its Bavarian equivalent – a curious coincidence in the light of his son's later career. As a result, my grandmother, while not exactly well off, was not precisely poor. [. . .]

But let us take a closer look at little Richard: in his short-sleeved jerkin, he strikes us as a delicate, pale and slightly built fellow by no means lacking in boisterousness – 'not a day passes when he doesn't leave the seat of his trousers on a fence,' his father complains in a letter. My mother's reminiscences stretch as far back as is humanly possible, but one will not, of course, find much in her memories of that period to throw light on Wagner's later character. Not even the most assiduous observer will detect anything specifically 'Wagnerian' in the fact that, satisfying his craving for 'something good', the young lad once stuffed his pockets full of hot cutlets and handed them over only when they began to burn him or that on running errands to Klepperbein's he regularly forgot the raisins, still less that, when a dog stole his bone, he chased it

1. Until such time as new documentary evidence comes to light, we shall never know for certain whether Wagner's father was the police actuary Friedrich Wagner (1770–1813) or the actor and portrait painter Ludwig Geyer (1779–1821). Wagner himself seems to have been in two minds on the subject, at least from the end of 1869 onwards; see Hollinrake 1970.

all the way through the town to the market place, where he received such a blow to his chest from a horse's hoof that his family were long concerned for the consequences.

Let us turn forward the clock a few years. Wagner is by now a worthy pupil at the Kreuzschule, learning to love and fear the Lord and, at the same time, getting up to all manner of japes. Initially keen on his fellow pupils' friendship, he gradually grows disenchanted with it (we shall shortly see why), while becoming increasingly attached to little Cäcilie, 'Cile', the 'pretty, dark-haired' girl who worships him to distraction and who regards all his pranks as the excrescences of wisdom. He is always with her whenever he 'has time' (or whenever he thinks he has), hatching plans and running around with her – not, of course, without being able to deny a certain feeling of condescension in his male pride. 'Be off with you, Cile, there are some boys coming,' he would sometimes say to her; 'if they see you with me, they'll call me a sissy!' And Cile was so well trained that she was gone in a trice.

At home the two children shared a single tiny room. By day, one of them would wait at the window for the other to return from school. At night they had a lot to put up with from each other, for, being so excitable, they slept only fitfully. Both had a holy dread of being on their own in the dark: Richard saw ghosts in every corner, and my mother's screams gave them tongue. The young boy was said to be particularly scared of the steep dark stairs leading up to the apartment and if he arrived home after dark he would ring the bell and try to entice down a servant girl with a light, in spite of having been forbidden to do so. 'Oh no, I was only sort of playing with it, and the stupid thing rang,' he once said on being told off yet again. Otherwise, of course, the stupid thing rang only when you tugged on its rusty crank with all your might. Once the two of them were late and had to make their way home in the dark from Blasewitz – and their journey took them past some churchyards. They did not know what to do, but help was at hand in the form of a passing carriage. They hailed it: they had no money, they told the driver, but they didn't weigh very much. The man saw sense, and Richard was rightly proud: 'Look, Cile, look – there's the churchyard with its ghosts, but ha ha, they can't get us now!'

His sister can still recall her brother suddenly shouting out in his sleep and talking, laughing and crying during the night, but she herself was no better. Once she ran breathlessly to their mother, saying that there was a 'big bogey' in her bed. This was a source of no little delight to the future tone-poet who, whenever he wanted to frighten her, would crawl under her bed and call out in a hollow, blood-curdling voice: 'Cile, Cile, there's a big bogey in your bed.' It rarely failed to work. This big bogey later became something of a family saying. I myself have two letters in which the now grown-up composer jokingly threatens his sister with it.[1] [. . .]

The children were happiest when their mother took them to the country: then their days were filled with sunshine. An early stay at Loschwitz remained lodged in their memory long after they had grown up. Even today, the house where they stayed on the Loschwitzer Grund continues to gaze back at me roguishly whenever I pass. Mother and elder sisters had plenty to do in the town, and so the children were nominally left in the care of the farmer's wife or of Dr Schneider's wife in Blasewitz. Here, next to the dog kennel, they built themselves a hut of planks in which to tell each other stories until they grew tired. In fact, no one seems to have worried unduly about them, and they did nothing but play foolish pranks, a number of which were later immortalized in delightful sketches by Kietz,[2] a pupil of Delaroche, who also produced the well-known pictures of the ailing Heine and of Schröder-Devrient. Before me I have a drawing showing 'Richel and Cile awaiting their Mama'. Just as Cäcilie had a great love of eccentricity in general, so she was inordinately fond of running around barefoot, but on this particular day, while they waited for their mother to return by boat that evening, it was frosty and her feet began to freeze. 'Wait,' said Richel; 'you take one of my boots, and we'll place our other two feet on top of each other.' This is how Kietz's sketch shows them. The boats that the children saw on the Elbe excited their imagination in no small way, and Richard even set about designing one for himself, a boat on which they planned no less an adventure than a pleasure cruise on the Loschwitz Brook. But the vessel's

1. *Family Letters* 196 and 233 (letters of 9 March 1853 and 31 July 1860).
2. Ernst Benedikt Kietz (1815–92) was one of the Wagners' closest friends in Paris. He studied with Paul Delaroche (1797–1856), remaining in the French capital until 1870, when he moved back to Germany. See illus. 3.

seaworthiness was not put to the test: 'You know, it doesn't really matter, we can just as well use a bathtub.'

A rather more tragic tale is that of the large pumpkin. The older sisters were back in town, the two youngsters out in the country. It was here that Richard hollowed out a huge pumpkin and cut eyes, nose and mouth into it. It was quite horrible to look at. 'Come on, Cile, let's go and frighten people with it.' Cile had noticed that their landlady's servants had taken Frau Geyer's porcelain cups – the ones with the large floral pattern – to use at their parties, and the future housewife was so indignant that she determined that, if the two of them went out, the unguarded living room should at least be left secure: 'Let's take the latch and door key with us.' And so they set out to frighten people, first to the village and then, since they had no luck there, up into the hills. They placed the key and latch inside the pumpkin – my, how they rattled! – and rolled it down to the bottom. What fun they had, chasing after the pumpkin, then clambering back up hill with it, and so on. Not until it was dark did they return home. 'What's got into you, you young good-for-nothings, taking the keys with you? Hand them over!' Oh dear, the keys, oh dear, – the pumpkin had lost them through its mouth. Luckily their mother was unable to leave Dresden that evening, so the farmer's servants had to make do with giving them a good dressing down. 'You good-for-nothings can sleep outside on the stove-bench,' they said when they were done. Richel and Cile had a good cry, then pulled off their clothes, except for the shirts that they were used to wearing in happier times when they still shared a bed, after which they lay down on the stove-bench, sobbed a little more, complained that they were freezing and finally fell asleep. It was already dark by the time that Richard's private tutor, Herr Humann, arrived from the town with instructions to see to the children, as their mother was prevented from coming. He stood there in solemn silence, an impartial judge, as the two children, roused from their slumbers, answered the charges and mounted their own defence. But slowly it dawned on him that he too would have to sleep on the stove-bench, at which point he lost his temper: 'Richard, you abject child, I'll give you a piece of my mind.' And his words poured out in a torrent, overwhelming the future composer, who cowered behind the stove and howled. But he had reckoned without little Cile. 'Sir! How dare you! It is no concern of yours – it was I who did it – and in any case – and . . .' Proud as Minerva, Cile, dressed only in her short smock, stepped between her brother and his teacher, her arms akimbo. This scene, too, Kietz has preserved for posterity. The reconciliation that is part of all good plays came when a bystander remarked that it was possible to climb into the house through an open window with the aid of a ladder, whereupon Cile and Richel picked up their clothes and were up in a trice, their tutor following with all the dignity he could muster.

'If only we hadn't put the key in the pumpkin,' Wagner wrote wistfully to his sister from exile some thirty years later, 'it would all have turned out so much better. Don't you agree?'[1]

An essential feature of Wagner's character – not only during his childhood – was his pronounced, almost passionate love of Nature. His principal pleasure was to run around out of doors, either singing and romping at my mother's side or, in winter, playing with his little hand-sledge. Sometimes they would go off to the Linkesches Bad, which in those days was outside the town, and in the meadow by the garden they could enjoy both Nature and music, the latter in the form of concerts in the park, which they were able to hear without paying. Or Mama Geyer gave them sixpence apiece – then they were well off indeed and could venture as far afield as the Plauenscher Grund or Loschwitz and buy a glass of milk to wash down the rolls they had brought with them. Curiously, although Richard was fond of looking at flowers and fruit, he could not bring himself to touch them. It was not, however, on walks or in collecting butterflies and other natural history speci-mens that his love of Nature found its most forceful expression, but in his self-sacrificial devotion to living creatures. Wagner's love of dogs played a major role in his life. It was more than a momen-tary pang of melancholy when, at his lowest ebb, he once said to my mother: 'Do you want to see the friends to whom I'm most grateful? There they are.' And he pointed to his dog and parrot.[2]
[. . .]

1. *Family Letters* 190 (letter of 30 December 1852).
2. The Wagners acquired Peps as a six-week-old puppy in September 1842; he died on 10 July 1855. Papo was a gift of the Hamburg impresario Julius Cornet (1793–1860) in March 1844. The parrot's death on 12 February 1851 assumed positively tragic proportions.

But let us now take a brief look at Richard's intellectual achievements. He was regarded at the time as a good pupil, although
more because he was bright than because he worked hard – only
later in Leipzig was he put off his lessons by the fact that, having
arrived from Dresden as a sixth-former, he found himself – to his
mortification – demoted to the fifth form. At that time, however,
he got on well in every subject, and there were few that did not
interest him. Greek was his greatest love, with Homer as his idol.
My mother, too, remembers him going on and on about Hector
and Achilles, but even more about the wicked sorceress Circe, the
doltish one-eyed cyclops and clever Odysseus, who led them all by
the nose. He was also fond of quoting lines from Voß's translation:
'Swiftly, with rumble of thunder'[1] was one of the expressions that
my mother remembered, presumably because it made the deepest
impression on her at that time. He was also keen on geography,
but felt nothing but loathing for French – I do not think he ever
really learnt it, in spite of his time in Paris. English he studied only
later.

As I have already mentioned, he got on badly with his classmates.
The sanguine and uniquely lively lad whose head was filled with a
thousand ideas and projects but who was so easily offended on
account of his almost feminine tenderness of feeling remained an
enigma to the average child, and here too we see the truth of the
saying: 'People are wont to mock what they don't understand.'[2] It
is impossible to reproach them for this, but it explains why he
took such little pleasure in their company and spent more and
more time with his sister. But the main reason for this may well
have been two incidents that I never heard recounted without a
good deal of feeling. The first of them I shall return to in a moment
in the context of *Der Freischütz*. The other relates to Wagner's first
patron's certificate.[3]

It was not, of course, a performance on the scale of the *Ring* or
even a firework display of the kind that Richard had sometimes
arranged until the police had had to intervene. It was no more than
a sort of shooting competition. At the time in question Richard and

1. *Odyssey* xi.598 in Johann Heinrich Voß's 1781 translation.
2. Goethe, *Faust* I, ll.1205–6.
3. Half a century later a system of patrons' certificates was devised to raise funds
for the first Bayreuth Festival.

Cäcilie were staying at the Three Crowns on the Bautzenerstraße. The little boxes that they kept under their beds and that contained all the money they had saved from breakfast had now grown fairly heavy. A great 'summer festival' was to be held for Richard's friends, with the competition as its high point. But they did not have enough money, and so a kind of club was set up to achieve this ideal aim: the subscription was set at threepence and everyone who contributed could advise on, and take part in, the pleasures in store. The treasures accumulated, and when all the paint and wood and brass foil and nails had been received, the Master proceeded to plan the festivities by first consulting his intendant – Cäcilie – on a suitable site for the festival. After all manner of arguments with their landlady, who had no time for such noble pursuits, they finally obtained her permission to hold the contest in her garden. Here was erected the pole that normally served as the shaft of a cart, and with his own hands Richard fashioned the proudest eagle from the meanest firewood, a bird which, festooned with trophies, soon cast its colourful lustre far and wide. The festival was due to take place the following day, but when the sun rose on the impresario the next morning as he stepped outside with his sister, his face radiant with happiness, in order to see his handiwork – it lay there in a pitiful heap on the ground. The other boys had brought it down with stones and now stood there, grinning contemptuously. 'We've paid our threepence, we can do what we like' was their response to Richard's anger and remonstrations. Of course, he and his sister once again dissolved in a flood of tears. Today, as I write these lines, I feel only a sense of undeniable disgust. It was Wagner's first experience of this kind. It was not to be his last.

Wagner had felt drawn to music from an early age, much though he hated having to learn the skills involved. From the pedantic piano teacher who found fault with his fingering and from the teacher who, when he expressed a wish to play overtures, complained that he was 'trying to dance before he could walk' and who declared that nothing would come of him – from the lessons of men such as these he would run away, slamming the door behind him and steadfastly refusing to atone. But he never forgot what my grandmother said on Geyer's death: 'He wanted to make some-

thing of you.' He recounted the story himself.[1] And if he thought
as much of becoming a scholar or a painter as of taking up music,
this latter was none the less one possibility among many. And how
he was seized by the enthusiasm sparked off everywhere by *Der
Freischütz*. When Weber, who was then the conductor at the
Dresden Opera, had finished rehearsing, he would pass through
the Jüdenhof. Then Richard would call his sister to the window:
'Look, there's the greatest man alive – you simply can't conceive
of how great he is.' And when Cäcilie saw the little bandy-legged
man hobbling along, with his large spectacles on his large nose
and wearing a long grey coat, she could initially see nothing 'great'
in him, but, like her brother, she too soon came to regard him with
absolute awe. The tricks that Wagner played to inveigle his way
into the theatre were particularly frequent in the case of *Der Freischütz*. The depth of Wagner's admiration for Weber is best illustrated, perhaps, by his actions in bringing back Weber's mortal
remains for burial in Dresden and the heartfelt words that he spoke
at his graveside.[2]

The boy could think of nothing but *Der Freischütz* at this time
– one example among many may suffice to show this. Richard
liked to mount amateur theatricals in his room and as soon as he
saw *Der Freischütz*, he absolutely had to stage it. It goes without
saying that it was the Wolf's Glen Scene that struck him as the
most suitable in this regard. Pasteboard and glue were pressed into
service to make the necessary props. His school friends had to
help. Scenery, curtains, fireworks and animals – everything was
produced, and my mother particularly admired a large boar with
enormous tusks that was rolled along on a board and looked
horribly like the Prince of Darkness in person. The performance
was to be given at a friend's house. Richard played the part of
Caspar, but the Max had not learnt his part, and when Richard
indicated his disapproval, he first laughed, then called him names.
And the others laughed and jeered, too. This was the second of
the bitter experiences that no gifted child can avoid.

Avenarius 1883: 1067–8, 1082–3

1. AS 11.
2. GS ii.46–8; PW vii.235–7; see also ML 296–9.

Wagner moved to Leipzig at the end of 1827 and the following autumn began harmony lessons with Gottlieb Müller (1800–63). His earliest compositions date from 1829. The first to receive a public airing was the 'Drum-Beat Overture' (WWV 10). Now lost, this piece takes its nickname from Wagner's claim that its most striking feature was a fortissimo drum beat on the second beat of every third bar (thus the account in his 'Autobiographical Sketch' of 1843; according to the revised version of this text that appeared in Wagner's collected writings, it was every fourth bar, while *Mein Leben* claims that it was every fifth bar). The conductor was Heinrich Dorn.

HEINRICH DORN (1804–92)

Dorn was well known in his day as a composer, conductor, writer and teacher. Active in Leipzig between 1829 and 1832, he later held appointments in Riga (1834–43), Cologne (1844–8) and Berlin (1849–69). He was an early champion of Wagner's works, both as a conductor and as a journalist, but the two men fell out over the circumstances of Wagner's dismissal from his post in Riga and they later lost no opportunity to snipe at each other in print. A high point of Dorn's career and a low point in his professional relationship with Wagner was the production of his opera, *Die Nibelungen*, under Liszt in Weimar in 1854, with Wagner's step-niece as the heroine; see also Newman i.76–8, 213–14, 236–9 and Leverett 1990.

It was as music director of the then Saxon Court Theatre at Leipzig between 1829 and 1832 that I made the young man's acquaintance. He had just started his musical studies under the Thomaskantor, Theodor Weinlig.[1] His elder sister, Rosalie[2] (later Dr Marbach's

---

1. Wagner studied with Theodor Weinlig (1780–1842) for some six months, starting in the autumn of 1831. His lessons with Müller, Weinlig and the violinist Robert Sipp (1806–99) belie his later claim that he was largely self-taught as a musician.
2. Rosalie Wagner (1803–37) married Oswald Marbach (1810–90) and died in childbirth.

wife), was the leading lady at the Leipzig theatre, while one of his younger sisters[1] had already married into one of the wealthy and hospitable Konversationsbrockhäuser, to whose house I, too, had access, with the result that we had several points in common, and it has already been pointed out elsewhere that it was I who conducted his first overture at the Leipzig theatre[2] and in doing so introduced him to the world of music, not, I may add, without violent dissent on the part of the orchestra which, led by the elderly Heinrich Matthäi,[3] had declared the whole work to be nonsense straight after the first rehearsal. I can still see the little octavo score, neatly written out in two different colours of ink and divided into three sections (for strings, woodwind and brass). It already contained in embryo all the large-scale effects that were later to excite the attention of the whole of the musical world, without, however, eliciting anything other than the most absolute bewilderment. Wagner was still bashful by nature at this time and not at all presumptuous, so that he laughed heartily at the spectacular failure of this maiden speech of his, which was greeted in total silence. He seemed to regard its fate as justified.

Dorn 1870: ii.1-2; see also WWV 10; AS 12 and ML 51-2

HEINRICH LAUBE (1806–84)

> Another family friend in the 1830s was Heinrich Laube, a leading literary figure of his day, now remembered as one of the principal voices of the radical, anti-Romantic Young German movement.

Ever since I had become caught up in life's maelstrom in Breslau as a result of my literary activities, experience had taught me to be wary of marriage. I was thirteen or fourteen and still living at home when I was suddenly struck by the thought that it was a crying shame that women were obliged to marry. Men, after all,

1. Luise (1805–72) gave up acting in 1828 when she married Friedrich Brockhaus (1800–65), a member of the firm of publishers best known for its encyclopaedic *Konversationslexikon*.
2. On 25 December 1830.
3. Heinrich August Matthäi (1781–1835).

are all frightful. I knew these men and, not entirely unreasonably, found them all ugly. This thought had often occurred to me since then, albeit with less emphasis on the idea of men's ugliness. But I had seen so many men who, unsuited to their wives, had driven the latter to take a lover who was granted all the husband's rights. Could not such adultery be prevented, I asked myself. Can the change of partner demanded by our irresistible likes and dislikes not find a legal form that goes beyond the divorce laws of the Protestants and the indissoluble bond between Catholics?

In this, I had been confirmed by the Saint-Simonists and, indeed, I was so obsessed by the idea that, soon after my arrival in Leipzig, I found myself at a ball and asked my nimble-footed dancing partner whether she, too, was of the opinion that our present marriage laws should be changed.

Fortunately the young lady to whom I put my impertinent question turned out to be quick-witted. 'Does it have to be now?' she asked with a laugh.

She was the sister of Richard Wagner, who at that time was still running around in the somewhat dubious guise of an impatient young musician. I visited the family home, and his anxious mother invariably asked me: 'Do you think anything will come of Richard?'

Wagner's mother was a small and sensible woman, whose conversation was not without its humorous turns of phrase. Her second marriage was to a painter – Richard was the youngest child of her first – and in the course of it she had learnt to tolerate the arts. Two of her daughters were actresses. But for this very reason she thought that a purely musical career was a highly risky business as a source of income for Richard. Richard himself was so irresponsible when it came to making money through music alone. His head was always in the clouds. He was then a carefree madcap of some nineteen summers, had received the sort of thorough musical education that had been common in Leipzig since Bach's day and exuded confidence. He demanded from me an opera libretto, and I even tried to meet his wishes: I began a work about Kosciusko,[1] but got no further than the opening act, the Imperial Diet at Cracow. Richard himself seemed to take no great pleasure in it.

Laube x.293–4; see also ML 70–71

1. The Polish patriot Thaddeus Kosciusko (1746–1817).

His mother's misgivings notwithstanding, Wagner resolved to make music his career. His first professional
appointment, obtained through his eldest brother's good
offices, was as chorus master in Würzburg (1833–4) and
was followed by posts as music director in Magdeburg,
Königsberg and Riga. It was in Bad Lauchstädt that he
met the actress Wilhelmine ('Minna') Planer (1809–66),
his senior by almost four years. There began a stormy
courtship that culminated in their marriage in November 1836. In 1825 Minna had been seduced and
abandoned by a guards captain, Ernst Rudolf von Ein-
siedel. Her daughter, Natalie Planer, was born in 1826.

NATALIE PLANER (1826–?99)

Natalie, who spent virtually her whole adult life
believing that she was Minna's sister, shared the
Wagners' home in Königsberg and elsewhere, her presence inevitably adding to the tensions of the
relationship. In 1890 she was discovered by Mary
Burrell living in a poorhouse at Leisnig. She proved
to be the possessor not only of a mass of Wagnerian
manuscripts but also a fund of reminiscences of 'poor,
kind Richard', who had continued to pay her an allowance even after Minna's death. While it is advisable to
treat some of her anecdotes with caution, there is no
doubt that they reflect the way in which she herself
remembered Wagner and, moreover, the way in which
she wished posterity to remember him. Certainly,
Wagner's own letters from this period confirm her
account of his desperation and jealousy – the jealousy
of the control freak. Here, in a letter of 24 November
1892, she answers Mary Burrell's enquiry about the
events of the summer of 1837.

As you know, Minna had married Richard on 24 November 1836
in the church at Tragheim,[1] which is the name of a district in
Königsberg, where he made Minna's life a veritable hell through
his unjust, immoderate & violent jealousy, & I myself often cried
out in fear & wept bitterly at the rough & brutal treatment that

1. Mistranscribed as 'Tropheimer Kirche' in Burrell 1953: 109.

he meted out to Minna, for I was still a child when I stayed with them in Königsberg. Poor Minna always burst into tears after such terrible scenes of jealousy, so much so that they often left her unconscious. Then, when his anger had passed, he was, of course, very sorry & with tender words he would ask her forgiveness, but the very next day the din would start up all over again & last all night. How often she begged him, imploring him & pleading with him from the bottom of her heart not to insult her with such unworthy suspicion & jealousy, which, deeply moved & with tears in his eyes, he would promise to do, without, however, keeping his word. Since this appalling & unworthy treatment went on & on, she said to him: 'Richard, I can't take any more of this; if you don't change, I'll leave you & go back to my parents. You can see that I'm serious: my bags are packed.' But Richard's rough & brutal treatment of her did not change, on the contrary, it got worse, until Minna could stand it no longer. And so, one afternoon, either on the last day of May or in early June 1837, weeping a thousand hot bitter tears, she left Königsberg with me, travelling by diligence to Dresden & not stopping till she was back with our parents. They were quite shocked & alarmed at Minna's sick, careworn & tearful appearance. But within days Richard came hurrying after her & early one morning – Minna was still in bed – threw himself on his knees at her bedside, nearly stifling her with his kisses. I know this very well, as I too was still in bed in the same room. Our mother, who was already up & who was furious at this rough treatment of Minna, had not wanted him to enter the room. But he had pushed her aside & forced his way in. Luckily for Richard, our father was still taking his morning walk, which he always did at this hour, otherwise I think he would have thrown Richard downstairs, he was so terribly angry that Richard had treated Minna so brutally & so roughly. Well, when he did get back, our father was none too welcoming & ordered Richard to leave the house at once. But our dear, kind, good-hearted mother felt so sorry for Richard in his despair & in his entreaties & tears that she sought to appease & calm our furious father. As a result he was finally allowed to stay & to be reconciled with Minna one more time.

NA

Wagner had been appointed music director in Königsberg on 1 April 1837, but the theatre went bankrupt
shortly afterwards, leaving him with no prospect of
paying off his mounting pile of debts. In June he nego-
tiated a new contract with Karl von Holtei (1798–1880)
as music director in Riga and took up his new appointment on 1 September. Heinrich Dorn claims credit for
the appointment.

HEINRICH DORN

We now became better acquainted, not least because our wives got
on so well together, and we spent some very pleasant hours
together. It was with great interest that I watched progress being
made on the first sketches of *Rienzi* and heard scene after scene
on the pianoforte. Wagner had written the part of Adriano for his
sister-in-law, Fräulein Planer,[1] who at these social gatherings had
to take all the female roles, while the men who were present and
who generally included the cellist from the theatre orchestra, that
great wit, Carl von Lutzau, sang whatever they could decipher
from the sketches, while bearded Russians stood aghast outside
the house as, late in the evening, they heard this hellish cacophony
wafting down from the rooms above them. That the strings of the
grand piano were scattered like chaff, so that ultimately all we
could hear was a flail-like wooden rattling as the metal strings on
the soundboard added their janissary strains (which, in view of the
score, was of no great consequence), goes without saying with as
inept a pianist as Wagner. Alas, his stay in Riga was to be only
short-lived. There were no serious objections to his conducting,
but, as an artist, he found it impossible to adapt to bourgeois life
once he was restricted by questions of debit and credit. Poor Holtei
had already had a lot to put up with as his conductor was forever
receiving summonses from his former residence in Königsberg.[2]

1. Amalie Planer (1811–?), who in 1839 married the Russian cavalry captain
(later general) Carl von Meck.
2. Although Wagner was safe from arrest in Riga, his creditors could, and did,
continue to appeal to his moral scruples both here and later in Dresden; see
Newman i.408–9. A number of the invoices owed by Wagner have survived in
the Latvian State Archives of History in Riga, 1378f., 1.apr., 9666 lieta.

But when Holtei's wife died and he grew tired of his old position and the tenor Johann Hoffmann,[1] who had come to Riga from St Petersburg in 1838, took over the running of the theatre at Easter 1839 and the committee alerted him to the fact that a number of businessmen in Riga were about to institute proceedings against Wagner for debt, the new director made short work of the matter and gave Wagner his notice, as it was impossible to run his theatre along orderly lines in such circumstances.

Dorn 1870: ii.3–4

NATALIE PLANER

Wagner's creditors began to close in on him and his passport was impounded. His adventurous escape from Riga in July 1839 is described by Natalie.

Wagner himself may not have been fully aware of the dangers of such a flight. It was only at the very last moment, by which time everything had been arranged & made ready for his escape, that Frau Minna, against whom no charges had been brought & who could have crossed the Russian border freely, unhindered & in safety, had learnt from her sister Amalie's fiancé, a relatively high-ranking Russian officer, that Wagner was in great danger, but as a true, loving & loyal German wife, she lost no time in agreeing to join him on this dangerous flight & not to abandon him in this time of great need & danger, but to remain at his side. God gave His blessing to her courageous & noble deed by allowing them to escape. Weary & utterly exhausted by the extreme exertion of their breakneck flight & by the great danger that they had overcome, they both finally reached the other side of the Prussian border in a pitiful, filthy Jewish carriage. Here their old friend[2] was waiting for them with a cart & their belongings, in order to take them to

1. Johann Hoffmann (1805–65) remained in Riga until 1844. After appointments in Prague and Frankfurt, he bought the Theater in der Josefstadt in Vienna in 1855 and was responsible for introducing *Tannhäuser* to Viennese audiences in 1857.
2. Abraham Möller, a Königsberg merchant who helped the Wagners on their flight from Riga.

the Kurisches Haff where a ship was lying at anchor in which they planned to sail for England. Here, too, their loyal friend had done everything to arrange the remainder of their journey with the captain, in spite of the latter's lengthy resistance, since, as refugees, they had no passports. Given the state of the roads & the ancient horses, this journey must have lasted more than two days. The following evening, before they reached their destination, they met with a serious accident when the driver, unfamiliar with the road, found himself in pitch darkness in a very unevenly surfaced farm-yard, where, attempting to retrace his steps, he overturned the carriage. Wagner's old friend was injured, Wagner himself was thrown from the carriage into the slurry pit & Minna was unfortu-nate enough to be trapped beneath the vehicle so that, seriously hurt, she was robbed of the greatest happiness that any young woman can know, that of incipient motherhood.[1] After the carriage had been righted with the help of some farmhands & Minna had been pushed back inside, a good-natured farm labourer agreed, in return for a generous tip, to light their way to the nearest ale-house. Fortunately, it was not far, so that the two men were able to walk along beside them. For all that this miserable ale-house was so dirty, the people there were unwilling to allow Richard to stay long enough even for him to wash & change his clothes, so pervasive was the smell that clung to him, & it was only by promising to leave them all his discarded clothes that he managed to persuade them to relent. The next day they had to rest on account of Minna's injuries but then set off again without delay in order to reach the boat in time. They arrived there in the evening but then had to hide in a tavern some considerable distance away, in order to be able to leave it at midnight & cover the whole of the distance to the boat by creeping along the ground through tall wet grass, so as not to be noticed by any of the coastguards who were keeping watch. They finally reached the boat, where the captain, who had been waiting for them, hurriedly concealed them in the very lowest hold behind barrels, crates & bales of goods, so they would not be found when the ship was inspected. In this

---

1. Although not otherwise authenticated, this version of events would account for the Wagners' childless marriage.

terrible state they had to remain for many agonizing hours until they reached the open sea & the captain could free them.

NA

SIR CHARLES HALLÉ (1819–95)

After an eventful crossing to London, where they spent a little over a week (12–20 August), visiting the Houses of Parliament and attempting to make contact with Bulwer-Lytton, the Wagners continued their journey to Paris, the capital of European music, where Wagner planned to make his fame and fortune. Among the expatriate Germans whom he met here was Charles Hallé.

Towards the end of the year 1839 Heller[1] brought one evening to my rooms a young musician, my senior by only six years, whose acquaintance he had made through Maurice Schlesinger, and who, as he told me in a side whisper, stood in great need of kindness and assistance. The name of this young musician was Richard Wagner, a name which at that time meant nothing to us, as we were in absolute ignorance of the talents he might or might not be endowed with. We knew that he was in great straits, had unsuccessfully applied for an appointment as chorus singer in a small theatre, and for his living made all kinds of arrangements for Schlesinger, even to an arrangement of Halévy's 'La Reine de Chypre' for *two flutes*, to which Heller suggested the addition of a big drum.[2] Wagner himself used to laugh at this occupation, the result of dire necessity; and we, never having seen or heard a note of his own compositions, took it almost for granted that he was not fit for much more. He was no pianist or he might have given us some idea of his own work. He rarely spoke of his aspirations,

1. The pianist and composer Stephen Heller (1813–88).
2. It was not until the winter of 1840–1 that Wagner began arranging popular operas for Maurice Schlesinger (1797–1871); see WWV 62. The arrangements of Halévy's *La reine de Chypre* (premièred at the Paris Opéra on 22 December 1841) comprise a vocal score, piano score, excerpts with piano accompaniment and transcriptions for string quartet and two violins. For an account of Wagner's finances during this period, see Spencer 1998.

but when he did so, it was usually in a strain which made us wonder if, as the phrase goes, he was 'all there.' We liked him as a most frank, amiable, and lively companion, modest and full of enthusiasm for all that is beautiful in art. And he felt evidently at home with us. He came often to the Rue Lafitte. Heller improvised, I played, or we played duets, and I remember that one evening when I had played to them Schumann's 'Carneval,' then quite new, we three indited a letter of thanks to the composer, which letter I saw more than forty years later in the hands of his widow.[1] In 1876, when I met him at Bayreuth, his first words alluded to the pleasant evenings with Heller at my rooms in Paris. What an immense change had taken place! What a difference there was between the man of 1839 and the man of 1876!

Schlesinger, the proprietor of the 'Gazette Musicale,' the most important musical paper in France, gave to the subscribers annually a few concerts with a view to increasing their number, and in the spring of 1840 he included in the programme an overture by his *then protégé*, Richard Wagner.[2] The overture was called 'Christoph Colomb,' and as it was the first time we were to hear a specimen of our friend's works, we were naturally very curious, and attended the concert with great expectations. The result was disastrous. Whether it was that the performance, for want of rehearsals, was most imperfect, or that the style was what we might now call *ultra-Wagnerian*, or for both these reasons joined together, the whole overture struck us as the work of a madman, and we had no opportunity to reconsider our judgment, as 'Christoph Colomb' has never again seen the light.

Hallé 1896: 59–61; see also ML 192–3

1. The letter, dated 26 November 1839, was signed by Hallé, Heller, Heinrich Panofka (1807–87) and Albert Franck and is now in the Sächsische Landesbibliothek, Dresden; see Boetticher 1979: 79–81.
2. Although a performance of the *Columbus* Overture was held on 4 February 1840, this was no more than a read-through by the Conservatoire Orchestra under Habeneck. The concert described by Hallé took place on 4 February 1841 at the Salle Herz.

FRIEDRICH PECHT (1814–1903)

Pecht was another German artist trying to make a name
for himself in Paris. Like Hallé, he committed his reminiscences to paper only at the end of his life and his
memory often played him false. None the less, he brings
a painter's eye for detail to the vignettes that make up
his memoirs.

Laube, whom I had got to know immediately after my arrival and
who had just returned from a tour of France, now planned to
spend the winter in Paris with his wife, so much did he admire the
French and French art – indeed, much to my own annoyance, he
constantly overrated them. To this end he had rented rooms in the
Boulevard des Italiens, where I often visited them both. One day I
was to show them round the Louvre. When I arrived, he said that
we would be joined by a young musician, the brother-in-law of
Friedrich Brockhaus, and his wife, and while we were waiting, he
explained that he had come here from Riga, hoping to have one
of his operas performed in Paris. His name was Richard Wagner.
– Soon the young man appeared, strikingly elegant and, indeed,
distinguished looking, in spite of the fact that his legs were much
too short,[1] with such an extraordinarily pretty woman on his arm
that she alone would have sufficed to make the couple interesting,
even if Wagner himself had not had so remarkable a head as
to prove involuntarily eye-catching. At first, he was unable to
concentrate on the pictures and his thoughts were clearly elsewhere,
but he then pulled himself together and soon revealed such a lively
wit that we rapidly became better acquainted, not least because,
hailing from Leipzig, he already had several points in common
with me, as I already knew three of his sisters. After wandering
round the gallery, we ate together in a restaurant and here he told
us about his adventures on his way here, the words tumbling out
uncontrollably – how he had set sail in a little boat and been driven
off course to Norway by the storm, how the whistling of the wind
in the frozen rigging had made such a strangely demonic impression
on him, sounding like the purest music, that once, when a ship

1. In the version of this text published in the *Allgemeine Musik-Zeitung* on 20–27
July 1894, Wagner's legs become 'somewhat short'.

had suddenly appeared before them in the storm and then vanished
again in the depths of the night as rapidly as it had come, he had
immediately thought of the Flying Dutchman. Since then he had not
stopped thinking of the music for such a work.[1] Attracted by the
irresistible appeal of his company, I soon got to know him better
and, since we shared all manner of interests (like him, I too was
seeking my fortune in Paris), I often visited him in the little fourth-
floor apartment that he had rented in the rue du Helder and
immediately furnished on credit.[2] He clearly had an innate gift for
running up debts, no doubt the result of his old actor's blood.

Pecht 1894: i.181–2

GIACOMO MEYERBEER (1791–1864)

The unprecedented success of *Robert le diable* (1831)
and *Les Huguenots* (1836) at the Paris Opéra proved a
stimulus to composers throughout Europe, and Wagner
was no exception. He first approached Meyerbeer in
February 1837 but by the time that Meyerbeer replied,
Wagner had already left Königsberg and the letter failed
to reach him. A chance meeting in Boulogne in August
1839 allowed Wagner to show the older composer the
first two acts of *Rienzi* and to enlist his support in his
assault on Paris. Meyerbeer duly provided Wagner with
letters of recommendation and from now on Wagner
turned to him whenever he was in need, each new
appeal for help couched in terms of increasingly cloying
sycophancy. He dedicated his arrangement of the vocal
score of *La favorite* to Meyerbeer and, as Heinz Becker
has pointed out, there are grounds for believing that his
article on *Les Huguenots* (SS xii.22–30) was written
during the winter of 1841–2 as a gesture of gratitude
but that Meyerbeer refused to allow it to be published
on the grounds that its obsequious tone showed neither
party in a favourable light (see Meyerbeer iii.396).

1. The earliest musical sketches for *Der fliegende Holländer* date from May–July
1840: see WWV 63.
2. The Wagners lived at 25 rue du Helder (no longer extant) between 15 April
1840 and 29 April 1841; prior to that they lived at 3 rue de la Tonnellerie (now
31 rue du Pont-Neuf).

Although the following letter from Meyerbeer to his secretary Louis Gouin of 15 July 1840 is not, strictly speaking, an eyewitness account, it may none the less serve to lay the foundations for later quotations from Meyerbeer's diaries.

I am enclosing a letter for Monsieur Wagner & would ask you to forward it to him as soon as possible. This young man interests me, he has both talent & enthusiasm, but fortune has not smiled on him: he has written me a long & very touching letter,[1] & it is because of this that I am asking you to ensure that he receives the help contained in the letter subjoined.

Meyerbeer iii.281

Meyerbeer's diaries for the months between October 1839 and December 1840 contain no fewer than thirty-four references to Wagner, whom he introduced to members of the French musical establishment and whose cause he championed in innumerable letters to colleagues. He was instrumental in ensuring that *Rienzi* was accepted for performance in Dresden and that *Der fliegende Holländer* was accepted in Berlin. When Dresden began to drag its heels, Wagner decided that the time had come for him to return to Germany and prosecute his cause in person.

1. SB i.392–7.

II (1842–49)

1842   12 *April* Wagner and Minna arrive in Dresden
June–July He takes her on holiday to Teplitz, returning
on 18 July with two prose drafts of *Tannhäuser* (at this
date still called *Der Venusberg*)
20 *October Rienzi* receives its triumphant first
performance at the Dresden Court Opera under the local
Kapellmeister, Carl Gottlieb Reißiger

> Act for inspection of asylums in Great Britain
> Mallarmé, Massenet and Sullivan born
> Mendelssohn, 'Scottish' Symphony
> Verdi, *Nabucco*
> Glinka, *Ruslan and Lyudmila*
> Lortzing, *Der Wildschütz*

1843   2 *January Der fliegende Holländer* premièred
Wagner borrows 1,000 thalers from Wilhelmine Schröder-
Devrient
His 'Autobiographical Sketch' is published in Laube's
Zeitung für die elegante Welt, 1 and 8 February
1 *February* Appointed Kapellmeister to the Royal Court
of Saxony
5 *March* Conducts new production of Gluck's *Armide* and
gains reputation as a Gluckiste
Writes 'biblical scene' *Das Liebesmahl der Apostel*, which
receives its first performance in Dresden's Frauenkirche
on 6 July
Spends summer vacation at Teplitz, where he later claims
that his reading of Jacob Grimm's *Teutonic Mythology*
'opened up a whole new world' (ML 260)
Between now and 13 April 1845 works intermittently on
the score of *Tannhäuser*

1 October Moves to larger apartment at 6 Ostra-Allee and begins to assemble library of classical and medieval works

Leipzig Conservatory opens under Mendelssohn
Grieg born
Donizetti, *Don Pasquale*
Kierkegaard, *Either–Or*
Feuerbach, *Principles of the Philosophy of the Future*
Dickens, *A Christmas Carol*

1844   Conducts Berlin première of *Der fliegende Holländer* on 7 January and Hamburg première of *Rienzi* on 21 March, but neither production is well received and Wagner's hopes of European recognition are blighted
25 June He concludes a deal with the local publisher, C. F. Meser, but falls further into debt as a result of lack of sales. At his suggestion, Spontini is invited to Dresden to superintend a production of *La vestale*
Also at Wagner's instigation, Weber's remains are brought back to Dresden from London on 14 December. On the 15th Wagner delivers an oration at the graveside

Nietzsche born
Verdi, *Ernani*
Heine, *Deutschland: Ein Wintermärchen*

1845   *13 April* Completes full score of *Tannhäuser*
Spends summer vacation at Marienbad, where he completes prose drafts of *Die Meistersinger von Nürnberg* (16 July) and *Lohengrin* (3 August)
19 October Tannhäuser premièred under Wagner
17 November Reads libretto of *Lohengrin* to Dresden Engelklub

The future King Ludwig II of Bavaria is born
Engels, *The Condition of the Working Classes in England*

1846   *2 March* Submits plans for reform of Court Orchestra
5 April In face of considerable opposition, conducts Beethoven's Ninth Symphony at annual Palm Sunday concert

Spends two months (15 May–?20 July) at Groß-Graupe,
working on the score of *Lohengrin*
His finances take a sudden and dramatic turn for the worse
when Schröder-Devrient demands repayment of the
money owed her. Wagner is granted a loan of 5,000 thalers
from the Theatre Pension Fund at 5 per cent interest. Under
the terms of the agreement, he is required to take out a
life-insurance policy at a premium of 5 per cent of the
capital. As a result, he now has to pay 300 thalers a year
to cover the interest and insurance – this out of an annual
salary of 1,500 thalers and even before he has started to
pay off his outstanding debts. A request for a loan of
1,200 thalers is turned down by Meyerbeer on 26
November
Wagner interrupts work on *Lohengrin* to write prose
sketch for a drama (opera?) on the life of Frederick
Barbarossa and to revise Gluck's *Iphigénie en Aulide*

> German academics meet at Frankfurt in May to discuss
> reunification
> Lortzing, *Der Waffenschmied*
> Berlioz, *La damnation de Faust*

1847   24 *February* Wagner's adaptation of *Iphigénie en Aulide*
is unveiled
28 *March* Repeat performance of Beethoven's Ninth
Symphony
Moves to cheaper rooms in Marcolini Palace
Reads Gibbon, Aeschylus and Hegel
24 *October* Conducts Berlin première of *Rienzi*

> Gold is discovered in California, leading to first Gold Rush
> Edison and Alexander Graham Bell born
> Mendelssohn dies (38)
> Verdi, *Macbeth* and *I masnadieri*
> Flotow, *Martha*

1848   9 *January* Wagner's mother dies
Between 22 January and 8 March he conducts three
orchestral concerts featuring works by Beethoven,
Cherubini, Gluck, Haydn, Mendelssohn, Mozart and

Palestrina (the *Stabat mater* in his own arrangement)
Insurrection in Sicily, Paris (overthrow of Louis-Philippe),
Vienna (Metternich forced to flee), Dresden, Berlin and
Frankfurt. In Dresden the populace is placated by empty
promises of reform on the part of Friedrich August II
28 April Full score of *Lohengrin* completed
11 May Submits 'Plan for the Organization of a German
National Theatre for the Kingdom of Saxony'
18 May German National Assembly meets at Frankfurt
14 June Wagner delivers address to the republican
Vaterlandsverein, 'How do Republican Aspirations Stand
in Relation to the Monarchy?'
Between 9 and 22 July visits Vienna in the hope of finding
support for his reformist plans
22 September Excerpts from Act I of *Lohengrin*
performed at concert to mark tercentenary of Dresden
Orchestra
4 October Completes *Die Nibelungensage (Mythus)*
15 October Article 'Germany and her Princes' appears
anonymously in Röckel's seditious *Volksblätter*
Prose draft of *Siegfried's Tod* completed on 20 October,
verse draft on 28 November

Pre-Raphaelite Brotherhood founded
Marx and Engels issue *Communist Manifesto*

1849   Works on scenario for five-act opera(?) *Jesus of Nazareth*
and writes speculative essay, *The Wibelungs*, on links
between Barbarossa, the Nibelung hoard and the Grail
10 February Anarchistic essay, 'Man and Existing Society',
possibly by Wagner, appears in Röckel's *Volksblätter*
16 February Liszt conducts performance of *Tannhäuser* in
Weimar, only the second staging outside Dresden
March Wagner is introduced to the Russian anarchist
Mikhail Bakunin
1 April Conducts Beethoven's Ninth Symphony at Palm
Sunday concert
Rhapsodical essay, 'Revolution', possibly by Wagner,
appears in *Volksblätter*, 8 April

30 April Friedrich August II rescinds constitution.
Following rumours that the Saxon government is calling
in Prussian troops, Dresden's population rises up. The king
and his ministers flee the city at dawn on 4 May and a
provisional government is set up. Fighting continues over
the next four days. On the 7th Wagner takes his wife to
Chemnitz and returns on the 8th to find the fighting almost
over. He flees the city with Bakunin and another of the
revolutionary leaders, Otto Heubner, but becomes
separated from them in Freiburg and thus escapes arrest

MARIE SCHMOLE (1832–?)

Marie Schmole was the daughter of the Dresden
costume designer Ferdinand Heine (1798–1872). She
was another of the eyewitnesses tracked down by Mary
Burrell and although doubts must surround the accuracy of her account, its bare outlines are sufficiently
confirmed by other reminiscences of the period to justify
its inclusion here, while its Romantic image of the
starving artist contributes to the picture of Wagner that
he and his friends were keen to promulgate.

Although I was only ten at the time, I clearly remember the first
occasion on which Wagner and his wife visited my parents. It was
in the summer of 1842. On coming home from school and looking
for my parents in the garden, I found them with a gentleman with
a refined-looking face and, what particularly impressed me, *bright
kid gloves*. Later, however, I noticed that they had often been
washed and were worn on the inside. Although living in extremely
straitened circumstances, he always set great store by his elegant,
neat appearance. The Wagners had known want and privations of
every kind and in full measure during their stay in Paris. Richard
would often slip out in the evening with a rolled up sheaf of music
and attempt to realize the value of what he had tossed off in haste.

When they lived in Meudon, they had sometimes passed by
gardens in the fading light and knocked down nuts from the trees
hanging over the walls, so hungry were they.

His wife, who was then very beautiful, conquered my heart, as
he did, with her friendly ways. When I was introduced to them, he
greeted me as Mariechen, who had survived several serious illnesses
while he was still in Paris. From then on, the Wagners came several
times a week to have supper with us in the garden, where Richard
particularly liked a large vine. Only later did I understand why his
gaze lingered so fondly over the simple dishes that decked the
table. I once heard Minna Wagner telling my mother that on many

days this was their first proper meal since breakfast. As we stood in front of the waiting fare, he would frequently say to his wife: 'Let's gorge ourselves, Minel.'

His greatest pleasure, as a prelude to the first course of cold meat, was new potatoes in their skins with herrings in a spicy sauce – 'picked herrings' he called it. On one occasion my mama jokingly remarked that he was eating too much butter and so the following evening he handed her a large knob of butter. On days like that he was as innocent and as happy as any child. As autumn approached, I often heard lively discussions about the start of rehearsals for *Rienzi*. There were times when Schröder-Devrient[1] reduced him to utter despair. As with almost all her new roles, she was often quite rude in rehearsal and incapable of thinking herself into the part. At one stage rehearsal, this brilliant but temperamental artist simply exploded. Wagner had repeatedly raised objections during a duet between Adriano (Schröder-Devrient) and Irene (Henriette Wüst):[2] Devrient had not sung it as he wanted. Whereupon she hurled the music at his feet, shouting: 'Let him sing this filth himself.' The poor man was deeply shocked and afraid of what might happen at the performance. It is no secret how wonderfully Devrient made up for her outburst and how magnificently she acted and sang Adriano.

Often Fischer, too,[3] took his meals with us and told us about the enthusiasm of the chorus, with whom he had already been rehearsing for some time. Later, whenever he spoke of the possible length of the opera, he would run his hands through his hair in comic despair, uttering many a 'hm, hm', but Richard was used to the Paris Opéra and thought nothing of spending five hours in the theatre. On the day of the first performance (20 October 1842), the Wagners had lunch with my parents, but of course they ate very little. Frau Minna kept pressing her hands to her heart and anxiously sighing, while Richard fidgeted on his chair, as he always

1. Now nearing the end of her career, Wilhelmine Schröder-Devrient (1804–60) was the leading dramatic soprano of her day. Wagner had first heard her as Bellini's Romeo a decade earlier. She went on to create the parts of Senta (1843) and Venus (1845).
2. Henriette Wüst (1816–92) remained a member of the Dresden ensemble until 1858.
3. Wilhelm Fischer (1789–1859) was the chorus master at the Dresden Court Theatre.

did when ill at ease, or he would jump up, run around the room and every five minutes take out his watch. Between four and five he could stand it no longer – neither could my father. The two men decided on a walk. It was not long, of course, before they found themselves near the theatre. Around five o'clock the square in front of the building began to come to life. Richard stood to one side, counting: 'Look, Ferdinand, there are three people over there – do you think they're going to the theatre? They are! And here come some more!' And so it went on, as the audience came pouring into the square from all sides. 'Heinemännel, I think it's going to be a full house! Don't you agree?' Finally the two friends could take no more. They went into the theatre and up on to the stage, but Richard could not stand it there for long. Just before the opera started, he slipped into a stalls box, but remained at the back. As the applause grew, so did his courage, but at the same time he became aware of the excessive profusion of riches with which his opera was filled. During the performance my father tracked Richard down to the dark corner of his box, and the longer the opera lasted, the more restless the composer became. He fidgeted on his chair, calling himself all manner of names: 'Such a blockhead! No, what an ass! No, what nonsense!' These were the honorary titles that he kept muttering to himself. His neighbours had no idea who their fidgety companion was – he had been called out in front of the curtain after the first act, but, in spite of the violence with which my father had propelled him on stage from the wings, the audience had seen only the tip of his nose, and so they now stared at him disapprovingly. Fearing further outbursts, my father dragged him out into the corridor. 'How stupid can you get? I could have written ten operas with all these tunes!' As the clock over the stage curtain moved towards ten, Wagner could bear it no longer. He clambered up the steps and stopped the clock, 'so that people at least won't see how late it is'. Even so, it is a well-known fact that, apart from one elderly gentleman in the stalls, *not a single spectator* left the theatre before the end of the opera. – And so Wagner had got what he wanted. His opera had been performed for the first time with a first-rate cast, with splendid scenery and costumes and on one of our leading stages. He had taken his first step towards his subsequent fame.

Burrell 1953: 165–8

ALFRED VON MEISSNER (1822–85)

Meißner was actively involved in the uprisings of
1848–9 before turning his hand to literature. He moved
to Dresden from Prague in 1845 and was introduced to
Wagner shortly afterwards.

Slightly less than average height and somewhat on the small side,
with staring eyes, pinched mouth and curved nose, a strikingly
broad and powerfully developed forehead and protruding chin, he
had a distinctly professorial air, not least because in an age when
men wore beards he was always completely clean-shaven. But early
struggles had left him unusually irritable, and there was already
something excitable, testy and venomous about him. *Tannhäuser*
had recently seen the light of day. The libretto had been praised
and the staging had been unusually brilliant, but the musical aspect
was found to be 'unsatisfactory'. Audiences missed any real sense
of character and the power of natural genius: it was all said to be
very artificial and tedious.

On our very first walk together we spoke at length, but exclusively about politics. Richard Wagner considered the current
political situation ripe for a total overhaul and looked forward to
the radical changes that were soon to take place as something
utterly inevitable. This transformation would come about with
little effort, for national and social institutions were only outwardly
intact. I remember his words exactly: a revolution had already
taken place in people's heads, the new Germany was ready and
waiting, like a bronze cast that needed only a hammer blow on its
clay shell in order for it to emerge. Meanwhile, Gutzkow had
joined us. He disagreed, stressing the force of lethargy, the power
of the old and the fear of the new, the masses' habit of serving and
obeying, and the lack of character in the vast majority. He
expressed a hundred reservations in that guarded way of his.

Wagner lost all control and broke off the discussion with a few
well-chosen words.

Meißner 1884: i.169–70

ROBERT SCHUMANN (1810–56)

The Schumanns moved to Dresden in December 1844 but found it difficult to relate to Wagner either socially or artistically.

17 March 1846. Chance encounter with R. Wagner in the Großer Garten. He possesses a tremendous gift of the gab and is full of oppressive ideas; it's impossible to listen to him for any length of time.

Schumann ii.398; see also Konrad 1987

EDUARD HANSLICK (1825–1904)

Hanslick first met Wagner in July 1845, was favourably impressed by *Tannhäuser* when he heard it in 1846 and wrote admiringly on the work in the columns of the *Allgemeine Wiener Musikzeitung*. But his classical training and love of formal beauty made him less responsive to Wagner's later works, which he criticized honestly and eloquently from his Chair in Aesthetics at the University of Vienna. His reputation has suffered unfairly at the hands of writers such as Newman, whose philistine attacks on him were pursued with the zeal of a private vendetta. Given Wagner's own wilfully wounding remarks on Hanslick, the latter's memoirs are notable for their self-deprecating and dignified tone. The following passage recounts the events of 3–4 September 1846.

After lunch Schumann invited me to walk with him and his family to the Großer Garten. Clara went on ahead with the eldest girl, Schumann led the other by the hand and I took charge of the third, Julie, an exceptionally pretty child, whom Schumann jokingly called my bride. We sat down for coffee at a large table beneath shady trees and I even found the notorious Saxon coffee excellent because I drank it at Schumann's side. I was now able to observe him in his role as a father, affectionate and contented. Here, too, he spoke very little, but his friendly, almost childlike eyes and his

smiling lips, pursed as though to whistle, seemed to betray a
touching eloquence all of their own. When I mentioned that I
was looking forward to seeing *Tannhäuser* the following evening,
he offered, to my great delight, to let me borrow for half a day
the autograph score that had just appeared.[1] Did he have much
contact with Wagner, I wondered. 'No,' retorted Schumann; 'for
me, Wagner is impossible; there's no doubt that he's an intelligent person, but he never stops talking. You can't talk *all* the
time.'

Early the next morning I hurried off to the Brühl Terrace, the
heavy score of *Tannhäuser* under my arm, breakfasting there and
skimming through the score with tremendous enthusiasm. Towards
midday I called on Wagner. He received me with great friendliness
and asked me to sit on the sofa for a while, as he had to audition
a young tenor called Brandes, a member of the far-flung family of
that name.[2] The latter suggested a whole series of operas from
which he wanted to audition, but Wagner did not have a single
vocal score to hand. Finally he thought that he would be able to
manage Tamino's aria from *Die Zauberflöte*. And of course he was
able to play it, albeit with a strikingly unpractised technique. The
tenor, it seemed, found favour and duly took his leave. Wagner
then got round to talking about all manner of things concerning
music and musicians in Dresden, including Schumann. 'On a superficial level we're on excellent terms; but you can't converse with
Schumann: he's an impossible person, he never says anything. I
called on him soon after my arrival from Paris and told him all
manner of interesting things about the Paris Opéra, about concerts
and composers – but Schumann just looked at me without moving
a muscle or stared straight ahead and said nothing. So I got up
and left. An impossible person.'

I had been much looking forward to the evening, and it proved
an unforgettable experience: *Tannhäuser* was given in the beautiful

---

1. One hundred copies of the full score of *Tannhäuser* were run off by a
lithographic process involving the gradual destruction of the specially prepared
paper on which Wagner wrote out the score by hand; see ML 300, Hopkinson
1973: 6 and WWV 70.
2. Wilhelm Brandes (1825–71), who began his career at the Vienna Court Opera
in 1847 and later assumed leading tenor roles in operas by Meyerbeer, Weber and
Wagner.

Dresden Court Theatre (subsequently burnt down), with Wagner conducting, his niece, Johanna Wagner,[1] as Elisabeth, Tichatschek[2] as Tannhäuser, Mitterwurzer[3] (the father of the famous actor) as Wolfram and Dettmer[4] as the Landgrave. The opera made a real impression on me and in places left me quite drunk. Schumann and his wife sat next to me in the stalls, but remained extremely quiet.

Hanslick 1894: i.69–71; see also Schumann iii/1.290, Newman 1931: 30–33 and Deas 1940

GUSTAV ADOLPH KIETZ (1824–1908)

The sculptor Gustav Adolph Kietz was the brother of Ernst Benedikt Kietz and got to know the Wagners in 1842. He was in regular contact with them during the 1840s and again for a time in the 1870s. Here he describes his meetings with them in the mid-1840s.

What an infinite amount I owe this dear man in terms of his teachings and the intellectual insights imparted both at home and on our walks together.

Wagner also had a choice library of valuable works in luxury bindings by which he set great store. Even so, he was happy for me to take his treasures back with me to my lonely bachelor's apartment, once he had initiated me into their spirit.

It was through him that I got to know Norse mythology, Wolfram von Eschenbach's *Parzival*, the old German heroic legends and other works besides. But he also talked a lot about German fairy tales. Whenever I could not follow him and had to ask, I

1. Johanna Wagner (1826–94) was the adopted daughter of Wagner's brother Albert (1799–1874) and, therefore, the composer's step-niece. After a distinguished career as a soprano, she took up acting in the 1860s, before returning to singing in the 1870s and creating the roles of Schwertleite and First Norn.
2. Joseph Tichatschek (1807–86) was a member of the Dresden Court Opera ensemble from 1838 to 1872; he created the roles of Rienzi and Tannhäuser.
3. Anton Mitterwurzer (1818–76) was the first Wolfram and Kurwenal (1865). His son was the famous Viennese actor Friedrich Mitterwurzer (1844–97).
4. Wilhelm Georg Dettmer (1808–76) was a member of the Dresden company from 1842 to 1849. He created the roles of Steffano Colonna and the Landgrave.

found all the instruction I could wish for, which he was kind
enough to provide.

At this point I should like to mention a comical incident that
took place in the Wagners' apartment in the Töpfergasse, where
they had moved from the Waisenhausstraße.[1]

One lunchtime I arrived to find him and his wife still in a state
of helpless mirth at a dubious pleasure they enjoyed almost every
lunchtime in this apartment when the local military band passed
beneath their windows. In order to give me a better impression
of the musical delights provided by the Riflemen's Battalion
as it passed the house, Frau Minna took up her position and
imitated the sound of the clarinets, while Wagner, laughing
all the while, accompanied her on the piano. She was such an
excellent mimic, her performance so virtuosic and the effect
so comical that at the end we all collapsed in a heap of laughter. On such occasions they were both as happy as sandboys.
[. . .]

For the winter of 1845/6 it was Wagner's keenest wish to introduce both his musicians and local audiences to the wealth of
wondrous beauties contained in Beethoven's Ninth Symphony. And
since it was his responsibility to organize the symphony to be
performed at the 1846 Palm Sunday concert, the income from
which would go to the pension fund for the members of the Royal
Orchestra, he suggested a performance of this wonderful work,
not for a moment suspecting the hornets' nest that he was stirring
up with his suggestion.

The members of the orchestra were reluctant to agree to his
choice as they were worried that it would result in reduced receipts
for their pension fund at a time when an increase was urgently
needed. They resolved to take their objections to the king himself[2]
in order to prevent the performance from going ahead, not least
because eight years previously they had performed the work under

---

1. After briefly staying in rented accommodation at 7 Töpfergasse, the Wagners
took rooms at 5 Waisenhausstraße at the end of July 1842; by late November
they were at 9 Marienstraße, where they remained until 1 November 1843,
when they moved to 6 Ostra-Allee.
2. King Friedrich August II (1797–1854) ascended the Saxon throne in 1836.
A distinguished botanist and landscape painter, he was Wagner's ultimate
superior.

Reißiger[1] in the palace in the Großer Garten and it had proved a complete fiasco. – Following this performance, this most glorious work had been declared 'carnival music sprung from the brain of a madman'.

Since Wagner would not be worn down but continued to insist on his resolve, a letter of protest, signed by Reißiger as well as by the two leaders and the members of the orchestra, was drawn up and submitted to the general administrator, Herr von Lüttichau,[2] with the most humble request that he add his own signature and pass on the letter to the king. But the king rejected the petition, as he had unqualified trust in Wagner's suggestions. Wagner fell out completely with the orchestral managers, and although he could not prevent them from filling the city with their tales of impending disaster, he made up his mind to prepare the audience by whetting their appetites and adding to their sense of expectancy so that increased attendance might guarantee a box-office success that was otherwise thought to be in danger. It was in a mood of almost religious reverence that Wagner set about restudying the Ninth Symphony, the full score of which he had sat up all night copying out while still a young man.

I still remember the tensions that reigned in the Wagner household each time that I lunched there. It was with the greatest agitation that he would tell me about the various obstacles that had been placed in his way with the obvious aim of putting a spoke in his wheel. The papers at that time, led by the widely read *Dresdner Anzeiger*, were full of the most mean-spirited and disparaging remarks about Wagner. But it was all to no avail. Undaunted, he went about his business, advancing step by step. His most embittered and oft-repeated complaint was directed at his leader, Karl Lipinsky,[3] whom he none the less valued very highly

1. Carl Gottlieb Reißiger (1798–1859) succeeded Weber as director of the Dresden Court Opera in 1826 and built up the company until it was generally acknowledged as the best in Germany. In *Mein Leben*, Wagner claims that his colleague was lazy, philistine and anti-progressive, but contemporary evidence does not bear this out.
2. A former forestry commissioner, August von Lüttichau (1786–1863) was intendant of the Dresden Court Theatre from 1824 until shortly before his death.
3. The Polish violinist Karol Józef Lipiński (1790–1861) toured extensively as a soloist before settling in Dresden in 1839.

as man and artist and who was widely respected in the Royal
Orchestra as an expert on Beethoven.

What infinite pains Wagner took in his attempts to explain the
work to his recalcitrant musicians and to do so, moreover, right
down to the very last nuance. He sang aloud the individual passages, took the wind section home with him and made them repeat
all the passages they did not understand until it was clear to them
what these notes were intended to say and express. And what a
pleasure it then gave him to return home one lunchtime, completely
exhausted, and say: 'Just imagine, Lipinsky was so pleased that he
kept on nodding his approval and finally took me in his arms!'
From this moment onwards the members of the orchestra willingly
accepted his corrections and ideas.

Wagner was always so exhausted by the rehearsals and so completely bathed in sweat that he would simply sit at the table with
a black silk cap drawn low over his head.

The performance, like the rehearsals that led up to it, took place
in the Old Opera House on the Zwinger. Under earlier Saxon
kings, the two large halls had been used for great court celebrations
and had such wonderful acoustics that Wagner never tired of
expressing his delight and amazement at them.

Needless to say, I avidly attended all the rehearsals. Before the
start I would wait outside for Wagner, with several of my friends
and fellow students in tow. He was happy to allow us to slip into
the hall behind him, even though admission was strictly forbidden.
From the first rehearsal onwards, I shall never forget my feelings
on observing Wagner take his place on the podium, close the great
score that lay open on his desk, place it beneath his chair and
begin to conduct and rehearse this vast, unfathomable work from
memory. And what unbelievable obstacles did he not encounter!
All the opposition and mistrust that had been harboured against
his abilities from the outset and that he had turned to trust and
enthusiastic admiration only through his energetic persistence
returned with each new correction. These were accepted only with
the greatest reluctance and, as before, he was once again treated
by his players as an amateur. How often we heard the gentlemen
exclaiming indignantly each time he broke off at the early
rehearsals: 'But we've got a D here, not a D flat.' To which Wagner
would reply calmly and with utter conviction: 'Then please correct

it, it's wrong, it must be D flat.' The players had no choice but to
obey him, albeit with reluctance. He paid particular attention to the
woodwind. The violinist Hüllweck, who was the son-in-law of
the then celebrated oboist Friedrich Kummer, later told me that
his father-in-law had admitted to him that at each of Wagner's
corrections he had whispered furiously to his neighbour: 'If only
the man knew what he was doing!' Only gradually, in the course
of the rehearsals, did it become clear to him what in fact was
involved here.

In order to strengthen the chorus, Wagner additionally drew on
the Dreyßig Academy and on singers from the Kreuzschule and
Seminary. There were around 300 singers all told, whom he was
able, in his unique way, to inspire to a pitch of real ecstasy. After
repeatedly breaking off and starting again, he finally succeeded in
making it clear to them that the passage 'Seid umschlungen, Milli-
onen' and, above all, 'Brüder, überm Sternenzelt muß ein lieber
Vater wohnen' should not be sung in any ordinary way but must
be hurled forth in utmost rapture. Wagner did not always find
willing acquiescence; but when, after untiring efforts, he finally
sang the passage to them with a sense of ecstatic joy that transported them all to a higher plane and continued to do so until his
own voice, previously audible above the others, could no longer
be heard, the resultant effect was so tremendous that it will forever
remain indelibly etched on the minds of all who experienced it.

How many times did Wagner's friend, that splendid baritone
Anton Mitterwurzer, not have to repeat the passage 'Freunde, nicht
diese Töne!'! He could not do it the way Wagner wanted and we
were startled to hear Wagner suddenly shout at him in a fit of ill
temper: 'That's not right! If you can't do it any better, forget it!'
Mitterwurzer said nothing but looked him in the eye – and then
sang this recitative with such enthralling magic as he can rarely
have displayed before.

In our dark corner of the gallery we could scarcely contain our
excitement at all that we heard, so powerfully did it affect us. The
days that we spent in Rietschel's studio following the final rehearsal
were given over not to our work but to repeating all we had heard.
I can still see our assistant Mühlhausen, who was occupied at this
time helping us to assemble the plaster cast of Rietschel's *Piety* in
the studio, striking his hands together in total amazement at our

odd behaviour and shaking his head in incredulity, saying, 'No, I don't believe it, I just don't believe it!', when Schilling, the creator of the Niederwald monument,[1] gave the cue for the timpani passage in the Scherzo and we all joined in. He clearly thought we had all taken leave of our senses. But it was not only young artists like ourselves who, in the frenzy of our enthusiasm, felt ourselves transported to what seemed a new world: the enthusiasm of the musicians in the packed hall, many of whom had travelled long distances to be there, grew from movement to movement. And when Niels Gade called on Wagner and assured him that he would willingly have paid twice over simply to hear the recitative on the basses once again,[2] I knew that we young people were quite right to feel so enthusiastic.

What splendid acoustics the wonderful old hall turned out to have! The very first notes of the symphony created the impression of music of the spheres descending from another, higher world, so ethereal and yet so clear, and so each movement gave way to the next. No one who lived to witness these hours will ever forget them. And to think that it is rumoured that Wagner, during the revolution, tossed a lighted torch into this hall, in which his ultimate dream had come true! What nonsense!

The performance took place on Palm Sunday before a packed house and against a background of widespread interest on the part of the general public. In spite of the significant expenses for the chorus, the income for the pension fund far exceeded anything previously known. It is sad and shaming that even on this occasion the most venomous baseness made itself felt, a baseness that grew in proportion to the enthusiasm felt for this wonderful work and its conductor. After all, it was Richard Wagner on the conductor's podium. For his enemies, it was all in a day's work to unleash against him all that envy and malice could dictate. [. . .]

As the Revolution drew ever closer, lunch with the Wagners took on a wholly new aspect. His delightful sense of humour, which

1. Johannes Schilling (1828–1910) is best remembered for his statue of Germania near Rüdesheim. Like Kietz, he was a pupil of Ernst Rietschel (1804–61), who was professor of sculpture in Dresden from 1832 until his death.
2. This anecdote is lifted, word for word, from GS ii.55–6; PW vii.246. It is not independently confirmed. Indeed, there is some suspicion that here and elsewhere Kietz used Wagner's published reminiscences in fashioning his own narrative.

had always provided the finest seasoning to every meal, appeared to have deserted him. There were often arguments between him and his wife as a result of his decisive actions and his arguments with his superior. On one occasion he burst out: 'It's terrible! While others have their adversaries only outside their own homes, I have my worst enemy sitting at my own table!' To which Frau Minna retorted: 'Oh, you men think you're so clever, but how foolishly you act!' The poor woman saw the threat to her husband's livelihood drawing ever closer and was afraid, both for his sake and her own, that they would revert to their sad situation in Paris, whereas Wagner was ruthless whenever his ideals and the welfare of his artists were at stake. She had *absolutely no inkling* of his greatness of intellect, which forged ahead along unsuspected pathways to ever new creations, yearning to escape the unworthy conditions into which he had gradually been driven.

Whenever he saw his wife's fear and concern after such outbursts, he would feel sorry for her and redouble the kindness towards her that was so much a part of his nature.

Kietz 1907: 20–21, 45–55 and 86–7; see also ML 328–33 and Kitzler 1904: 8

KARL GUTZKOW (1811–78)

A political journalist, Gutzkow became a leading light of the Young German movement with his novel *Wally die Zweiflerin*, a work that earned him a month's imprisonment for bringing the Christian religion into disrepute. Further novels and politically tendentious plays followed, culminating in *Zopf und Schwert* (1844) and *Uriel Acosta* (1846), both of which were premièred in Dresden, where Gutzkow held the post of literary adviser to the Court Theatre between 1845 and 1848. From the outset Wagner resented his interference in the running of the theatre. Writing from the vantage point of the mid-1870s, Gutzkow here describes the tensions that existed between Wagner, Reißiger and Lüttichau.

One thing that one has to admire about Reißiger is that it was he who, as Weber's successor and admirer and as a highly educated, multifaceted, strict theoretician and church composer, with a

knowledge of Gluck, Mozart, Haydn and Beethoven that was
second to none, had to bear the initial brunt of what we later
learnt to call the 'music of the future', with all its manifold preten-
sions. The chaos of ideas that is currently running up that makeshift
theatre at Bayreuth in an attempt to render more palatable the
manuals of Norse mythology (manuals that are now awash in
music) struck this decent, valiant and invariably courteous man
with the force of a volcanic eruption. In the innermost depths of
his being he hated what he least wanted to appear to hate. For he
had no wish to seem to be jealous. He did not want to show that,
for him, there was no comparison between his latest opera, *Der
Schiffbruch der Medusa*, and *Tannhäuser*. 'I admire the man, I
appreciate his talent, I really do,' he would often exclaim at meetings, singling out the most beautiful passages and the artistry
of many a Wagnerian structure. 'But you can't keep banging
your head against a brick wall.' Reißiger was the first of the
martyrs to be cast aside by the high-spirited adherents of the new
school.

One day angry Achilles returned from his ships in the Friedrichstadt[1] and attended one of our advisory sessions. What may have
induced him to come I do not know, but I shall never forget the
occasion. As a general rule, the intendant's mind was a tabula rasa
on the question of our various artistic duties. What had been
agreed the previous week was forgotten by the next. He would
then take out a diary in an attempt to gain his bearings. He had
jotted down the names of Gluck, Shakespeare and Bauernfeld and
made a careful note of what the producers and conductors had
thought possible and what they had promised to put on between
Easter and Whitsuntide, between Whitsuntide and Ascension and
between Ascension and the First Sunday in Advent. This he called
'mapping out the land'. It was like using brightly coloured little
flags to mark out the course of a railway line. When he presented
us with the results of all these diagrams, we felt clouds of opium
envelop us, fondly dreaming that we had actually achieved a result,
while the *Lyratöne* poet and former editor of the *Abend-Zeitung*,

---

1. In April 1847 the Wagners moved to cheaper rooms in the Marcolini Palace
in the Friedrichstadt district of Dresden.

Theodor Hell,[1] quietly nodded off, invariably waking up with the words 'Yes, Your Excellency'. It was at one of these meetings, when the diary was once again covered with the most beguiling visions, that Richard Wagner was to express his opinion on the possibility of transcribing a role in an opera by – well, at all events by someone other than himself. The feeling that we were all one big happy family again encouraged the intendant to allow the poet–composer to preface his remarks with a summary of all the main ideas of his as yet unpublished essay *Opera and Drama*. We listened in silence. Possessed of a Saxon's gift of the gab, Wagner was soon in full flight. 'So do you think that Frau Kriete . . .', the intendant finally broke in with the merest hint of impatience, as Wagner, warming to his theme, began to define the difference between rhythm and melody. 'But just as Gluck went back to the purer forms of antiquity . . .', Wagner continued, unperturbed. 'Do you think that Frau Kriete . . .', his superior asked somewhat more insistently. 'Please! Please!' begged his older colleague in an undertone, but the creator of *Tannhäuser*, speaking by now with the tongues of angels, would not be put off his stride, conscious as he was of already approaching the more recent period and Frau Kriete's vocal register. 'But the transcription,' the intendant finally exclaimed, looking at the clock, 'would it be possible for Frau Kriete . . .'. 'It was very much in his handling of the human voice that Gluck had the advantage over the Piccinnists.' 'But, Christ Almighty, all we want to know is whether Frau Kriete can sing the part,' screamed the intendant, forcefully interrupting a complex argument and a wealth of ideas that had driven him to distraction. This first reappearance of the 'second conductor' at one of our directorial discussions proved to have no sequel. To my dispassionate eye, Wagner seemed to have entered into the most curious psychological match, a sort of marriage of convenience between intellect and imagination.

I should add that the idol of all the uncertainties of our age was by no means ill-disposed to me. Already widely acclaimed at this

---

1. Theodor Hell was the pen name of Theodor Winkler (1775–1856), who edited the Dresden *Abend-Zeitung* from 1817 to 1843, providing Wagner with a source of income during his years in Paris by publishing many of his articles. From 1841 he was deputy director of the Dresden Court Theatre. In 1821 he had published a volume of poetry under the title *Lyratöne*.

time, he came to see me one day and invited me to follow him
down the path that he himself had taken, saying that the second
and fourth acts of my play, *Uriel Acosta*,[1] showed my ability to do
so. Here, he went on, I had certainly not questioned the notion of
combining opera and drama. I thanked him, while continuing to
doubt the possibility of a lasting union between these two different
branches of art; in art, every hybrid form, I said, went against the
grain with me. Opera must remain opera, drama drama. The latter,
after all, had to appeal to the intellect and judgement, while at the
same time stirring the heart in a very specific and explicit manner;
in this it differed from music, which was only ever concerned with
universalities and uncertainties and which was vague and unclear,
even though both forms, I admitted, must appeal to the imagination. If I had then had any inkling of *Götterdämmerung* and *Das
Rheingold*, of *Der Ring des Nibelungen* and the Bayreuth Theatre,
I would have said that to appeal only to the imagination is to
appeal merely to the senses and renders a nation effeminate. My
experience of music was far from superficial, as the excellent piano
playing of my wife – a pupil of Aloys Schmitt – had kept me in
daily touch with the world of music, and so I often said quite
openly, if not to Wagner, at least to others, that the *Tannhäuser*
Overture seemed to me like a wearisome and often tasteless canon;
I compared it to that Shakespearean canon that could 'hale souls
out of men's bodies';[2] the perpetual sextuplets were nerve-jangling.
With the exception of its charming polonaise, *Tannhäuser* struck
me as tedious. But I remember once asking the composer himself
on the Dippoldiswalder Platz: 'Why didn't you include Klingsohr
in your Wartburg contest? Surely he's part of the story.[3] You'd
have a powerful bass role à la Bertram in *Robert le diable* and, in
terms of the plot, there'd be a demonic representative to work on
Tannhäuser in dramatic form. It really isn't dramatic for everything
to come from Tannhäuser alone and from his reminiscences.' Fol-

1. First performed in Dresden in December 1846, Gutzkow's tragedy deals with
the clash between a free-thinking individual and the intolerance and bigotry of
orthodox religion – in this case, Judaism; see also Bauer 1998: 83–5.
2. *Much Ado about Nothing*, ii.3: 'Is it not strange that sheeps' guts should hale
souls out of men's bodies?'
3. The black magician, Clingesor/Klingsohr, figures in two of Wagner's sources,
the late thirteenth-century *Wartburgkrieg* and Hoffmann's *Der Kampf der
Sänger*.

lowing this openness on my part, no further meeting of minds took place between us. But at every performance of a Wagner opera that I attended (I was later present at the first performance of *Lohengrin* in Weimar) I heard the most outrageously premeditated applause, the first manifestation of the claque that has now been organized throughout the whole of Germany and for which Wagner, Liszt and others will one day have to answer before the tribunal of art. Behind me in the audience, a German–Russian family literally went wild in their demonstrative fanaticism, making a quite unbelievable contribution to the cult of Wagner and setting the tone for this infatuation in Dresden. Women from the upper echelons of society, those who are sensual by nature and men of an effeminate stamp made it their special concern to cultivate Wagner's music in a similar way elsewhere.

Gutzkow 1875: 316–20

EDUARD DEVRIENT (1801–77)

> Eduard Devrient began his professional career as a singer, taking the part of Christ in Mendelssohn's revival of the *St Matthew Passion* in 1829 and four years later singing the title role in the first performance of Marschner's *Hans Heiling*, for which he also wrote the libretto. Following the loss of his singing voice, he turned to acting and writing. He became a member of the Dresden Court Theatre in 1844 and although he resigned as a producer in 1846, he continued to act with the company until 1852, when he moved to Karlsruhe to run the Ducal Theatre. Here he remained until 1870, his path once again crossing Wagner's when the latter hoped to have *Tristan und Isolde* staged in the town. The plan came to nothing, a failure that Wagner paranoically ascribed to Devrient's machinations.

26 August 1846. Spent evening at Hiller's.[1] Argued violently at table with Kapellmeister Wagner, who took the naturalistic line,

1. The conductor, composer and teacher Ferdinand Hiller (1811–85), whose salon was a meeting place for Dresden's intelligentsia.

according to which the mind is only a product of the physical organism.

14 August 1847. Spoke with Kapellmeister Wagner; he's at war with Lüttichau, refuses to accept Gutzkow's interference in the Opera. It's all got rather out of hand. He still has the idea of opening the king's eyes to the state of the theatre. The fool! As if kings were interested in seeing things clearly.

8 March 1848. Concert at the theatre. I spoke with Wagner and heard him utter the first encouraging words about my book.[1] He has read the first volume and says I have a great future ahead of me. He's a good sort, always bursting with hopes for the state of Germany: I have no such hopes.

1 April 1848. Wagner called on me at 5 o'clock, we went for a walk through the Großer Garten. He told me about a new plan for an opera based on the Siegfried legend.

7 April 1848. Met Wagner and Röckel.[2] Went with them to the Terrace. Things have still not hotted up sufficiently for Wagner.

26 April 1848. Met Wagner and Röckel and argued furiously over politics. They see knavery and treachery in everything, whereas it is nothing but incompetence and pitiful petty-mindedness in the face of the age in which we live. At least we finally agreed on this. – Then to the committee. They're still arguing over the electoral lists. Then suggestions were made to get round delays to the money supply as quickly as possible, otherwise the unemployed workers will attack us in our own homes. – Lüttichau's stupid circular[3] has already been denounced in the *Dresdner Journal* and Reißiger

1. *Geschichte der deutschen Schauspielkunst*, a history of the German theatre begun in 1848 and completed in 1874.
2. August Röckel (1814–76) was assistant conductor to Wagner from 1843 to 1848. He edited the short-lived but seditious *Volksblätter* and took an active part in the uprisings of 1848 and 1849 for which he was sentenced to death, commuted to life imprisonment. He was released in 1862 and devoted the remainder of his life to journalism. He, too, ultimately fell out with Wagner, in his case for blowing the gaff on the true nature of Wagner's relationship with Cosima von Bülow.
3. Lüttichau had written to all the members of the Court Theatre, asking them to give Reißiger their completed voting papers for the elections to the Frankfurt Assembly, an invitation that was taken to suggest collusion between the two men.

portrayed as a veritable lickspittle of the party of reaction. If only he hadn't dropped his guard. But this Vaterlandsverein is a veritable Committee of Public Safety.[1] With a brazenness without equal it openly instructs its members not to vote for anyone that it has not indicated itself. It declares itself ready to listen to every denunciation, publishes a regular list of suspects, puts up posters publicly stirring up the soldiers against the officers and violates all feelings of reserve and custom in the most outrageous manner. We shall soon have entire lists of people and things that are banned. – I see no way of overcoming this nonsense except for some wiser counsel to prevail and for both associations to be merged.[2]

19 May 1848. Wagner came with Röckel and read me his scheme for reorganizing the orchestra. He has already been to the ministry with his plan for reorganizing the theatre. What will Lüttichau say and do? We argued over several points such as the partial abandonment of entr'acte music at comedies. I then told Röckel about my objections to his suggestion for arming the people.

1 June 1848. Post-prandial visit from Kapellmeister Wagner; we again argued over politics in a quite barbarous way. He wants to destroy in order to rebuild, I want to transform what already exists in order to create a new world.

19 June 1848. Received letter from Kapellmeister Wagner, he asks me to intercede and ensure that king and court forget his mad manifesto. People misunderstand him completely and are embittered. I replied to his letter.[3]

1. The Vaterlandsverein, of which Wagner and Röckel were members, was a radically republican association and, as such, opposed to the monarchical Deutscher Verein of which Devrient was a member. Established in April 1793, the Committee of Public Safety was effectively the war cabinet of the French Revolution, whose aims it pursued with increasing single-mindedness, eventually becoming synonymous with the Terror itself.
2. Devrient himself led the way by joining the Vaterlandsverein on 13 May 1848.
3. Wagner had delivered an impassioned speech to the Vaterlandsverein on 14 June, arguing that only by destroying 'the demonic concept of money' was it possible to achieve 'the total emancipation of the human race' and calling for a republic to be established under Friedrich August II. (This apparent anomaly in his thinking, whereby a republic should have a king as its ruler, is generally greeted with a pitying smile on the part of Wagnerian writers and held out as an example of his impracticality, but precisely the same idea is central to Kant's

20 June 1848. Spoke with Lüttichau at lunchtime about Wagner, he judged the affair leniently and indulgently and had already sent away a deputation from the orchestra demanding the conductor's dismissal. The king has said nothing about the affair, perhaps he knows nothing.

14 July 1848. I was told of Kapellmeister Wagner's financial problems, of which I had previously been less than fully informed.[1] How can such a dreamer destroy his life like this?

21 July 1848. Received letter from Kapellmeister Wagner in Vienna,[2] asking me to call on his wife, but my visit proved to be in vain. He is throwing himself at my mercy, I am to sort out his life for him, comfort his wife. A wayward hothead who always begins by making things worse for himself and who then, when it is too late, calls on others to help him. What is to be done? [. . .]

23 July 1848. Visit from Kapellmeister Wagner. He showed me how hopelessly bogged down he is in debt: the only solution I can see is for him to declare himself insolvent. He takes his relations with the theatre far too seriously, which only adds to his exasperation. He is very pleased with the political situation in Vienna.

Devrient 1964: i.357–442

Perpetual Peace of 1795, Friedrich Schlegel's *Essay on Republicanism* of 1796 and Julius Fröbel's 1848 pamphlet *The Monarchy and the Sovereignty of the People*.) Wagner's speech, the text of which was published as a special supplement to the *Dresdner Anzeiger* on the 15th, appears to have been a conscious attempt to merge the aims of the Vaterlandsverein with those of the Deutscher Verein, as advocated by Devrient in his diary entry of 26 April 1848. As a result of this speech and the uproar that it caused, a performance of *Rienzi* planned for 17 June was cancelled. Wagner wrote to Lüttichau on the 18th in an attempt to justify his actions; and on the 19th he wrote to Devrient, asking him for his advice.

1. See chronology for 1846; according to an otherwise unsubstantiated claim by Friedrich Pecht (1894: i.293), Wagner's debts when he fled Dresden in May 1849 amounted to more than 20,000 thalers, nearly thirteen times his annual salary.
2. Wagner had obtained leave of absence to spend two weeks in Vienna, ostensibly to recover from a gastric complaint but in reality to gain a professional foothold in the city at a time when his position in Dresden was growing increasingly precarious. He arrived in Vienna on 9 July and was back in Dresden by the 23rd. By now his position was hopelessly compromised and plans to stage *Lohengrin* in Dresden were abandoned.

EDUARD HANSLICK

Hanslick recalls Wagner's visit to Vienna in July 1848.

Richard Wagner came to Vienna for a few days, clearly lured here
by political events. I spent an evening with him and Professor Josef
Fischhof of the Vienna Conservatory in a little café garden by the
Danube. Wagner was all politics: with the victory of the Revolution, he was convinced, would come a total rebirth of art, society
and religion and a new type of theatre and music. He asked who
were the leaders of the democratic movement in Vienna, and Friedrich Uhl took him to one of their meetings. It soon turned out that
he had been wanting to see the democratic member of parliament,
Dr Adolf Fischhof, not Professor Fischhof, who taught the piano
and who was not a little surprised to hear Wagner speak only
about politics, with not a word about music.

Hanslick 1894: i.134–5

FRIEDRICH UHL (1825–1906)

The long-standing editor of *Der Botschafter* and the
Wiener Zeitung, Friedrich Uhl left his own account of
Wagner's visit to Vienna's Democratic Union in July
1848. Originally published in the *Wiener Fremden-Blatt*
on 6 December 1891, it was taken over into his urbane
and self-conscious memoirs of 1908.

Wagner would not take no for an answer but continued to insist
on becoming better acquainted with the democrats on the Danube,
and so one evening I took him to the 'Roman Emperor', a hotel
in the Renngasse, where the Democratic Union was holding one
of its meetings. We took our seats. The president got to his feet,
positioned himself next to a large table and launched into a
muddled speech. He spoke the words 'A repooblic is t'best form
of state' with peculiar clarity, whereupon I looked at Wagner. He
smiled sadly. 'Have you had enough?' I asked. 'Yes,' he answered,
and with that we left. The president of the Democratic Union was
a vinegar seller from Cracow who was completely uneducated and

who learnt by rote the speeches that were written for him by his brother, the spiritual leader of the extremists, who because of his profession – he was a rabbi – did not dare to appear in public. From then on, Wagner and I rarely touched on the subject of politics, although he asked me to write reports on Vienna for the *Dresdner Zeitung*, which he edited with Johannes Minkwitz and Röckel, a request that I was happy to meet.[1] I saw a great deal of him at this time: for hours on end we would walk to and fro on the Stephansplatz, while he developed his ideas and plans for the 'theatre of the future'.

Uhl 1908: 57–8

EDUARD DEVRIENT

12 October 1848. In the evening Kapellmeister Wagner came. I'd invited him in spite of Therese's objections.[2] Although he may now be in ill odour politically speaking, that is no reason to snub him socially. He read us his compilation of the Siegfried legends; it showed great talent. He wants to turn it into an opera, but nothing will come of it, I fear. Nordic myth finds little sympathy, not least because it is unknown; and these rough-hewn giants must be left to the imagination, theatrical reality belittles them and turns them into mere playthings. Also, Wagner always casts his net too wide and works in his modern ideas. He accuses me of not falling in with his plans to revolutionize the theatre. He says that if I'd written something on the subject, the revolution would have long been over. How he would like to misuse me to his own advantage, for the sake of his darling plans!

21 October 1848. Kapellmeister Wagner brought me the draft of an opera, his head is again bursting with big ideas on socialism. Now a united Germany is no longer enough for him, what he wants now is a united Europe, united humanity.

1. Uhl seems to be confusing the radical *Dresdner Zeitung*, which was edited by Heinrich Eduard Minckwitz and Ludwig Wittig and to which Bakunin contributed, with the even more radical *Volksblätter*, which was edited by Röckel and (in his absence) by Wagner.
2. Devrient's wife, Therese, née Schlesinger (1803–82).

2 December 1848. Kapellmeister Wagner read me his finished libretto to *Siegfried's Tod*. The fellow's a poet through and through. A fine piece of work. Alliteration, as used by him, is a real find for opera poems; it ought to be raised to the level of a general principle. I was able to suggest a number of changes. I consider this his best poem, certainly his most dramatic. Afterwards we spoke at length about language, the education of the people, Christian development and of course came on to the state, whereupon he mounted his hobby horse, the destruction of capital. But there's no doubt that he has the best mind of anyone I know in Dresden.

15 February 1849. Kapellmeister Wagner told me about an extremely violent argument he's had with Lüttichau in the course of which the latter said the most dreadful things. He wants to get rid of him, but is first determined to humiliate him as much as he can, that much is clear. The poor fellow was very demoralized.

19 February 1849. At midday went to see Lüttichau. [. . .] He told me at length about his relations with Kapellmeister Wagner. He is clearly sorry to have behaved so inconsiderately towards him, and the success of *Tannhäuser* in Weimar has filled him with renewed respect. I was able to put in a good word for Wagner, and he entrusted me with the task of getting the two of them back on a friendly footing. After supper I had an opportunity to do so.

31 March 1849. Met Kapellmeister Wagner on the Terrace, another discussion about his theories for changing the world. He still thinks that only by destroying property is it possible to civilize mankind. I maintain that nothing can be achieved by such a superficial arrangement, but only through a new religious rebirth in Europe, by means of which selfishness – the source of all our social evils – will be reduced. He thinks of putting an end to all deficiencies, believes in the absolute and original perfection of the human race, a perfection lost only as a result of the state. What folly to regard six thousand years of human development as an error caused by the outward mechanism of the state. Finally he had to agree with me that only moral amelioration can put an end to our misery and that this would produce the right types of state, based on the law of love.

Devrient 1964: i.450–74

Revolution came to Dresden in May 1849. In the absence of any first-hand accounts detailing Wagner's involvement in the uprising, the full extent of his complicity will probably never be known. For years after his death, Bayreuth did what it could to play down his involvement, and friends such as Kietz took this as their cue and cut their biographical cloth accordingly. By the same token, the enemies that Wagner had made during his years in Dresden were only too ready to seize their chance to level charges whose veracity was never challenged in the courts. None the less, there were prima facie grounds for issuing a warrant for Wagner's arrest and there is no doubt that, had he returned to Germany and been arrested, he would, if found guilty, have suffered a long term of imprisonment. In 1856 he petitioned the king of Saxony for an amnesty and at this point a document was drawn up, itemizing the case against him.

SUMMARY OF EVIDENCE

1. The former Kapellmeister Wagner was intimately acquainted with the leaders of the rising, Bakunin,[1] Heubner, and Röckel.

2. About six weeks before the outbreak of the insurrection secret meetings took place on several occasions at the house of the law-student Neumann, who lived in the Menagerie Garden (so called). Bakunin, who was known as Dr Schwarz, had rooms at that time in Neumann's house. The object of these meetings has not been ascertained, but they are believed to have been connected with the rebellion, as stores of firearms and ammunition are said to have been found on Neumann's premises. Wagner is charged with having been present at these meetings.

---

1. The Russian anarchist Mikhail Bakunin (1814–76) did not arrive in Dresden until March 1849 (see Carr 1975: 185), a date that calls into question Shaw's otherwise attractive thesis that Siegfried is 'the ideal of Bakoonin' (Shaw 1898: 48). Bakunin's famous comment, under cross-examination on 19 September 1849, that 'I immediately recognized Wagner as a fantast and although I spoke with him a lot, including politics, I never committed myself to any joint action with him', needs to be seen against the background of his desire to prevent Wagner from sharing his own fate (Kersten 1926: 102).

3. Wagner is further charged with having lent his garden for the purpose of a conference on the question of arming the populace, in which Röckel, Lieutenants Schreiber and Müller, Professor Semper,[1] and others took part.

4. The notorious brassfounder Oehme, one of those most deeply implicated in the rebellion, and known more particularly for his attempts to burn down the Royal Palace, asserts that just before Easter 1849 Wagner and Röckel gave him an order for a considerable number of hand-grenades; these were said to be wanted for Prague, and were sent to the office of the *Dresdener Zeitung*. It seems, however, that they were never dispatched to Prague, as Oehme declares that on May 4, 1849, Wagner commissioned him to fill the grenades, which were still at the office of the *Dresdener Zeitung*.

5. Shortly before the outbreak of the rebellion Röckel travelled to Prague, where he endeavoured to arrange for a general armed rising against the various Governments. Meanwhile the Dresden rebellion had broken out, and Wagner wrote to Röckel, informing him of the fact and urging him to return. This letter[2] compromises Wagner in the gravest manner.

6. While the rebellion was in progress Wagner is alleged
(a) to have been in the Town Hall on the day of the election of the so-called Provisional Government, and to have incited Bakunin to accompany him;
(b) to have been seen on the Kreuzturm; and
(c) to have accompanied revolutionary reinforcements from Zittau.

Lippert 1930: 22–3; see also ML 390–413; Kietz 1907: 88–107; Schumann 1913: i.449–55; Devrient 1964: i.476–85; Carr 1975; Gregor-Dellin 1983: 168–80; and Kramer 1999

---

1. Gottfried Semper (1803–79) was one of the leading architects of his day. At the time in question he was professor of architecture at the Dresden Academy. Following his involvement in the Dresden Uprising, he fled first to England, then to Switzerland, where he renewed acquaintance with Wagner.
2. Letter of 2 May 1849: SL 144–5.

III (1849–58)

1849   *13 May* Wagner arrives in Weimar and the following day
attends a rehearsal of *Tannhäuser*. On the 15th he is
received at Eisenach by the Grand Duchess Maria
Pawlowna and visits the Wartburg for the first time. He
returns to Weimar on the 17th to find that a warrant has
been issued for his arrest. Travelling on an expired
passport and with funds provided by Liszt, he makes his
way to the Swiss border and arrives in Zurich on 28 May.
A brief foray to Paris (2 June–6 July) serves only to confirm
him in his dislike of the city. He returns to Zurich and
writes *Art and Revolution* (completed late July). Minna
joins him in early September
4 November Completes *The Artwork of the Future*

German National Assembly moves from Frankfurt to
Stuttgart, where it is dissolved by troops on 18 June, thus
marking the end of attempts at unification under a
parliamentary system
Communist riots in Paris in June are soon put down and lead
to repressive legislation
Strindberg born
Chopin dies (39)
Nicolai, *Die lustigen Weiber von Windsor*
Meyerbeer, *Le prophète*

1850   Julie Ritter in Dresden and Jessie Laussot in Bordeaux
offer Wagner an annual allowance. He conducts the first
of many concerts in Zurich
28 January Completes prose draft of *Wieland der Schmied*
and immediately sets off for Paris in a further attempt to
make an impression there. Attends performance of *Le
prophète*, before 24 February

March He is invited to visit the Laussot family in Bordeaux, where he falls in love with Jessie. His plans to elope with her are thwarted by her husband and he returns to Zurich on 3 July

August Begins musical sketches for *Siegfried's Tod* but soon abandons them

28 August Lohengrin premièred in Weimar. Garbled reports of the inadequacies of the staging persuade Wagner to think in terms of a festival of his own

His anti-Semitic essay 'Jews in Music' appears in the *Neue Zeitschrift für Musik*, 3 and 6 September

4 October Conducts *Der Freischütz* at the Aktientheater in Zurich, the first of seventeen opera performances between now and February 1855

Begins his longest theoretical essay, *Opera and Drama*, which he completes on 10 January 1851

> Friedrich Wilhelm IV of Prussia summons parliament in Erfurt in an attempt to marginalize Austria. Austria reacts by reviving the old Bundestag in Frankfurt. Following Russian intervention, Prussia subordinates herself to Austria
> French troops restore Pius IX: he responds by revoking the constitution
> Freedom of the press curtailed in France
> Louis-Philippe (76), Wordsworth (80) and Balzac (51) die
> Schumann, *Genoveva*
> Tennyson, *In Memoriam*

1851   Completes *Opera and Drama* (10 January), *A Theatre in Zurich* (17 April), 'On the Goethe Foundation' (8 May) and *A Communication to my Friends* (August, rev. November)

Writes prose draft and libretto of *Der junge Siegfried* (completed 24 June) and prose sketches for *Das Rheingold* and *Die Walküre* (October/November)

Spends two months at hydropathic centre at Albisbrunn (15 September–23 November)

> Censorship of Prussian press revived. German Diet abolishes fundamental rights
> *2 December* Louis-Napoléon carries out *coup d'état*

The Great Exhibition opens in London
Verdi, *Rigoletto*
Liszt, *Mazeppa*

1852   Appalled at the reactionary situation in Europe, Wagner –
       who had looked forward to 1852 as the year of
       revolutionary change – refuses to acknowledge the new
       year and dates his letters 32 December 1851, etc.
       Continues to conduct concerts and operas in Zurich,
       including four performances of *Der fliegende Holländer*
       in a revised version
       February Is introduced to the recently retired silk
       merchant Otto Wesendonck and his twenty-three-year-
       old wife, Mathilde, and in May to François and Eliza
       Wille, whose circle of friends includes Georg Herwegh,
       Theodor Mommsen, Gottfried Semper, Gottfried Keller
       and the young Conrad Ferdinand Meyer
       Completes prose draft of *Das Rheingold* on 31 March and
       that of *Die Walküre* on 26 May. The verse draft of *Die
       Walküre* is completed on 1 July, that of *Das Rheingold* on
       3 November
       In response to demands from German theatres to stage
       Tannhäuser, Wagner writes his instruction booklet *On
       Performing 'Tannhäuser'* in August, following it up with
       a similar guide to *Der fliegende Holländer* in December
       Revises *Der junge Siegfried* and *Siegfried's Tod* in
       preparation for publication of poem the following February

          Censorship of press in France. Louis-Napoléon proclaims
          himself emperor, 2 December

1853   Wagner publishes fifty copies of the poem of the *Ring* at
       his own expense and reads the work on consecutive
       evenings at the Hôtel Baur au Lac in Zurich, 16–19
       February
       Conducts three concerts of excerpts from his own works,
       18, 20 and 22 May
       Writes polka and sonata for Mathilde Wesendonck
       2–10 July Liszt visits Wagner in Zurich and introduces
       him to his symphonic poems

24 *August* Wagner leaves for Italy on a holiday paid for
by Otto Wesendonck, but ill-health drives him back to
Zurich by 10 September
6 *October* Meets Liszt in Basel and accompanies him to
Paris, where he meets Cosima Liszt, 10 October. Back in
Zurich by 28 October
1 *November* Begins composition draft of *Das Rheingold*

> Russia invades Danubian Principalities, precipitating Crimean
> War
> Verdi, *Il trovatore* and *La traviata*
> Liszt, *Festklänge*
> Brahms, First Piano Sonata

1854 Completes composition draft of *Das Rheingold* on 14
January and begins that of *Die Walküre* on 28 June,
while simultaneously working on the full score of *Das
Rheingold*
Financial problems increase. Minna's health deteriorates
Reads Schopenhauer's *The World as Will and
Representation*, September–October, and later claims that
'Only now did I understand my own Wotan' (ML 510)
Conceives idea of writing opera on the medieval Tristan
legend

> Trade unions banned in Germany
> Jacob and Wilhelm Grimm publish the first volume of their
> dictionary (completed in 1954)
> Humperdinck and Janáček born
> Tieck (79) and Schelling (79) die
> Meyerbeer, *L'étoile du Nord*
> Dorn, *Die Nibelungen*
> Berlioz, *L'enfance du Christ*
> Liszt, *Orpheus* and *Hungaria*

1855 *17 January* Completes revised version of *Faust* Overture
and conducts performance on 23rd
March–June Spends four months in London, conducting
eight concerts for the Old Philharmonic Society
Continues to work on *Die Walküre*
Frequent attacks of erysipelas

11 September Fall of Sebastopol
Kierkegaard dies (42)
Verdi, *Les vêpres siciliennes*
Whitman, *Leaves of Grass*

1856　*23 March* Completes full score of *Die Walküre*
16 May Conceives Buddhist drama of renunciation, *The Victors*
Writes new Schopenhauerian ending for *Ring*, May
Petitions King Johann of Saxony for amnesty
September Begins first composition draft of *Siegfried*
13 October Liszt arrives for six-week visit, followed by
Carolyne Sayn-Wittgenstein and her daughter. Liszt plays
from his recently completed symphonic poems
19 December First dated musical sketches for *Tristan und Isolde*

Sigmund Freud, Bernard Shaw and Oscar Wilde born
Heinrich Heine (58) and Robert Schumann (46) die

1857　*15 February* Writes open letter to Marie Wittgenstein on
Liszt's symphonic poems
Later (ML 547) claims that it was on Good Friday 1857
that he conceived the idea of writing a music drama on
Wolfram's *Parzival*
28 April Moves into 'Asyl', a small house paid for by
Otto Wesendonck in the grounds of the latter's as yet
unfinished villa
9 August Breaks off composition of *Siegfried* at end of
Act Two
Visits from Eduard Devrient, Ferdinand Praeger and, in
September, Hans and Cosima von Bülow on their
honeymoon
18 September Verse draft of *Tristan und Isolde* completed
1 October Begins first complete draft of music
Sets five poems by Mathilde Wesendonck (completed 1
May 1858)

Garibaldi founds Italian National Association, August
Elgar born
Glinka dies (52)

Verdi, *Simon Boccanegra*
Flaubert, *Madame Bovary*
Baudelaire, *Les fleurs du mal*

1858   Tensions in Zurich persuade Wagner to go to Paris for
        three weeks, 15 January–6 February. Berlioz reads him
        the poem of *Les Troyens*
        7 April Minna intercepts a letter from Wagner to Mathilde
        Wesendonck. The atmosphere continues to worsen and,
        after a series of visits from, among others, Tichatschek,
        Niemann, Hans and Cosima von Bülow, the Comtesse
        d'Agoult and Karl Klindworth, Wagner decides to leave
        the Asyl and travel to Italy, 17 August

        14 January Plot to assassinate Napoleon III
        Liszt resigns his post at Weimar
        Leoncavallo and Puccini born
        Offenbach, *Orphée aux enfers*
        Cornelius, *Der Barbier von Bagdad*

MARIE HOHENLOHE (1838–1920)

Marie Hohenlohe was the daughter of Liszt's in-
amorata, Carolyne Sayn-Wittgenstein (1819–87). Here,
from the vantage point of 1889, she recalls Wagner's
arrival in Weimar following the suppression of the
Dresden Uprising.

Liszt had recently heard *Tannhäuser* in Dresden under Wagner's
own direction,[1] and the work had immediately struck him as a
revelation emanating in some mysterious way from a world of
transcendent beauty. He was determined to put it into production
in Weimar without delay and had invited Wagner to attend the
rehearsals.[2] Wagner came and talked of nothing but music. Not
once did he boast that he and his friend Semper had been seriously
implicated in the May Uprising in Dresden. It was later said that
he had been persuaded to take part only out of anger at the fact
that his intendant, Baron Lüttichau, had refused to allow him some
extra clarinets to reinforce the orchestra in *Tannhäuser* and that
Semper had helped to build the barricades only out of his professional pride as an architect. Even if this version of events is
somewhat fanciful, there is no doubt that both men acted less out
of any profound political conviction than from mere thoughtless-
ness. The *Tannhäuser* rehearsal had just ended when Liszt received
a note from the Grand Duke announcing that a warrant had been
issued for his visitor's arrest. The government would turn a blind
eye to his presence in Weimar until the following morning in order
not to have to hand him over. He should use this time to make
good his escape. No one was more astonished at this news than
Wagner. Liszt immediately equipped him with a passport in the

1. A confusion with the performance of *Rienzi* that Liszt heard in Dresden on 29
February 1844; see Walker ii.112–13.
2. The production had opened on 16 February 1849. Wagner turned up
unannounced at a rehearsal for the May revival.

name of a stranger, together with some money, and made all the necessary arrangements for him to reach the Swiss border unharmed.

Hohenlohe 1938: 11–12

> Wagner arrived in Zurich on 28 May and two days later was issued with a travel permit:

Herr Richard Wagner of Leipzig, *compositeur de musique*
Age: 36
Height: 5′ 5½′[1]
Hair: Brown
Eyebrows: Brown
Eyes: Blue
Nose: Medium
Mouth: Medium
Chin: Round
Destination: France
Valid for 1 year

Fehr i.6

> At Liszt's instigation, Wagner travelled directly from Zurich to Paris but was so appalled by his renewed exposure to French culture that he returned to Zurich on 6 July. The following piece appeared anonymously in the *Grenzboten* on 5 October 1849 and describes

1. The original reads '5 Fuß 5½ Zoll'. The Zurich *Fuss* at this time was the equivalent of 0.32811 yards (see Alexander 1850: 38). A complication arises over the *Zoll*. Historically, the Zurich *Fuss* was divided into 12 *Zoll* until 1828, and into 10 thereafter. But, as Alexander points out (156), most Swiss continued to use the old measurement, with the result that new legislation became necessary. This was not formally enacted until 24 December 1851 and did not come into effect until 31 December 1856 (see Hallock and Wade 1906: 97). Under the old system, Wagner would be 5 feet 4½ inches tall. If we assume that the bureaucrats responsible for issuing him with his permit adopted the newer system of measurement, his height would work out at 5 feet 5½ inches. As other eyewitnesses report, Wagner was of medium or slightly below medium height, certainly not the 'snuffling gnome from Saxony' described by Thomas Mann (1985: 50). The average height of army recruits born in the years around 1813 was 5 feet 7.67 inches or 171.88 cm, while that of the male population at large was around 2.5 cm shorter; see Floud and others 1990: 148 and 155.

him in his new habitat. The leading journal of German
and Austrian liberalism, the *Grenzboten* was owned and
edited by Gustav Freytag (1816–95) and Julian Schmidt
(1818–86). Although Newman claims that it 'distinguished itself during the remainder of Wagner's life by
its attacks on him' (ii.242), the present article, with its
editorial footnote, hardly bears this out.

'German Refugees in Switzerland'

Take, if you will, your courage in both hands and come with me
to another of Switzerland's capitals, Zurich, the so-called Athens
of the Alps. Of all the towns in Switzerland, this is the one that
has always been the most open to foreigners, and it is here that the
greatest number of refugees are to be found, albeit very few of
their leaders. We see them everywhere. Their main meeting place,
however, is the Café litteraire [*sic*] on the Weinplatz, whose land-
lord, Herr Groß, once freed Robert Steiger from prison in Lucerne.[1]
Here, where Zurich's liberals have long foregathered, let me first
show you the Saxons. They form a little group around the former
member of the provisional government, Karl Todt; the man has
grown very old and attempts in vain to silence unwelcome inner
voices. Beside him is the pitiful figure of another former member
of the Diet, Herr Jäckel, the happy owner of the well-known 'blue
coat', who cowers beside Todt like a misshapen question mark.
Kapellmeister Wagner, by contrast, the inspired composer of
Tannhäuser, still keeps his head above water and refuses to be
cowed by fate. With him, his enthusiasm was genuine, with no
reservations of any kind – of how many others, apart from him,
is it still possible to say this?*

Die Grenzboten, viii/41 (5 October 1849), 73

1. See Dierauer 1917: v.683–4.

* In no insurrection, perhaps, have so many honourable, if confused, elements
played a part alongside base ones as they did in the case of the Dresden Uprising:
men of considerable learning and honest character, for whom one may feel sorry,
but whom one cannot condemn for an emotion by which we were all seized to
a greater or lesser extent (ed.)

GIACOMO MEYERBEER

Wagner spent his early years of exile wrestling with aesthetic questions in an attempt to define the role of the Wagnerian music drama within the society of the future. In *Art and Revolution* (1849), *The Artwork of the Future* (1849), 'Jews in Music' (1850) and *Opera and Drama* (1850–1), he set forth his vision of an artwork divorced from the empty virtuosity that he saw as the bane of contemporary opera. In this, Meyerbeer served as a whipping boy, with Wagner's ideological antipathy fuelled by resentment at his former dependency and by the phenomenal success of *Le prophète* at a time when his own works were virtually unperformed. 'Jews in Music' was published pseudonymously in the influential and widely read *Neue Zeitschrift für Musik* on 3 and 6 September 1850. Meyerbeer is not mentioned by name here, but the reference to him is unmistakable. Although a French translation appeared in both *Le diapason* (in three instalments between 3 and 10 October 1850) and *La France musicale* (in four instalments between 13 October and 10 November 1850, on this occasion with Meyerbeer's name added by the editor as a subheading), Meyerbeer appears to have been unaware of this attack on him. Wagner returned to the offensive in *Opera and Drama*, which was published in three volumes in late November 1851, and on this occasion he named names. Meyerbeer's diary entry of 24 November 1851 reads:

I was also very demoralized to learn from Burguy[1] that Richard Wagner has attacked me violently in his new book on the future of opera. I subsequently turned up a manuscript essay by this same Richard Wagner, written in his own hand (10 years ago), which he gave me to publish and in which he praised me extravagantly; it is called: On the Standpoint of Meyerbeer's Music.[2]

Meyerbeer v.454; see also Katz 1986; Rose 1992; Bauer 1998: 94–9; and Oberzaucher-Schüller 1998

1. Burguis was Amalia Beer's secretary.
2. 'On Meyerbeer's *Huguenots*': SS xii.22–30; for the dating of this essay, see p.30 above.

MARIE HOHENLOHE

In the autumn of 1853 my mother and I attended a music festival in Karlsruhe conducted by Liszt. A meeting in nearby Basel was arranged between the two composers, whom Wagner's exile had brought much closer together. They were now inseparable. An enthusiastic group of disciples accompanied Liszt[1] – we had no wish to be missing on such an important occasion. I remember that it was already evening by the time we reached Basel, where Wagner was waiting for us impatiently. There were noisy scenes in the hotel where we all assembled. I became increasingly withdrawn, while eagerly assimilating all the sparks that were leaping up around me. My excited silence caught Wagner's attention – he guessed my deeper feelings – and from then on he called me 'the Child'. When he spoke to me, his voice sounded soft and gentle, as though from subdued emotion, and my eyes filled with tears. Normally he bubbled with jokes, wild ideas and comic remarks. We spent three memorable days in Basel. The friends made music all day long, playing their compositions and singing the tenderest and most sublime of works in their hoarse and wavery voices until their enthusiasm knew no bounds and men's tears were shed in abundance. In the evening Wagner read us the poem of the *Ring of the Nibelung*, of which he had just had printed a small number of copies for his friends. I was only sixteen and understood little of the 'Wälsungs' sufferings', but Wagner's vibrant voice affected me deeply, and I gained an inkling of its underlying poetry. The next day he was due to travel to Paris with Liszt. When he finished reading *Die Walküre*, I was barely able to suppress my tears and stammered that it was sad not to hear the remaining poems. My mother, who was happy to be taken along to Paris, immediately said that 'the Child' must go there too in order to hear the end of the work. And so we went with them. In Paris we found Liszt's three children, the offspring of his lengthy liaison with the Comtesse d'Agoult. He had adopted them and given them his name and was solely responsible for their education. They now lived under the watchful eye of my mother's former governess, an

1. They included Hans von Bülow (1830–94), Joseph Joachim (1831–1907), Peter Cornelius (1824–74), Richard Pohl (1826–96), Dionys Pruckner (1834–96) and Ede Reményi (1828–98).

old and strait-laced adherent of the *ancien régime*. I was the same age as the two girls, who were still somewhat unsophisticated and who gazed at the hostile world with the startled eyes of a hind. Blandine was the elder of the two, prettier, plumper, more ready to please – by no means pretentious and already fairly content with her lot. Poor Cosima, on the other hand, was in the throes of adolescence – tall, angular and fair-skinned, with a large mouth and long nose, the very image of her father. Only her long golden hair was of rare lustre and great beauty. And her poor child's heart seethed with all the fury of a volcano. Dark passion and boundless vanity pulsated through her veins – and now and then the Parisienne's inborn mockery played wantonly on her thin lips. Her brother Daniel was the youngest of the three, a tender-hearted child, who always looked so sad with his dreamy eyes and who already seemed marked out by the pulmonary illness that was to kill him only a few years later.

Following a frugal meal with Liszt's children in the simply furnished little salon in the Rue Casimir-Périer, Wagner read us the rest of the *Ring*. The children understood barely enough German to grasp the meaning of the words. But they too were affected by our own emotion. Daniel's laurel wreaths which, in keeping with French custom, he had received at school were hanging on the wall. Half in jest I took one down and placed it on Wagner's head. I can still see Cosima's ecstatic expression as the tears ran down her pointed nose. At that time Wagner had no eyes for the ugly child who was one day to become his Isolde.

Hohenlohe 1938: 13–14

FERDINAND PRAEGER (1815–1891)

The German composer, pianist and writer on music, Ferdinand Praeger, settled in London in 1834 and was soon in demand as a teacher. From 1842 he acted as London correspondent of the *Neue Zeitschrift für Musik* and in 1851–2 toured Europe, performing in Paris, Leipzig, Berlin and Hamburg. His overture *Abellino* was conducted by Berlioz in July 1855, and a concert of his works was organized by his pupils in

London on 10 July 1879. His reminiscences of Wagner, published in English and German in 1892, were immediately branded a fabrication by the praetorian guard at Bayreuth. While it is regrettably true that Praeger falsified documents in an attempt to exaggerate the importance of his role in Wagner's life, it is clear that what really antagonized the Bayreuthians was his account of Wagner's prominent part in the Dresden Uprising of May 1849 – and this at the very time that Bayreuth was attempting to underplay that involvement. At all events, there is something distinctly comical about Chamberlain's expostulation that 'our Master has scarcely been dead for ten years and already all manner of fables, fairy tales and legends have sprung up around his proud and simple life' (1894: 2). And for Chamberlain, currently overseeing one of the most egregious attempts in the history of musicology to misrepresent an artist by systematically censoring his correspondence, to criticize Praeger for his actions suggests either a pot-and-kettle blindness to his own complicitous activities or a deliberate attempt to divert attention. While Praeger's text needs to be treated with caution, it remains a fact that he saw Wagner on seventeen documented occasions during the latter's stay in London: they went to the theatre together (the pantomime *Mother Goose* and Boucicault's *Corsican Brothers*), visited Gravesend and Brighton and would have gone to Bath had Praeger not been unwell. Throughout his letters of this period, Wagner refers to his frequent meetings with Praeger and places him at the head of his list of acquaintances in London. Praeger also stayed with Wagner in Zurich in July 1857, saw him in Paris during the winter of 1860–1, visited him at Tribschen in July–August 1871 and attended the 1882 Bayreuth Festival.

During the winter of 1854–5 Wagner received an invitation to conduct the Old Philharmonic Society's forthcoming season of concerts, an invitation that he accepted with some hesitation and very soon came to regret.

Wagner arrived at midnight precisely on Sunday, the fifth of March. If I had not already acquired through the graphic letters of August Roeckel an insight into the peculiarities of Richard

Wagner's habits of thought, power of grasping profound questions of mental speculation, whilst relieving the severity of serious discourse by the intermingling of jocular ebulitions [*sic*] of fancy, I was soon to have a fair specimen of these wondrous qualities. One of the many points in which we found ourselves at home, was the habit of citing phrases from Schiller or Goethe, as applicable to our subjects of discussion, as often ironically as seriously. To these we added an almost interminable dictionary of quotations from the plays and operas of the early part of the century. These mental links were, in the course of a long and intimate friendship, augmented by references to striking qualities, defects, or oddities, our circle of acquaintances forming a means of communication between us which might not inaptly be likened to mental shorthand. Nothing could have exceeded the hilarity, when, upon showing him, at an advanced hour, to his bedroom,[1] he enthusiastically said, 'August was right; we shall understand each other thoroughly!' I felt in an exalted position, and dreamed that, like Spontini, I had received a new decoration from some potentate which delighted me, but the pleasant dream soon turned to nightmare, when I could find no room on my coat to place the newly acquired bauble. The next morning I found the signification of the dream. Exalted positions have their duties as well as their pleasures, and it became my duty to acquaint Wagner that a so-called 'Necker' hat (*i.e.* a slouched one) was not becoming for the conductor of so conservative a society as the Philharmonic, and that it was necessary that he should provide himself with a tall hat, indeed, such headgear as would efface all remembrance of the social class to which his soft felt hat was judicially assigned, for, be it known, in some parts of Germany the soft slouched hat had been interdicted by police order as being the emblem of revolutionary principles. I think it was on the strength of the accuracy of this last statement that Wagner gave way, and I at once followed up the success by taking the composer of 'Tannhäuser' to the best West End hatter, where, after an onslaught on the sons of Britannia and their manias, we succeeded in fitting a hat on that wondrous head of the great thinker. I could not help sarcastically joking

1. Wagner spent his first night at the Praegers' at 31 Milton Street (now 65 Balcombe Street), Paddington. The following day he moved into rooms at 22 Portland Terrace (demolished in around 1905) to the north of Regent's Park.

Wagner on his compulsory leave-taking with the 'revolutionary' hat for four months, – the time he was to sojourn amongst us, – by citing from Schiller's 'Fiesco' the passage about the fall of the hero's cloak into the water, upon which Ver[r]ina pushes him after it with the sinister words, 'When the purple falls, the duke must follow.' As to Richard Wagner's democratic principles, I observed that the solitude of exile had considerably modified them. This I noticed to my surprise and no less pain, for, when I anxiously inquired after our poor friend, August Roeckel, he shrugged his shoulders and said, 'Perhaps he tries to revolutionize the prison warders, for the "Wuhlers" ' (uprooters, a name of the period) 'are never at rest in their self-elected role of reformers!' I, who knew the unambitious, self-sacrificing nature of the poor prisoner, felt a pang of disappointment at Wagner's remark, and had often to suffer the same when the year 1849 was mentioned.

We drove from the hatmaker straight to the city to inquire after a box containing the compositions Wagner had been requested to bring over with him.[1] The box had arrived, and then we continued our peregrinations back to the West, alighting at Nottingham Place, the residence of Mr. Anderson.[2] The old gentleman possessed all the suave, gentle manner of the courtier, and all went well during the preliminary conversation about the projected programme, until Mr. Anderson mentioned a prize symphony of Lachner as one of the intended works to be performed. Wagner sprang from his seat, as if shot from a gun, exclaiming loudly and angrily, 'Have I therefore left my quiet seclusion in Switzerland to cross the sea to conduct a prize symphony by Lachner? no; never! If that be a condition of the bargain I at once reject it, and will return. What brought me away was the eagerness to head a far-famed orchestra and to perform worthily the works of the great masters, but no Kapellmeister music; and that of a "Lachner," bah!' Mr. Anderson sat aghast in his chair, looking with bewildered surprise on this unexpected outbreak of passion, delivered with extraordinary volu-

1. The *Tannhäuser* Overture and excerpts from *Lohengrin* were played at three Philharmonic concerts.
2. George Frederick Anderson (1793–1876) was Master of the Queen's Musick from 1848 to 1870 and treasurer of the Philharmonic Society from 1840 until his death. He lived with his wife, the concert pianist Lucy Anderson, née Philpot (1797–1878), at 34 Nottingham Place.

bility and heat by Wagner, partly in French and partly in German. I interposed a more tranquillizing report of the harangue and succeeded in assuring Mr. Anderson that the matter might be arranged by striking out the 'prize' composition, to which he directly most urbanely acceded.[1] Wagner, who did not fail to perceive the startling effect his derisive attack on the proposed work had produced on poor Mr. Anderson, whose knowledge of the French language was fairly efficient in an Andante movement, but quite incapable of following such a *presto agitato* as the Wagner speech had assumed, begged me to explain the dubious position of prize compositions in all cases, and certainly no less in the case of the Lachner composition, and Wagner himself laughingly turned the conversation into a more general and quiet channel. After thus having tranquillized the storm, the interview ended more agreeably than the startling episode had promised. I, however, then clearly foresaw the many difficulties likely to occur during the conductorship of a man of Wagner's Vesuvius-like temper, and the sequel amply proved that I had not been unduly prejudiced in this respect. Yet in all his bursts of excitability, a sudden veering round was always to be expected, should it chance that the angry poetmusician perceived any ludicrous feature in the controversy, when he would turn to that as a means of subduing his ebullition of temper, and falling into a jocular vein, would plainly show he was conscious of having exceeded the bounds of moderation. I was glad that we had passed the Rubicon of our difficulties for the present, for I was fully aware that whatever difficulties might arise with

1. Although doubt has been cast on this anecdote by Ellis and others, it is confirmed by the Minutes of the Directors' Meeting of the Philharmonic Society held on 6 March: 'Mr Anderson stated that he had desired this Meeting to be called, in consequence of Mr Wagner have [*sic*] expressed a wish that the Symphonies inserted in the programme of the first Concert should be changed. Mr Wagner, who was present, explained his reasons for this; and on deliberation, it was agreed to substitute Haydn's Symphony No· 7 (Grand) for the Prize Symphony of Lachner.' The programme of the concert on 12 March was: Haydn's Symphony no. 99, 'Soave sia il vento' from *Così fan tutte*, Spohr's Dramatic Concerto, 'Ocean, thou mighty monster' from *Oberon*, Mendelssohn's *Fingal's Cave* Overture, Beethoven's 'Eroica' Symphony, a duet from *Der Vampyr* and the Overture to *Die Zauberflöte*. Praeger adds that 'it was these "full" programmes, reminding him of the cry of the London omnibus conductors, "full inside," which led him [Wagner] humorously to speak of himself as "conductor of the Philharmonic Omnibus" ' (Praeger 1892: 257).

regard to Wagner's relation to the other directors, they would be easily overcome by Mr. Anderson's support, for it was he who unquestionably ruled the 'Camarilla,' or secret Spanish council, as Wagner styled the 'seven,' when any work proposed by them for performance met with disapproval. I never could well understand how the Lachner episode became known, but it is certain that it did, for the German opposition journals, and there were many, made great capital out of the refusal of Wagner to conduct a prize symphony.

Our next visit was an unclouded one. We went to call on Sainton, who was as refined a soloist as he was an intelligent and energetic orchestral leader.[1] His jovial temperament, Gasconic fun (born at Toulouse), his good and frank nature, pleased Wagner at once. Charles Lüders, a German musician, 'le frère intime' of Sainton, formed the oddest contrast to his friend's character.[2] Quiet, reflective, and somewhat old-fashioned, he nevertheless became an ardent admirer of Wagner's music, and proved that 'extremes meet,' for in his compositions, and they are many, known in Germany and in France, the good Lüders tenaciously clung to the traditions of a past period. We soon identified him in gentle fun with the 'contrapuntista.' Notwithstanding the marked contrast of the quartette, Wagner, Sainton, Lüders, and myself, we harmonized remarkably well, and many were our pleasant, convivial meetings during the time of Wagner's stay in London. As Sainton had always been very intimate with Costa,[3] and was his recognized deputy in his absence, he accompanied us on the first visit to the Neapolitan conductor, Wagner expressing a wish to make Costa's acquaintance. This was the only visit of etiquette Wagner paid. He sternly refused to pay any more, no matter to whom, and I gladly desisted from advocating any, though he suffered severely in consequence from a press which stigmatized him as proud and unsociable.

We went home to dine. What a pleasant impression did the

---

1. Prosper Sainton (1813–90) settled in London in 1845 and taught the violin at the Royal Academy of Music.
2. Charles Lüders (?–1883) shared rooms with Sainton at 8 Hinde Street, off Manchester Square.
3. Sir Michael Costa (1808–84) conducted the Philharmonic concerts between 1846 and 1854. It was his defection at the end of the 1854 season that led, by a somewhat tortuous route, to Wagner's appointment; see Spencer 1982.

master give us of his childlike jollity. Full of fun, he exhibited his remarkable power of imitation. He was a born actor, and it was impossible not to recognize immediately who was the individual caricatured, for Wagner's power of observation led him at all times to notice the most minute characteristics of all whom he encountered. A repast in his society might well be described as a 'feast of reason and flow of soul,'[1] for, mixed in odd ways, were the most solid remarks of deep, logical intuition, with the sprightliest, frolicsome humour. Wagner ate very quickly, and I soon had occasion to notice the fatal consequences of such unwise procedure, for although a moderate eater, he did not fail to suffer severely from such a pernicious practice. This first day afforded a side-light upon the master's peculiarities. Never having been used to the society of children, he was plainly awkward in his treatment of them, which we did not fail to perceive whenever my little boy was brought in to say 'good-night.'

As soon as we had discovered a fitting apartment at Portland Place, Regent's Park, within a few minutes' walk of my house, the first thing he wanted was an easel for his work, so that he might stand up to score. No sooner was that desire satisfied than he insisted on an eider-down quilt for his bed. Both these satisfied desires are illustrative of Wagner. He knew not self-denial. It was sufficient that he wished, that his wish should be granted. When he arrived in London, his means were limited, but nevertheless the satisfaction of the desires was what he ever adhered to.

He had not been here a day before his determined character was made strikingly apparent to me. In the matter of crossing a crowded thoroughfare his intrepidity bordered close upon the reckless. He would go straight across a road; safe on the other side, he was almost boyish in his laugh at the nervousness of others. But this was Wagner. It was this deliberate attacking everything that made him what he was; timorousness was not in his character; dauntless fearlessness, perhaps not under proper control, naturally gave birth to an iconoclast, who struck with vigour at all opposition, heedless of destroying the penates worshipped by others.

The rehearsal and the introduction of the band of the Philharmonic was a nervous moment for me. I knew the spirit of

1. Alexander Pope, 'To Mr. Fortescue', l.127.

opposition had found its way among a few members of the orchestra; indeed, it numbered one at least, who felt himself displaced by Wagner's appointment. However, Wagner came. He addressed the band in a brotherly manner, as co-workers for the glory of art; made an apt reference to their idol, his predecessor, and secured the good-will at once of the majority. I say advisedly the majority only, because they had not long set to work when he was gently admonished by some that 'they had not been in the habit of taking this movement so slowly, and that, perhaps, the next had been taken a trifle too fast.' Wagner was diplomatic; his words were conciliatory, but, for all that, he went on his way, and would have the *tempi* according to his will. At the end he was applauded heartily, and henceforth the band apparently followed implicitly his directions. [. . .]

After the first concert, we went by arrangement to spend a few hours at his rooms. Dear me, what an evening of excitement that was! There were Wagner, Sainton, Lüders, Klindworth[1] (whom I had introduced to Wagner as a pupil of Liszt), myself and wife. Animal spirits ran high. Wagner was in ecstasies. The concert had been a marked success artistically, and Richard Wagner's reception flattering. On arriving at his rooms, he found it necessary to change his dress from 'top to toe.' He had perspired so freely from excitement that his collar was as though it had that moment been dipped in a basin of water. So while he went to change his attire and don a somewhat handsome dressing-robe made by Minna, Sainton prepared a mayonnaise for the lobster, and Lüders rum punch made after a Danish method, and one particularly appreciated by Wagner, who, indeed, loved everything unusual of that description. Wagner had chosen lobster salad, I should mention, because crab fish were either not to be got at all in Germany, or were very expensive. When he returned he put himself at the piano. His memory was excellent, and innumerable 'bits' or references of the most varied description were rattled off in a sprightly manner; but more excellent was his running commentary of observations as to the intention of the composer. These observations showed the thinker and discerning critic, and in themselves were of value

1. Karl Klindworth (1830–1916) had been a member of Liszt's circle in Weimar since 1852, but was now living in London, where he remained until 1868, when he took up a teaching appointment at the new Moscow Conservatory.

in helping others to comprehend the meaning of the music. What he said has mostly found its way into print; indeed, it may be affirmed that the greater part of his literary productions was only the transcription of what he uttered incessantly in ordinary conversation. Then, too, he sang; and what singing it was! It was, as I told him then, just like the barking of a big Newfoundland dog. He laughed heartily, but kept on nevertheless. He cared not. Yet though his 'singing' was but howling, he sang with his whole heart, and held you, as it were, spellbound. There was the real musician. He felt what he was doing. He was earnest, and that was, and is, the cause of his greatness. [. . .]

Reflections upon the habits and customs of a past generation sometimes introduce us to situations that produce in the mind wonder and perhaps a feeling of disgust. Who can picture the composer of that colossal work of intellect, the 'Nibelung Ring,' sitting at the piano, in an elegant, loose robe-de-chambre, singing, with full heart, snatches and scenes from his 'adored' idol, Weber's 'Euryanthe,' and at intervals of every three or four minutes indulging in large quantities of scented snuff. The snuff-taking scene of the evening is the deeper graven on my memory, because Wagner abruptly stopped singing, on finding his snuff-box empty, and got into a childish, pettish fit of anger. He turned to us in deepest concern, with 'Kein schnupf tabac mehr also Kein gesang mehr'[1] (no more snuff, no more song); and though we had reached the small hours of early morn, would have someone start in search of this 'necessary adjunct.' When singing, the more impassioned he became, the more frequent the snuff-taking. Now, this practice of Wagner's, one cultivated from early manhood, in my opinion pointedly illustrates a phase in the man's character. He did not care for snuff, and even allowed the indelicacy of the habit, but it was that insatiable nature of his that yearned for the enjoyment of all the 'supposed' luxuries of life. It was precisely the same with smoking. He indulged in this, to me, barbarous acquirement more moderately, but experienced not the slightest pleasure from it. I have seen him puffing from the mild and inoffensive cheroot, to the luxurious hookah – the latter, too, as he confessed, only because

1. Presumably it was Praeger's posthumous editor, rather than Praeger himself, who garbled the German here.

it was an Oriental growth, and the luxury of Eastern people harmonized with his own fondness for unlimited profusion. 'Other people find pleasure in smoking; then why should not I?' This is, briefly, the only explanation Wagner ever offered in defence of the practice – a practice which he was fully aware increased the malignity of his terrible dyspepsia.

There was in Wagner a nervous excitability which not infrequently led to outbursts of passion, which it would be difficult to understand or explain, were it not that there existed a positive physical cause. First, he suffered, as I have stated earlier, from occasional attacks of erysipelas; then his nervous system was delicate, sensitive, – nay, I should say, irritable. Spasmodic displays of temper were often the result, I firmly feel, of purely physical suffering. His skin was so sensitive that he wore silk next to the body, and that at a time when he was not the favoured of fortune. In London he bought the silk and had shirts made for him; so, too, it was with his other garments. We went together to a fashionable tailor in Regent Street, where he ordered that his pockets and the back of his vest should be of silk, as also the lining of his frock-coat sleeves; for Wagner could not endure the touch of cotton, as it produced a shuddering sensation throughout the body that distressed him. I remember well the tailor's surprise and explanation that silk for the back of the vest and lining of the sleeves was not at all necessary, and that the richest people never had silk linings; besides, it was not seen. This last observation brought Wagner up to one of his indignant outbursts, 'Never seen! yes; that's the tendency of this century; sham, sham in everything; that which is not seen may be paltry and mean, provided only that the exterior be richly gilded.'

Praeger 1892: 228–52; see also Ellis v.41–446

MALWIDA VON MEYSENBUG (1816–1903)

Banned from Berlin as a result of her revolutionary contacts, Malwida von Meysenbug settled in London in 1852 and found work there as a governess to the family of the radical Russian writer Alexander Herzen

(1812–70). Here she recalls attending Wagner's second
Philharmonic concert on 26 March.

The thrill I felt at that concert can only be compared to a similar
impression I remember having had at a musical performance in my
youth when I heard the singer Schröder-Devrient. Through this
incomparable artist, I got the first real revelation of the essence of
dramatic art. The same was revealed to me now by an orchestral
performance which seemed to unfold for the first time the mysterious language of the tone world; something I had long known
and loved came to me as a new gift in its proper light and setting.
This was especially the case with the overture to the *Freischütz*.
Being an ardent admirer of Weber's, I had often heard all of his
operas, but the *Freischütz* I had heard from childhood, so to speak,
and knew it almost by heart. Now it seemed as if I heard the poetic
tone picture of the Overture for the first time, and [it] suddenly
became clear to me that only now did I hear it as it should be
heard. The whole Forest myth with its magic, its horrors and its
sweet innocence and poetry, stood transfigured before my sight.

The personality of the conductor came as little into consideration
as in the reading of his books. I was sitting too far back to be able
to get a correct idea of him; I only had the feeling that a wave of
harmony flowed visibly from his baton over the orchestra, making
the musicians play more beautifully than they had ever been able
to do before. Of all the music I had heard in England, so rich in
concerts, this concert stood out preëminently.

One can imagine with what delight I accepted an invitation from
Anna,[1] a short time after this, to spend an evening at her house
with Wagner. Nothing else could have persuaded me to leave my
beloved children the second time for two days and a night.
However, I could not deny myself this long-desired pleasure.

The very reserved, cool manner with which Wagner received our
warm reception of him estranged me somewhat at first. Then,
however, I realized that it was due naturally to his unsympathetic
reception in England. An antagonism between him and the English,
who were saturated with a Mendelssohn cult, had been apparent
from the beginning, and this was the cause of such absurdities in

1. Anna Althaus, the wife of Friedrich Althaus (1829–97), who worked as a
general practitioner in Hampstead. The meeting took place on 31 March.

musical accounts and criticisms of the season as: 'One could not possibly expect anything from a conductor who even directs Beethoven symphonies by heart.'[1]

Almost immediately, our conversation turned to the works of a philosopher whose name arose like a shining star out of the oblivion in which he had been left for more than a half a century. This was Arthur Schopenhauer. Well did I remember having seen in Frankfurt-am-Main, a little man in a gray cloak with several collars, then called 'chenille,' who, followed by a poodle dog, took his walk on the Main quay daily at the same hour as I. I also remembered that I had been told that this man was Arthur Schopenhauer, the son of the popular authoress of the same name, and that he was an absolute idiot. An acquaintance of ours, then a Senator of the free city of Frankfurt, and a highly esteemed man, who sat at the table d'hôte with him daily, loved to ridicule him and tell anecdotes about him to prove his stupidity.

Since then I had heard no more about him until now, when news from Germany was brought that his works, although published long ago, were now being read and that he was considered by some as the greatest philosopher since Kant, and by others even much greater. I do not know how Frederick had heard that Wagner shared this last opinion. He turned the conversation upon Schopenhauer and asked Wagner for an explanation of the fundamental principles of the Schopenhauer philosophy.

In the conversation following this, I was particularly struck with the expression 'the negation of the will to live,' which phrase Wagner declared to be the final result of Schopenhauer's view of life. Accustomed to looking upon the will as a power of moral self-determination, although I could never quite solve the contradiction

1. Writing in *The Times* on 14 March, James Davison (1813–85) noted that Wagner conducted the 'Eroica' 'without a score before him, which says more for his memory, we think, than for his judgment'. Henry Finck reports that Wagner was given to understand that to conduct without a score 'was considered a slight on the classical composers; and after a rehearsal of one of Beethoven's symphonies, he yielded in so far to the pressure brought to bear on him as to promise to bring along a score at the public performance. He did so. After the performance the parties who had urged him to use a score crowded around him with congratulations on the excellent result of their advice – until one of them happened to glance at the score on his desk, which proved to be – Rossini's *Barber of Seville*!'; Finck i.451.

between its obvious slavery and its freedom as declared by
Christian dogma, this phrase describing the highest ethical task of
mankind was to me absolutely incomprehensible. Had I not always
looked upon the directing of the will toward uninterrupted moral
perfection and action as the final goal of existence? However, this
sentence echoed in me like something before which I dared not
stand as before a riddle. The answer must be somewhere within
me. It attracted me with inspiring awe as though it must be a key
to the gate toward which my life was tending and behind which
the light of final perception would appear to me.

The evening passed without a more congenial feeling arising
between Wagner and any of us. I felt distressed about this meeting,
and it hurt me all the more because I had been prepared to meet
the author of those works and the director of that concert with
such ardent enthusiasm. Not wishing this impression to remain, I
wrote him a few lines later, inviting him to come out to Richmond
as Herzen would also be happy to meet him. Unfortunately I
received a regret, giving his approaching departure, and business
incident to it, as the reason.

Meysenbug 1937: 210–13

KARL KLINDWORTH (1830–1916)

> The pianist and teacher Karl Klindworth was living in
> London at the time of Wagner's visit and was later
> entrusted with the task of preparing vocal scores of all
> his principal works. Towards the end of his life he
> adopted Winifred Williams (1897–1980), who married
> Siegfried Wagner in 1915. The present passage is taken
> from an interview published in 1898.

He used to grumble tremendously at the length of the programmes. He found it impossible to properly prepare such an
amount of work with the too limited time at rehearsal. I remember
how distressed he was at the lethargy of the orchestra. He said,
with arms uplifted to the band: 'You are the famous Philharmonic
orchestra. Raise yourselves, gentlemen; be *artists*!' He waged war
with the Directors for doing such absurd things as putting down

an operatic air quite unsuitable to the artistic standard which the
Philharmonic Society should follow and to the singer to whom it
was assigned. '*Where* are the Directors?' he furiously asked at the
rehearsal. Wagner said that, outside his immediate circle of friends,
there were only two people in England who cared anything about
him, and they were the Queen and the Prince Consort.

Klindworth 1898: 516

QUEEN VICTORIA (1819–1901)

Together with Prince Albert, Queen Victoria attended
the penultimate Philharmonic concert on 11 June 1855
and was introduced to Wagner during the interval. She
noted afterwards in her diary:

June 11. We dined early with Feodore, her girls, our Boys, & all
the Ladies and Gentlemen going to the Philharmonic where a fine
concert was given, under the direction of the celebrated composer
Herr Richard Wagner. He conducted in a peculiar way, taking
Mozart's & Beethoven's Symphonies in quite a different time time
[*sic*], to what one is accustomed. His own overture to 'Tannhäuser'
is a wonderful composition, quite overpowering, so grand, & in
parts wild, striking and descriptive. We spoke to him afterwards.
He is short, very quiet, wears spectacles & has a very finely
developed forehead, a hooked nose, & projecting chin. He must
be 3 or 4 & 30.[1]

Royal Archives, Windsor

---

1. Wagner notoriously described the queen as '*not* fat, but very small and not at
all pretty, with, I am sorry to say, a rather red nose: but there is something
uncommonly friendly and confiding about her, and though she is by no means
imposing, she is nevertheless a kind and delightful person' (SL 348; letter of 12
June 1855). The full programme, which was planned in consultation with Windsor
Castle, was Macfarren's *Chevy Chase* Overture, an aria from Spohr's *Jessonda*,
Mozart's 'Jupiter' Symphony, 'Ocean, thou mighty monster' from *Oberon*, the
Tannhäuser Overture, Beethoven's Eighth Symphony, Cherubini's *Ave Maria*, a
duet from Paer's *Agnese* and the Overture to Cherubini's *Anacreon*.

ROBERT VON HORNSTEIN (1833–1890)

The young German composer Robert von Hornstein first met Wagner in May 1853 and returned to Switzerland in July 1854 in the hope of hearing him conduct at Sion. Although his hopes were dashed by Wagner's refusal to conduct the concert in question, he attached himself to the composer and between then and May 1856 was able to observe him at close quarters. Here he begins by describing Wagner's second-floor rooms at 13 Zeltweg, into which the Wagners had moved in April 1853.

Wagner's apartment consisted of a suite of rooms. At one end was his bedroom, beside it his study. Here were to be found a large grand piano and his library. The inevitable high desk was beside the piano. There was also a sofa on which he would recline and read. Beside it was the dining room. Then came his wife's room. In this room was the parrot that would whistle the opening of Beethoven's Eighth Symphony.[1]

The rooms were elegantly furnished. The floors were covered with carpets and the rooms divided by portières. It was said that he paid a minimal rent and that the wealthy Herr Escher of Linth[2] regarded it as an honour to house him. The rent was said to be merely pro forma. On the whole, things were not going badly for him. Since his flight to Switzerland he had been in receipt of an annual allowance of 800 thalers from Ritter's mother.[3] One of his Zurich friends, Councillor Sulzer,[4] a wealthy bachelor, was a huntsman and fish farmer who helped to keep Wagner's table well

1. Jacquot, aka Knackerchen, was Papo's successor and was acquired in 1854. He followed Minna to Dresden when Wagner's household broke up in 1858.
2. The property was currently owned by Clementine Stockar-Escher (1816–86), an amateur portrait painter. The rental was 800 francs per annum. As Fehr points out (i.295–9), Wagner's finances went through one of their periodically parlous phases in the summer of 1854 as a belated result of the outlay of furnishing the rooms at 13 Zeltweg in the style to which he was accustomed. At this point Otto Wesendonck wrote off Wagner's debts to the tune of 7,000 francs.
3. Julie Ritter (1794–1869) had got to know Wagner in Dresden and supported him during the 1850s. Her son Karl (1830–91) was one of a whole series of young men who attached themselves to Wagner in their search for a surrogate father.
4. Jakob Sulzer (1821–97) was cantonal secretary of Zurich and one of Wagner's closest and most supportive friends.

stocked. The wines all came from Wesendonk's cellar.¹ Brockhaus
was said to have paid him a decent fee for *Opera and Drama* and
Art and Revolution.² The royalties on *Tannhäuser*, *Der fliegende
Holländer* and *Lohengrin* were beginning to flow in. Of course,
there were many occasions when he handed over these works once
and for all for a pittance.³ But there can have been no shortage of
money entering his house, and so even today I cannot understand
how he could keep on running up debts. Wesendonk paid them
off for him from time to time. By the time he moved to Lucerne,⁴
it is said that Zurich's shopkeepers would not have let him go if
Karl Ritter had not settled his bills to the tune of several thousand
francs.

It is true, he lived well. His table was well appointed. But one
could hardly speak of luxury. Even when he had relatively large
numbers of people round, the fare was comparatively simple, and
I have already explained who provided these meals. His wife,
moreover, ensured that things did not get out of hand. How small
was their household! Wagner himself, his wife and her married
sister, a simple, undemanding person,⁵ the parrot and a little dog.
He set a certain store by elegance. But there was no question of

1. Otto Wesendonck (1815–96) and his wife Mathilde (1828–1902) settled in
Zurich in 1851 and were introduced to Wagner the following year. For reasons
best known to himself, their son decided to spell the family name Wesendonk, a
decision that has bedevilled writings on Wagner ever since.
2. *Opera and Drama* (1851) and *Art and Revolution* (1849) were published by
J. J. Weber and Otto Wigand respectively. Wagner's fee for the former was 20
louis d'or (483 francs), for the latter only 5.
3. With the exception of isolated productions of *Der fliegende Holländer* in Riga
(3 June 1843, under Heinrich Dorn), Cassel (5 June 1843, under Louis Spohr)
and Berlin (7 January 1844, under Wagner), this work had still to find a place
for itself in the regular repertory, although Wagner's production in Zurich in
April–May 1852 led to performances in Breslau (26 January 1853), Weimar (16
February 1853) and Schwerin (6 April 1853). *Tannhäuser* and *Lohengrin* fared
somewhat better as a result of Liszt's pioneering work in Weimar. By the mid-
1850s *Tannhäuser* had been taken into the repertory of more than forty German
opera houses, while *Lohengrin* soon made up for lost ground. None the less,
Wagner's fees from these performances were often risibly low, not least because
of his need to raise money quickly. For 22 productions of *Tannhäuser* between
26 January 1852 and 1 February 1855 he received a total of only 362 louis d'or
(8,750 francs).
4. In March 1859.
5. Natalie Planer, Minna's illegitimate daughter, did not in fact marry until 1868.

'whole catalogues of night gowns' or of 'blackamoors and liveried servants'. Where did the money go? Throughout his life he suffered from fits of generosity and sympathy, when he would give away a thaler instead of a groschen; this did not pay the bills. And, notwithstanding his tendency towards prodigality, he also had fits of avarice to which Ritter drew my attention. One day he was beside himself with rage over a copyist's bill. It was the copy of a large score. Ritter and I did not find it particularly excessive, but there was nothing we could do to calm him.

Even later in Munich, accounts of Wagner's household generally belonged to the realm of fancy. Hiller once told me in Cologne that he knew of around half a million francs that he had managed to extort from sundry sources. Even today I cannot understand where the money went to. Wagner's biographers may cudgel their brains on the subject, I simply cannot work it out.

I was invited to dine with them several times a week, with myself as their only guest. On these occasions Wagner could be utterly charming, particularly if he had spent a productive morning composing. Once he arrived slightly late with shining eyes and flushed face. 'I've just been working on my vaudeville,' he said with a laugh. He meant his trilogy. It was the Ride of the Valkyries that was created that morning.[1]

There were times when I arrived somewhat earlier and waited in the next room while he sat at the piano and composed. There was no door between us. He knew that I was there, but it did not disturb him in the least. In this way I saw a considerable part of *Die Walküre* being written. Some of it he would show me in the form of a sketch – I am thinking, for example, of the music accompanying the handing over of the mead in the opening act, a passage that captivated me immediately.

Now and then he would play us whole acts, including ones from earlier operas. In the presence of the Ritters, Wesendonks, Heims[2]

---

1. Wagner started work on the complete draft of Act Three of *Die Walküre* on 20 November 1854.
2. Ignaz Heim (1818–80) was a song composer and conductor of the local choral society. His wife Emilie (1830–1912) was a singer. A read-through of Act One of *Die Walküre* took place in Wagner's rooms on 26 April 1856. The pianist was Theodor Kirchner (1823–1903).

and myself, he performed the first act of *Die Walküre* for us. Frau Heim, an excellent singer, supported him. It was a strange première.

He himself did not sing at all badly, achieving much with little voice. It was a fairly average voice, though he felt more comfortable in a higher register. Much the same could be said of his piano playing. Without being properly trained, he could none the less achieve all he wanted.

That evening he was very happy. On such occasions he was kind and avoided cutting capers. Unfortunately this was not always the case. He could also be quite unbearable.

The presence of Frau Wesendonk always put him on edge. It seemed that he could not bear it when she paid him no attention.

I remember one particular evening, when more or less the same company had gathered in his rooms for supper. It was one that left a bitter aftertaste. No music was performed that evening. He was used to holding the floor. On that evening each of us spoke with his or her neighbour. Suddenly he uttered a scream, so that everyone jumped to attention. It was brief but piercing, like a pistol shot. Everyone stared at him, whereupon he announced with the utmost calm that he was particularly fond of *The Golden Pot* by Amadeus Hoffmann and now intended to read it to us. He read it from start to finish. By now it was very late. At the end of the reading, Wesendonk permitted himself a by no means inappropriate remark on this type of Romanticism, for which he admitted to having no time. At this, Wagner flew at him in a rage and it was only thanks to Wesendonk's restraint that the evening did not end in a row.

But a further surprise was in store. Towards the end he broke into a jeremiad to the effect that he was being pursued by creditors on account of the junk all around him. The next day Wesendonk paid his bills. It needed all the fanatical devotion that is typical of young people to forget the impression that this made.

Conversely, he was enchanting whenever he went walking with Ritter and me. Witty insights flew through the air. He regaled us with tales from the rich storehouse of his experiences. Many a word of wisdom there was to be heard. Idiosyncratic views on people, relationships, art and politics were aired. His whole good-naturedness, of which he had a plentiful supply, came to the fore. There was something touching about his love of animals. Whenever his fellow feeling was stirred, he was utterly disarmed. He had long since ceased to love his wife and was consumed with passion for another. He grew violent, sullen, offensive, but never crude. He could have wounded his wife with a single word. He never did so. I shall later describe a scene that affords the best possible illustration of this.

His way of speaking would vary immensely. Sometimes he spoke briefly, aptly, succinctly. But then he would start to stutter and choke; there was something effortful about his search for the right expression. He would also begin to mutter between his teeth, not completing his sentences, but leaving his listeners to guess at what he was saying, or making some gesture as though to explain his meaning. Then he was the exact opposite of Schopenhauer, for whom everything was so vividly expressed that it was always impossible to imagine a different way of saying it. No other words seemed possible.

He could be boisterously cheerful, even childish. Then he would start to slide round the floor like a schoolboy. When he was really high-spirited, he spoke the earthiest Saxon dialect. He always had a Saxon accent. Even French, which he spoke fairly badly, he intoned in a Saxon way. I did not like to hear him speak on official occasions. At such times he would work himself up to a pitch of emotion which, I felt, ill became him. They were generally propaganda speeches that never failed to make their mark on those at whom they were aimed. This he understood.

On one of our walks he spoke about fame. 'You young people strive for fame and honour and envy me my successes. What does one get from these honours? You get used to them so quickly and always want more.' [. . .]

His musical hero was, and remained, Beethoven or, to be more precise, late Beethoven. To break a lance for middle-period Beethoven at the expense of the later works struck him as reactionary. I once did so, and he got very worked up.

Even so, he had a great and sincere love of Mozart, which I always found very touching.

Although he could be as touchy as a lady-in-waiting, he did not mind us taking certain liberties. He allowed Ritter to speak some particularly telling home truths. After grumbling briefly, he was his usual affable self. When he asked complainingly why he, of all men, did not have a large fortune – his desire was to own millions – I retorted: 'It still wouldn't be enough for you. You'd find things to complain about Lake Zurich and have it filled in.' 'You don't understand me,' he said, annoyed. And that was that.

He was by no means averse to telling lascivious jokes. Once, when he had told one in the presence of his wife and sister-in-law, he turned as red as any young girl. It suited him to blush.

He told us amusing stories about his life in the theatre. His director at Ballenstedt[1] had an affected son. In Wagner's presence he once said in the most stilted German: 'Dearest papa! May I not join the boys in the streets? We do so want to whittle some swords for ourselves.' Good old Reißiger once said to him: 'My dear colleague, why is it that your operas are so popular and mine are not? After all, they have plenty of tunes!'

He once gave the Berlin critic Ernst Kossak[2] a copy of the text of *Lohengrin* to read. With the sweetest of smiles, the latter said: 'Ah, it is *so* nice.'

And it was with a mischievous smile that he described the 'Corinthian' barricades of his friend Gottfried Semper. At the baptism of a child of Frau Wesendonk[3] I found myself standing next to Wagner. We were at the back. He was exceedingly sullen. Suddenly he muttered to himself: 'It's like attending your own execution.' It was not a remark that suggested an intimate relationship. We were all convinced, in any case, that his relations never went beyond certain bounds. [. . .]

The scene at Wagner's that I touched upon earlier was as follows: I was alone with Wagner at table. Sulzer had sent a splendid fish. Frau Wagner, who always mothered me, drew my attention to the paltry morsel that I had taken and placed a better piece before me. This resulted in an unbelievably stupid scene that was remarkable

1. The Ballenstedt festival was held on 22–3 June 1852 and amounted to a celebration of the music of the New German School. It was run by Liszt and a local hotelier. The director referred to here may have been Hermann Langer (1819–89), who at the time was director of the Leipzig University Choral Society; see Kirchmeyer 1993.
2. Ernst Kossak (1814–80) founded the *Echo* and the *Zeitungshalle*. Wagner met him in Berlin when rehearsing *Rienzi* in October 1847.
3. Guido Wesendonck was born on 13 September 1855 and died on 13 October 1858. In his Annals, Wagner noted: 'Refused invitation to become godfather as it would be unlucky' (BB 125).

even for a man as unpredictable as Wagner. He flew into a rage and shouted at his wife: 'You and your Hornstein! As long as *he* is well provided for! You couldn't care less what your husband gets.' He carried on like this at some length until his wife could take no more and ran from the room in tears, with her sister hard on her heels. And once again he began to fuss, this time that their howling had put him off his meal and so on. I watched in silence as these events unfolded. The whole stupid episode ended with Wagner gradually calming down and asking me to go and comfort his wife; he could not bear passive resistance. I went in search of his wife and sister-in-law and with some difficulty calmed them down. 'Oh, he's a wicked man, a wicked man,' sobbed Frau Wagner. Finally we all sat down again round the table. 'I'm worried about Herr Hornstein,' she wailed. 'What must he think of us?' 'Ach, Hornstein,' he retorted. 'Don't take it amiss. I didn't mean it.' 'Oh, I know you well enough by now,' was my answer. And with that this insane episode came to an end and the roast was served.

Hornstein 1908: 135–45

> In *Mein Leben*, Wagner describes Hornstein as 'a very comical person' and a 'young booby', losing no opportunity to cast aspersions on his intellectual abilities and sexual preferences (ML 506–7). His scorn sprang from Hornstein's refusal to share with him his inheritance in 1861, a refusal grounded in an incident that Hornstein, in an attempt to spare Wagner's feelings, suppressed from his autobiography but which his son felt impelled to publish following the appearance of *Mein Leben* in 1911.

I should add that I often told Ritter and his wife of my regret that I was not in a position to return Wagner's invitations. On each occasion I received the same answer from Ritter: 'Wagner does not expect that now. He knows your circumstances and will follow it up later. He is waiting for a more opportune moment.' I did not like to think that these attentions were not based simply on feelings of friendship. I let Ritter know my sentiments in this regard. 'Oh, there is no question that Wagner likes you a lot and

has a high opinion of your talent,'[1] said Ritter, 'but it is so much
a part of his nature to have these ulterior motives that he is
incapable of making an exception here.'

This was to become even clearer to me. I was told that it was
the done thing to take along a few bottles of wine whenever one
was invited to Wagner's. I never had occasion to convince myself
of this, and even if I had been convinced, I would not have had it
in me to enter so distinguished a house with my coat pockets
bulging with bottles. Wagner's birthday had come round once
again.[2] An invitation to dinner arrived. I was expecting a sizeable
gathering and was extremely surprised to find only Herr
Baumgartner, the conductor of the local Liedertafel, who had made
a name for himself in Switzerland with some attractive and popular
male-voice choruses.[3] At least Wagner will not now begrudge
himself a quiet birthday, I thought to myself. Our little gathering
was extremely relaxed. We reached the dessert. Like a shot, Wagner
suddenly asked his sister-in-law to bring him the wine list from a
nearby wine bar. With some hesitation she carried out this unexpected errand. The wine list arrives. Wagner reads out the names
of the different makes of champagne, together with their prices,
and finally gives instructions for a bottle of middling quality to be
brought. We all felt very uncomfortable. The bottle of champagne
was emptied and Wagner turned to his two guests, a contemptuous
smile playing around his lips as he raised his voice and said: 'Shall
I now give a thaler to each of the gentlemen present?' His wife
and sister-in-law rushed to the door, aghast, much as the ladies of
the court rush from the Wartburg in *Tannhäuser*. Baumgartner and
I were dumbfounded and I think that we both must have felt like
emptying our glasses over our dear host's head. But this was not
such a good idea and so, after a moment's silence, we simply burst
out laughing. We thanked our affable host with a laugh and left.
The women of the house were nowhere to be found. When we

1. As late as November 1856 Wagner wrote to the Winterthur publisher, Jakob
Melchior Rieter-Biedermann (1811–76), recommending Hornstein's sonatas for
publication.
2. 22 May 1856.
3. Wilhelm Baumgartner (1820–67) was another local *lieder* composer whose
works Wagner championed, on this occasion in the columns of the
Eidgenössische Zeitung; see SS xii.286–8.

reached the street, Baumgartner declared that he would never again accept an invitation from Wagner, and for my own part I was already firmly resolved to leave Zurich as soon as was reasonably possible. I also discovered that, like me, Baumgartner had never been in the habit of turning an invitation from Wagner into a picnic.

I went straight to Ritter and, with some warmth, told him the whole story. Ritter was furious. The sensitive Frau Ritter kept changing colour. 'Something's got be done,' exclaimed Ritter as he paced the room. 'But what? I have it! I'll send him a crate of champagne at once.' I was not entirely sure that this would have the intended effect, but Ritter knew what he was doing and it was not long before Wagner came in through the door and launched into the following bizarre explanation: it was not us that he had meant, but the German princes. 'They're performing my operas and are keen on me. But what do I get in return? It doesn't occur to *them* to send me a crate of wine.' And so he went on. But his visit was ill-timed. By now we were pretty furious and he was forced to listen to things that he would rather not have heard. He went very quiet. Finally we began to feel sorry for him and by the time that he left we were outwardly reconciled. But the wound remained and I was now firmly convinced that I could remain in Zurich no longer. The only question now was how I could leave without causing a stir. It was decided that I would remain a few more weeks and not avoid Wagner's house entirely but simply visit him less frequently. And this is what I did. When I took my leave of him, there was no further talk of all this. I had to recount this whole tiresome story as it provides the key to my later behaviour, when Wagner tried to obtain money from me in so shameless a way following my father's death. The correspondence bound up with this extortionate appeal to my purse led to a permanent rift between Wagner and me.

Hornstein 1911: 7–12

MATHILDE WESENDONCK (1828–1902)

Mathilde Wesendonck and her husband Otto settled in
Zurich in 1851 and became acquainted with Wagner
soon afterwards, with Mathilde providing artistic
inspiration while her husband paid his bills. Towards
the end of her life, Mathilde recalled her relationship
with Wagner.

It was not until 1853 that our relations became more friendly and
more intimate. It was then that he began to initiate me into his
aims. He began by reading me his 'Three Opera Poems',[1] which I
found enchanting, followed by the introduction to them and gradually by all his other prose writings, one by one.

I was fond of Beethoven, and so he played me the sonatas; if a
concert was planned at which he was to conduct one of Beethoven's
symphonies, he was tireless in playing the relevant movements both
before and after the rehearsal until I felt quite at home with them.
He was delighted whenever I was able to follow him and his
enthusiasm fired my own. If I appeared at a morning rehearsal at
ten, he would exclaim: 'The very stones must marvel! Frau W. astir
by ten o'clock!'

In 1854 (between 28 June and 27 December) he wrote and
completed the sketches for Die Walküre. The short prelude bears
the letters G....... S.. M........[2]

It was at about this time that Wesendonck gave him an American
gold pen. They were still very rare at that time, but infinitely
better than today's! With this gold pen he wrote the whole of the
orchestral score of Die Walküre, which – quite apart from its
inestimable value in other respects – is a veritable masterpiece of
calligraphy. This score was Wesendonck's property, he had pur-
chased it from the Master. Later, at the Master's request, he
presented it to His Majesty King Ludwig II of Bavaria and in

1. In 1851 Breitkopf & Härtel published the libretti of Der fliegende Holländer,
Tannhäuser and Lohengrin together with Wagner's self-apologia, A
Communication to my Friends, by way of an introduction.
2. Presumably 'Gesegnet sei Mathilde' ('Blessed be Mathilde'); see illus. 10.
Strictly speaking, Mathilde is referring here to the first complete draft of the
opera, which occupied Wagner between these dates.

return received a handwritten letter from the king in token of his gratitude.

A *Faust* Overture that he wrote in Paris in January 1840 and revised in Zurich in January 1855 he intended to dedicate to me. Suddenly, however, he was struck by the thought that this was impossible. 'I cannot possibly pin this terrible motto on you', he exclaimed:

> The god who dwells enthroned within my breast
> Can stir my inner vision's deepest springs,
> But he who binds my strength to his behest
> Brings no command to sway external things.
> Thus life has taught me, with its weary weight,
> To long for death, and the dear light to hate.[1]

As a result he contented himself with giving me the score and adding a few words: 'To the dear woman.'[2]

Once, on a joint excursion to Brunnen, he played excerpts from the 'Eroica' and the C minor Symphony on a cottage piano in the dining room. It was already beginning to grow dark. The next morning, at breakfast, by contrast, I was greeted with the strains of *Lohengrin*.

In 1852 [*recte* 1854] he introduced me to the philosophy of Arthur Schopenhauer and in general was concerned to draw my attention to every important product of the worlds of literature and science. Either he read himself or he discussed their contents with me.

What he composed in the morning he would play on my grand piano in the afternoon, checking over what he had written. It was the hour between five and six; he called himself 'the sandman'.

There were times when he was not satisfied with something and tried to find another way of expressing it. This was the case with the Valhalla motif. I said: 'Master, that's good!' But he replied: 'No, no, it's got to be even better.' For a while he strode impatiently up and down the salon, then finally ran out. He did not appear

1. *Faust* I, ll.1566–71, tr. Philip Wayne.
2. The initials 's.l.F.' ('seiner lieben Freundin') appear at the end of the autograph score of the revised version of the work, now in the Bayreuth Archives. The other works dedicated to Mathilde are the Sonata in A flat major WWV 85 and the first complete draft of *Tristan und Isolde* WWV 90.

the following afternoon and stayed away the next day and the next. Finally he came in, very quietly and unobserved, sat down at the piano and played the glorious motif just as it had been before. 'Well?' I asked. 'Yes, you're right, I can't improve it!'

And so it is to him alone that I owe all that has been best in my life. [. . .]

The years that he spent in Zurich were a time of self-reflection for Wagner, a time of work and inner mellowing, which cannot be ignored without breaking the thread of his overall development. When he left, he was no longer the man that he had been when he arrived.

He never knew 'desolation'. He brought excitement where it had not previously existed. If ever he entered a room, visibly tired and weary, it was wonderful to see how, after a brief rest and refreshment, the clouds would lift from his face and a radiance suffuse his features whenever he sat down at the piano.

The beautiful, spacious apartment in the Escherhäuser[1] had become unbearable because of the many pianos in the neighbouring apartments. He had come to an arrangement with a smith who lived opposite, under the terms of which the latter was not allowed to hammer during the mornings (when Wagner was working) as he was composing Siegfried's Forging Song. Hence his longing for a home of his own, a longing that was finally to be satisfied in April 1857.

He was a great lover of Nature. In his garden he would watch the warbler's little nest,[2] a rose on his desk could make him happy, and the Forest Murmurs in *Siegfried* tell of the whispering treetops in the forests in the Sihl Valley, where he went on long walks, often in the company of the poet Georg Herwegh.[3] Their conversation would then turn on the philosophy of Arthur Schopenhauer.

1. Wagner's rooms at 13 Zeltweg were part of a larger area owned by the Escher family and known locally as the Escherhäuser.
2. Probably a garden warbler (*Sylvia borin*), although the German ('Grasmücke') may also refer to the lesser whitethroat (*Sylvia curruca*) and even the blackcap (*Sylvia atricapilla*).
3. Georg Herwegh (1817–75) deserted to Switzerland in 1839 and made a name for himself writing revolutionary poems, although his reputation suffered following the revolutions of 1848–9. It is generally believed to have been Herwegh who introduced Wagner to the writings of Schopenhauer.

For a time his musical aides-de-camp were Tausig[1] and Hans von Bülow. The latter's gratitude, selflessness and willingness to make sacrifices of every kind knew no bounds. But Tausig, too, was touching in his attempts to read the Master's wishes in his eyes. Once, while he was staying at the Wagners' villa, he played dominoes for an hour with the Master's excitable, ailing wife in order not to disturb Wagner's afternoon nap.

Gottfried Semper's appointment to the Zurich Polytechnic was an event of the happiest kind; Wagner read Gottfried Keller's *Der grüne Heinrich* and *Die Leute von Seldwyla* to us with consummate mastery. His favourites were 'Spiegel das Kätzchen', 'Die drei gerechten Kammacher' and 'Romeo und Julia'.[2]

It was with Frau Eliza Wille at Mariafeld that he discussed everything that moved him most deeply as man and artist.

I should finally like to mention the truest of the true, his family friend, Jakob Sulzer, who was also responsible for Keller's appointment as cantonal secretary.

There was no shortage of visitors from Weimar. And the Countess d'Agoult did not think it beneath her to travel to Zurich from Paris 'Pour faire connaissance des Grandes [*recte* grands] Hommes'.[3]

Richard Wagner loved his 'Asyl', as he called his new home in the Enge near Zurich. He left it with feelings of pain and grief – left it of his own free will! Why? An idle question! From this period dates *Tristan und Isolde*! 'The rest is silence and heads bowed in reverence!'

Wesendonck 1896: 93–4

1. The Polish pianist and composer Carl Tausig (1841–71) arrived in Zurich, on Liszt's recommendation, in May 1858. He was involved in setting up the Bayreuth Patrons' scheme in 1871 but died of typhus only weeks later.
2. The leading Swiss writer Gottfried Keller (1819–90) became a member of Wagner's circle in Zurich following his return from Berlin in 1855. The last three titles are novellas taken from the collection *Die Leute von Seldwyla*, which was published in two volumes in 1856. In general, Wagner preferred the works of dead writers.
3. The Comtesse Marie d'Agoult (1805–76) visited Wagner in Zurich in late July 1858.

IV (1858–64)

1858 *17 August* Wagner leaves the Asyl and travels to Venice, where he arrives on the 29th and stays with Karl Ritter at the Palazzo Giustiniani on the Grand Canal. Minna returns to Dresden in early September. Works on Act Two of *Tristan und Isolde*, which he completes in full score on 18 March 1859

1859 *24 March* Leaves Venice as the political situation worsens
Moves to Lucerne, where he completes the full score of Act Three of *Tristan und Isolde* on 6 August
Sells publication rights of *Ring* to Otto Wesendonck for 6,000 francs per work, but then, with Wesendonck's agreement, negotiates sale of *Das Rheingold* to Franz Schott for 10,000 francs
10 September Moves to Paris, where Minna joins him in mid-November and where he hopes to stage model productions of his operas

France declares war on Austria and defeats the Austrians at Magenta and (with Sardinian help) Solferino. Franco-Austrian armistice, 8 July
German National Association formed with aim of uniting Germany under Prussia, September
Spohr dies (75)
Darwin, *The Origin of Species*
Verdi, *Un ballo in maschera*
Gounod, *Faust*
Dickens, *A Tale of Two Cities*
George Eliot, *Adam Bede*
Tennyson, *Idylls of the King*

1860 Three concerts at Théâtre Italien feature orchestral

excerpts from Wagner's works, 25 January, 1 and 8
February. Deficit written off by Marie Kalergis
March Wagner received by Rossini
At the instigation of the wife of the Austrian ambassador,
Napoleon III gives instructions for *Tannhäuser* to be
staged at the Opéra
Wagner conducts two concerts in Brussels, 24 and 28
March
Unable to repay Wesendonck the 6,000 francs advanced
for *Das Rheingold*, Wagner sells him the rights to the
unwritten *Götterdämmerung*
15 July Partial amnesty allows Wagner to return to all
parts of Germany except Saxony. A brief visit to Hesse and
Baden-Baden between 12 and 19 August leaves him deeply
disillusioned
September Writes essay '*Zukunftsmusik*'
24 September Rehearsals for *Tannhäuser* begin at the
Opéra, but are delayed when Wagner succumbs to typhoid
fever. Completes revised version of Venusberg Scene

> Garibaldi proclaims Victor Emmanuel King of Italy, 26
> October
> Brahms, Joachim and others publish a manifesto attacking the
> New German School
> Wolf, Albéniz, Gustave Charpentier, Mahler and Paderewski
> born
> Schröder-Devrient (55) and Schopenhauer (72) die

1861   *Tannhäuser* staged at Paris Opéra, but the first three
performances (13, 18, 24 March) are disrupted by
politically motivated disturbances, and Wagner withdraws
the score
Discussions in Karlsruhe over possible production of
Tristan und Isolde
11 May Hears *Lohengrin* for the first time at a rehearsal
in Vienna
Restless summer, commuting between Paris, Germany and
Vienna
2–9 August Attends inaugural meeting of Allgemeiner
Deutscher Musikverein in Weimar

September Moves to Vienna in the hope of performing *Tristan und Isolde* there

Decides to write *Die Meistersinger von Nürnberg* in an attempt to pay off his mounting burden of debts and returns to Paris, late December

> Kingdom of Italy proclaimed, 17 March
> Outbreak of American Civil War
> Prince Albert (42) and Marschner (66) die
> Hebbel, *Die Nibelungen*
> Dickens, *Great Expectations*
> George Eliot, *Silas Marner*

1862 Completes libretto of *Die Meistersinger* and travels to Mainz to read it at Schott's house, 5 February. Takes lodgings in nearby Biebrich, where Minna arrives unexpectedly. After 'ten days of hell', the couple decide to live apart

28 March A full amnesty is granted to Wagner, allowing him to return to Saxony

Starts work on the Overture to *Die Meistersinger*

Visitors to Biebrich during the summer include Hans and Cosima von Bülow, Ludwig and Malwina Schnorr von Carolsfeld (whom Wagner coaches in the roles of Tristan and Isolde) and August Röckel, recently released from prison

Wagner's debts increase as a result of his lack of progress on *Die Meistersinger* and Schott's resultant refusal to pay him

1 November Overture to *Die Meistersinger* premièred at the Leipzig Gewandhaus before a small but enthusiastic audience

3–7 November Sees Minna for the last time

Gives up rooms at Biebrich and moves to Vienna for series of concerts of excerpts from his own works, 26 December, 1 and 11 January. The copyists for the concert include Cornelius, Tausig, Weißheimer and Brahms

> *September* Bismarck becomes Prussian premier and makes 'Blood and Iron' speech
> Delius and Debussy born

Halévy dies (62)
Verdi, *La forza del destino*
Hugo, *Les misérables*
Turgenev, *Fathers and Sons*

1863   Losses on Viennese concerts covered by local members of
the aristocracy. Embarks on series of concerts of his own
works in Prague (8 February), St Petersburg (19, 26
February, 6, 21 March, 2, 5 April), Moscow (13, 15, 17
March), Budapest (23, 28 July), Prague (5, 8 November),
Karlsruhe (14, 19 November), Löwenberg (2 December),
Breslau (7 December), Vienna (27 December)
May Moves into villa at Penzing in the suburbs of Vienna
and furnishes it on the proceeds of his Russian concerts

    Polish insurrection crushed
    Mascagni and Munch born
    Delacroix (64) and Jacob Grimm (78) die
    Bizet, *Les pêcheurs de perles*
    Berlioz, *Les Troyens à Carthage*
    Renan, *La vie de Jésus*
    Manet, *Déjeuner sur l'herbe*
    Whistler, *Symphony in White*

1864   Wagner's financial situation grows increasingly desperate
and on 23 March he flees Vienna in order to evade his
creditors. Stays with Eliza Wille at Mariafeld, 26
March–28 April. Travels to Stuttgart, where on 3 May
he is run to earth by King Ludwig II's private secretary

LÉON CARVALHO (1825–97)

Wagner arrived in Paris in mid-September 1859 with the
aim of organizing model performances of *Tannhäuser,*
Lohengrin and *Tristan und Isolde.* The French impresario Léon Carvalho had been hoping for some time to
stage *Tannhäuser* at the Théâtre Lyrique and so Wagner
arranged a private audition at his rooms in the Avenue
de Matignon.

I can still see Wagner rigged out in a blue jacket with red frogging
and a yellow smoking cap trimmed with green torsades. He was
waiting for me in his salon, where two grand pianos had been set
up for the performance of his work. With a fire and spirit that I
shall never forget he played me the first part of *Tannhäuser*; then,
dripping with sweat, he disappeared, only to return coiffed with a
red bonnet decorated with yellow braid. His blue jacket had been
replaced by a yellow one highlighted in blue. In this new get-up
he sang me the second part of his opera. He howled, flung himself
about, hit all manner of wrong notes and, to cap it all, sang in
German! And his eyes! The eyes of a madman! I did not dare
contradict him, he frightened me!

Tiersot 1935: 179; see also Gasperini 1866: 53–4

Although Auguste de Gasperini (1825–69) agrees in
essence with this somewhat colourful account, he is
wrong when he claims that this was the last that Wagner
saw of Carvalho. The latter continued to take an interest
in *Tannhäuser,* even after the débâcle at the Opéra in
March 1861. Meanwhile, Wagner had decided that he
stood a greater chance of making an impression in Paris
if he arranged a series of concert performances of
excerpts from his works along the lines of those held in
Zurich in 1853. Three concerts were given at the
Théâtre Italien on 25 January and 1 and 8 February

1860. The programme, which was essentially the same
for all three concerts, comprised the overtures to *Der
fliegende Holländer* and *Tannhäuser*, the preludes to the
opening acts of *Tristan und Isolde* and *Lohengrin* and
orchestral and choral excerpts from *Tannhäuser* and
Lohengrin. The audience included Auber, Baudelaire,
Berlioz, Champfleury, Gounod, Joncières and Reyer.
The timpanist was Jules Massenet.

JULES MASSENET (1842–1912)

Massenet's reminiscence dates from the very end of his
life and may not be entirely reliable.[1]

In the orchestra they were either for or against Wagner; two parties
had formed, and violent arguments raged between them. One day,
after the rehearsal, a veritable battle broke out at the back of the
stage, which had been turned into a concert hall. The music had
had such a powerful effect on me that I had burst into tears.
Wagner was not sure what was happening and, as a result of the
exertions involved in the rehearsals, was extremely agitated and
on edge. He fought his way to the noisy group at the back and asked
what was going on. For a whole minute the disputants found
themselves in a state of great embarrassment, until one of them
pointed at me and said: 'Here's someone who would go through
fire and water for you.' Wagner looked at me, placed his hand on
my shoulder and said in a tone of voice that clearly betrayed his
emotion: 'That's good, young man, thank you!' He had guessed
what the argument was about. The concert was a genuine success;
in particular the pieces from *Lohengrin* left a deep impression.

Massenet 1961: 5

---

1. He also claimed to have spent ten days with Wagner at Villiers-sur-Marne,
working with the tenor Gustave Roger (1815–79) on the translation of
Tannhäuser, but his account diverges at too many points from the version offered
by Léon Leroy (Leroy 1884) to be considered trustworthy.

VICTORIN DE JONCIÈRES (1839–1903)

The composer Victorin de Joncières recalls the first concert.

In the grand-tier boxes sat Auber, seemingly bored and indifferent, with his two female aides-de-camp; Berlioz, corseted into his tightly buttoned frock coat, his neck imprisoned in a high black silk cravat that was fashionable in the years around 1830 and from which his haughty head emerged like that of a bird of prey, with his disproportionately broad brow beneath its mop of grey hair, his piercing eyes and his fixed, sardonic grin; and, further away, Fiorentino, the influential critic of *Le constitutionnel*, his fat prelate's hand stroking his luxuriant beard that spread out over his white waistcoat.

In the orchestra stalls sat Gounod, the young composer whom the recent production of *Faust* at the Théâtre Lyrique had brought to wider notice and who could be seen talking to Carvalho, while the latter pulled at his auburn side-whiskers; the blond-haired Reyer, whose only works to have been seen at that date were a one-act comic opera *Maître Wolfram* and a ballet *Sacountalâ* and who was chatting to his collaborator, Théophile Gautier, the latter distinguished by his leonine mane and flowing beard. Azévédo, the intractable critic of *L'opinion nationale*, less filthy than usual, was alternately cleaning his nails and picking his teeth with the point of a penknife.

At the back of a ground-floor box lurked Hans von Bülow, the new Messiah's fervent apostle, who had rehearsed the chorus for a whole month in the Salle Beethoven. He was accompanied by his young wife, the blonde Cosima, Liszt's daughter,[1] who ten years later was to divorce him and marry the composer of *Tristan und Isolde*. With them could also be seen Émile Ollivier, one of *Les Cinq*,[2] who married Mme Bülow's sister, a

1. Cosima (1837–1930) was in fact in Berlin, mourning the death of her brother, Daniel, who had died on 13 December 1859.
2. The French lawyer and politician Émile Ollivier (1825–1913) was a member of the opposition and, together with Louis Darimon (1819–1902), Jules Favre (1809–80), Jacques-Louis Hénon (1802–72) and Ernest Picard (1821–77), formed the group known as 'Les Cinq' in 1857, obtaining a number of constitutional

charming creature who died only a few years later in the very flower of her youth.

And, more or less everywhere, were Germans who had come to support their compatriot's cause, professors from the Conservatoire, Ambroise Thomas, Reber, Carafa, Leborne, Elwart and so on and so forth.

For my own part, I was lucky to have obtained a seat in one of the fourth-tier boxes placed at the disposal of composition pupils at the Conservatoire. I had enrolled in Leborne's class only a few months previously, having definitively quit the École des Beaux-Arts and abandoned painting for music.

Whenever I saw my former comrades from the atelier in their sumptuous private mansions, I often asked myself whether I had taken the right decision.

On stage, a tiered platform had been constructed for the musicians; the chorus, on a lower level, occupied the position normally taken by the orchestra at opera performances.

Suddenly all conversation ceased and a palpable silence ensued: a man approaching fifty, small in stature, a voluminous head shaded by long hair proudly thrown back, a domed forehead surmounting two flashing eyes, thin-lipped and with a protruding chin framed by brown side-whiskers, passed through the ranks of musicians with a rapid, nervous tread. He was followed by a servant dressed in the showy livery of the second act of *La traviata* who, with comic gravity, carried an ebony baton upon a silver tray. Wagner feverishly clambered on to the conductor's little podium, removed his white gloves, which he tossed into the tray with a disdainful gesture, and took up his commander's baton, while the valet bowed deeply, then withdrew. This little scene, which would no doubt have impressed a naïve German audience, produced a slight murmur of mirth that was rapidly quelled by the conductor's three sharp taps on his music stand, as he gave a signal for the orchestra to begin.

And the amazing tempest of *The Flying Dutchman* unleashes

concessions from Napoleon III. In January 1870 he accepted Napoleon's invitation to form a new government and was thus responsible for declaring war on Prussia in July 1870. He married Liszt's daughter, Blandine (1835–62), in 1857.

its strident squalls on an audience literally stunned by so unexpected a storm: cloudbanks form, then burst in torrents of water, lightning rends the darkened sky and the rumbling of thunder is mixed with the moans of the wind. All at once the storm subsides and a wistful melody rises above this appalling cataclysm: it is the ballad that Senta will sing, Senta the maid who loves the accursed Dutchman and who is faithful to him unto death. This touching melody, archaic in outline, returns again and again throughout his torment, now curtailed and weakened, now whole and triumphant, before fading away at the end, borne aloft by the harps,[1] in the starry heights of infinity.

It is clear that the vast mass of listeners understood very little of this splendid symphonic piece, a piece so moving in its twofold expression of the picturesque and the psychological. If people applauded, it was more from politeness than conviction. Wagner bowed very low, the slowness of his gesture designed to prolong the applause. 'He's a cunning old fox,' said one of my neighbours, quite rightly, 'he knows every trick in the book.'

Joncières 1898: 9–11; see also Gasperini 1866: 55–8

CHARLES HALLÉ

In July 1860 Wagner was granted a partial amnesty, allowing him to return to every part of Germany save Saxony. In August he availed himself of that opportunity to visit Minna in Bad Soden, where she was taking the waters. Other towns that he visited on this week-long stay were Frankfurt (where he saw his brother Albert), Heidelberg, Baden-Baden (where he was able to thank Princess Augusta of Prussia for her help in obtaining his amnesty) and Mannheim. In Heidelberg he met Hallé for the first time since the early 1840s.

1. Two harps were used in Paris in 1860, although the number was later reduced to one; see WWV 63 VIII b.

In after years I met Wagner seldom, and each time found it more difficult to recognise in him the genial, modest young companion I had known so well. His manner of speech had become bombastic, often not to be 'understanded of the people.' In 1862[1] we met by accident in the ruins of the old castle of Heidelberg. In the previous winter I had given concert performances of Gluck's 'Iphigenia in Tauris,' in Manchester, London, and other towns with remarkable success. This apparently had interested Wagner greatly, and rather surprised him. He spoke of it at length, and concluded by saying: 'The English are an extraordinary people – *und dennoch weiss ich nicht ob es je bei ihnen zu dem Seufzer kommt, ohne den der Blumenduft der Kunst nicht in den Aether steigt.*' I have quoted this wonderful sentence in the original German, but it may be roughly translated: 'Still, I do not know if ever they arrive at the sigh, without which the aroma of the art does not ascend into space.' Dr. E. Becker, for so many years librarian to H.M. Queen Victoria, was with me on that occasion, and immediately wrote down the sentence in his pocket-book. We never understood it, but felt it was worth preserving.

Hallé 1896: 61–2

LUCIEN PETIPA (1815–98)

In March 1860 Napoleon III issued an imperial ukase requiring *Tannhäuser* to be staged at the Opéra. Although Wagner refused to bow to pressure to provide a ballet in Act Two, thereby incurring the anger of the members of the Jockey Club who regularly dined before the performance and turned up at the theatre only in time to ogle their favourite ballerinas in the traditional second- or third-act ballet, he substantially rewrote the Venusberg Scene in Act One in an attempt to redress what he saw as a dramatic

1. Either a misprint or a lapse of memory: in a letter to his wife dated 17 August 1860 Hallé reports that he has just met Wagner in Heidelberg (Hallé 1896: 257). The Manchester performance of *Iphigénie en Tauride* that he mentions here took place on 25 January 1860. Wagner's own performing version of *Iphigénie en Aulide* had opened in Dresden on 24 February 1847.

imbalance in the piece. His choreographer was Lucien Petipa.[1]

Wagner was living in the Rue d'Aumale when I first went to see him with Monsieur Nuitter.[2] He had just finished the music for the Bacchanal,[3] and he wanted me to hear it and to explain the choreographic effects that he hoped to obtain. The moment we arrived, the composer sat down at the piano. He played with an enthusiasm and a fury that no words can begin to describe. His hands ground the keys. At the same time he flung himself around, shouting the names of the groups as they entered and attempting to conjure up the scenes of this terrible Bacchanal. 'Arrival of the fauns and satyrs, – they turn everything upside down, – the disorder reaches its climax,' the composer screamed at me, hands still pummelling the ivory keyboard, as these musical ravings continued to mount. He banged out a series of chords that caused the whole room to shudder, then suddenly exclaimed: 'A clap of thunder rings out, we're all dead.' At that very moment, a cart full of cobblestones disgorged its load in the street, producing a prolonged and terrible noise. Stupefied, Wagner turned round and we all looked at each other, our eyes wide open. We needed a few moments to recover from our emotion. This is how I was initiated into the new music.

1. Several writers have claimed that it was Lucien's brother, Marius (1818–1910), but the latter spent most of his career in St Petersburg, first as principal dancer and, from 1862, first ballet master. Lucien made his début in *La sylphide* and created the role of Albert in *Giselle*. Among the operas that he choreographed in Paris were *Les vêpres siciliennes* (1855), *La reine de Saba* (1862), *Don Carlos* (1867) and *Hamlet* (1868).
2. Wagner initially took rooms at 4 avenue de Matignon but moved to 16 rue Newton on 20 October. After spending a large sum of money refurbishing this latter property, he was obliged to leave it when the street was dug up as part of Haussmann's plans for rebuilding Paris. Between 15 October 1860 and July 1861 he lived at 3 rue d'Aumale, within walking distance of the Opéra. Charles-Louis-Étienne Truinet (1828–99) was one of the leading opera translators of his day (he wrote under the anagrammatical *nom de plume* of Charles Nuitter) and was drafted in to help with the translation of *Tannhäuser* after a whole series of earlier attempts to produce a translation had come to nothing; for eyewitness accounts of these preliminary skirmishes, see Roche 1863: xvi–xix; Leroy 1884: 41; and Abbate 1984: 133–209 and 428–30.
3. Wagner began work on this scene in mid-December 1860 and completed the full score on 28 January 1861.

[...] For the group of the Three Graces, I went to the Louvre to copy the classical marble. I have even kept the drawing. But it was really a waste of time to be so conscientious, as each dance lasted only a few minutes. I say 'dance', but it would be truer to speak of *tableaux vivants*. [...] Wagner was very happy with what we did to his Bacchanal.[1] He wasn't easy to please. What a devil of a man! At the rehearsals he would go and stand at the back of the auditorium. When he wanted to come down to the orchestra pit to make some remark to the artists, instead of taking the corridor, he would step over the seats, walking as much on his hands as his feet, and risking breaking both arms and legs. One day he leant too far over the orchestra and burnt himself on one of the footlights. You can understand how so demanding a man was bound to annoy many people.

Petipa 1895: 3

MALWIDA VON MEYSENBUG

Malwida von Meysenbug renewed contact with Wagner during the winter of 1859–60, becoming better acquainted with him following her return to Paris in the autumn of 1860.

When we were settled, I went to the Wagners. They no longer had the cheerful little house of the previous winter, but were on the second floor of an apartment house in one of the noisiest, darkest streets of Paris. This change had been necessary for pecuniary reasons. It hurt me dreadfully to see it. I felt how terrible it must be for Wagner to live in such an unsympathetic place.

Before entering the house, I could hear strains of music. I was ushered into the parlor; Mrs. Wagner greeted me, whispered a welcome and offered me a seat. Wagner himself was busy at the grand piano with a young singer who was studying the shepherd's

1. But see ML 629–30 and Bauer 1998: 110–13.

song from *Tannhäuser*.[1] In this way I heard the music I had so longed to hear. When they had finished practising, Wagner came up to me, welcomed me most cordially, saying: 'How fortunate that you have come. You will never hear a better performance than the one to be given here; it is going to be splendid.'

I now divided my life between my household duties with Olga[2] and my visits to the Wagners. To my sorrow, I began to realize more and more that my friend Wagner was not happy in his married life. I had felt the winter before that his wife was little suited to him, that she was not capable of raising him above the many petty and sordid cares and conditions of life, nor of lessening them with greatness of soul and feminine charm. This man, so utterly dominated by his dæmon, should always have a high-minded, understanding woman by his side – a wife who would have known how to mediate between his genius and the world, by understanding that these are always hostile one to the other.

Frau Wagner never grasped this. She wanted to mediate by demanding from the genius concessions to the world which he could not and should not make. From her inability to grasp the essence of genius and its relations to the world, there arose constant friction in their daily life. This was augmented by their not having any children – usually the one reconciling and softening element in marriage. Nevertheless, Frau Wagner was a good woman, and, in

1. Presumably Mélanie-Charlotte Reboux (1834–76), a student from the Conservatoire to whom Wagner, according to Gasperini (1866: 60), took a fancy, even though she was 'manifestly unequal to the task set her. This young person sang out of tune as gaily as you please at the rehearsals. It was still worse at the first performance, when she would have ruined everything, if the battle had not been lost in advance'. Gasperini's memory or judgement must have been at fault, as Reboux went on to create principal roles in Gounod's *Mireille* (1864) and Boito's *Mefistofele* (1868). Other parts in her repertory were Juliette and Valentine.
2. Malwida's ward, Olga Herzen (1850–1953). It may be worth offsetting this paragraph with Wagner's own contemporary assessment of his relations with Malwida in a letter to Mathilde Wesendonck of [12 February 1861]: 'My acquaintances include a democratic old maid, a certain Fräulein von Meysenbug, who is at present staying here as governess to some Russian children. She is unbelievably ugly, but she has this in her favour, that when she was first introduced to me some years ago in London, I treated her very badly in a fit of ill-temper provoked by her effusive ideas on improving the world. This memory stirred me now, and, as a result of my remorse, she now feels more at ease in my presence'; SL 505.

the eyes of the world, decidedly the better and the more unhappy of the two. My sympathies were more for Wagner, however, for whom love should have been the medium of reaching all human hearts. Instead, she made his cup of life more bitter still. [. . .]

In the meantime, the rehearsals of *Tannhäuser* were going on, and Wagner asked me to come to the first complete orchestral rehearsal. There were only a few favored ones in the large Opera House – Wagner's wife and I were the only women. Thus I heard for the first time this music played by a complete orchestra. I was affected as by something sublime and sacred and touched as by some great truth. Everything went beautifully and after the glorious sextette,[1] where the Minnesingers greet Tannhäuser just back from the Venusberg, the orchestra stood up and cheered Wagner enthusiastically. It was one o'clock in the morning before the rehearsal was over.

Wagner was very happy and excited, for all seemed to promise such glorious things, and he invited me and his wife to have supper in the Maison d'Or on the Boulevard des Italiens. We sat in a small room by ourselves. This was a very happy hour. Wagner told us how he had explained the ideally beautiful part of Elizabeth to young Marie Sachs.[2] He had chosen her for the role on account of her magnificent voice, although she was only a beginner. He had explained to her among others the place where she had to answer Wolfram's question with a silent gesture: 'I thank you for your tender friendship, but my path leads there where no one can accompany me.'

Shortly after this rehearsal, the prospects of great success were dimmed. The killjoy hobgoblins which delight in frustrating an ideal moment in the life of man were busy blowing clouds of envy and ill humor from all sides. Political scandal-mongers were dissatisfied that Princess Metternich should have been the one to introduce this work of art, so foreign to the French temperament. The press was dissatisfied because Wagner did not, like Meyerbeer

---

1. *Recte* septet.
2. The Belgian soprano Marie Sasse (1834–1907) made her début as Gilda in 1852. Other roles in her repertory included Countess Almaviva and Eurydice, which she sang to Viardot's Orpheus in Berlioz's version of Gluck's opera. She later created Sélika in *L'Africaine* (1865) and Élisabeth de Valois in *Don Carlos* (1867); see Sasse 1895: 3 and Sasse 1902: 148–53.

and others, give its representatives fine dinners to bribe their tastes. The claque, usually engaged by every composer, foamed with rage because they were banned by Wagner.[1] In the orchestra, too, different factions arose; the incapable conductor[2] had suddenly become hostile. We, the friends and followers, were deeply distressed that Wagner had refused in the beginning to direct the opera himself, as we all had so ardently wished him to do.[3] And lastly – this was the principal thing – the young Paris lions, the men of the Jockey Club, were indignant that there was no ballet of the usual type and at the usual time – that is, in the second act.[4]

It was a known fact that the ladies of the ballet had their wages increased by these gentlemen and that the latter were accustomed to go to the opera after dining, not to hear beautiful harmonies, but to see the most unnatural and most terrible production of modern art, the ballet. After the performance, they became better acquainted with the dancing nymphs behind the scenes.

What did these aristocratic rakes care about a performance of a chaste work of art, which celebrated the victory of sacred love over the frenzy of emotions? Not only did they not care, but they must hate and condemn it even before hearing it. It was the divine judgment on their boundless depravity. These men were the principal instigators of the intrigues which doomed the performance to failure. They had the baseness to buy small whistles beforehand, by means of which they intended to air their opinion of Art.

Thus the clouds gathered even more threateningly, and with fear and trembling, I went to the dress rehearsal. I also took Olga because I wanted her to learn to love music in its best and highest form. The dress rehearsal took place without any outward disturbance. The large audience consisted mostly of friends, among whom was the Princess Metternich – she was enthusiastic. It was a heavenly evening for me, for it was the fulfillment of what I had long

1. Wagner later relented on this point, but by then the damage had been done.
2. (Pierre-)Louis(-Philippe) Dietsch (1808–65) was resident conductor at the Opéra and a composer in his own right, although there is no truth to the claim that his opera Le vaisseau fantôme, first staged at the Paris Opéra on 9 November 1842, was in any way indebted to Wagner's libretto for Der fliegende Holländer; see Millington 1986 and Bloom 1987.
3. As a foreigner, Wagner was not eligible to conduct his own work.
4. For a touchingly naïve reminiscence by one of the Jockeys, the Prince de Sagan (1832–1910), see Sagan 1895.

wished for. Although I felt that there was much to be desired in
the performance and that Wagner would not be satisfied, yet much
of it was very beautiful – as for instance the rôle of Elizabeth, as
sung by Sachs – and I now had an idea of the whole, which fully
confirmed my anticipation. The magic worked on little Olga, too,
as I had hoped it would; she sat lost in awe and enthusiasm, not
becoming tired, although it was very late before the rehearsal was
over. On coming out of the opera, I met Wagner, who was waiting
for his wife. I saw by his face that he was not satisfied and how
little he expected a victory over the hostile forces working against
him.[1]

One more day of thrilling anticipation passed by and then came
the day of the actual performance. I sat in a box with several
women and Czermak.[2] The overture and the first act went off
without any disturbance, and, although the setting of the ghostly
dance of the gods in the Venusberg fell far short of Wagner's idea,
and the three Graces appeared in pink ballet dresses, I nevertheless
heaved a sigh of relief and hoped that our fears were ungrounded.
However, at the change of scene, during the ravishing poetic pro-
gression from the dreary Bacchanalia below, to the peaceful
morning stillness of the Thüringian valley, at the sounds of the
shawm and the Shepherd's song, suddenly a long-prepared attack
broke out, and loud hissing and shouts interrupted the music.
Naturally, Wagner's friends and those of the audience who wanted
to hear it to the end before judging it, did not remain silent.
As these were stronger in numbers, they were victorious and the
performance continued; the singers remained undisturbed, doing
their best.

Unfortunately, it was not long before the noise began again.
Likewise the protest against it, which retained the upper hand; thus
the performance was finished, though because of these frightful
interruptions, it was impossible for anyone to get a correct
impression of the whole.

Words cannot express my excitement and indignation; as other
admirers were likewise indignant. Czermak was so furious that it
was difficult to restrain him from laying hands on some of the

1. On 25 February Wagner had asked to be allowed to conduct the dress rehearsal
and first three performances, but his request was turned down.
2. The Czech painter Jaroslav Czermak (1831–78).

leaders of the opposition. These gentlemen did not hesitate, but sat in full view, holding in their gloved hands the little whistles which, on a given signal, sounded shrill notes.

The following day I went to the Wagners'. I found him perfectly composed, so much so, that even the papers most violently opposed to him in the fight which had broken out in the press, admitted that he had conducted himself in a most dignified manner during the storm of the evening performance. He wanted to withdraw the score and prevent a second performance, because he realized that there could be no real success with such an audience as that of the Paris Opera. We, his close friends, were opposed to this and were anxious for a repetition as we felt positive that it would be successful. In our great excitement we did not stop to consider that this was now an absolute impossibility.

The time for the second performance drew near. The hostile party had armed itself still more. So had the friendly party. The fight was much more bitter than the first time. I was in a box with Wagner's wife and the Hungarian woman who had introduced us. Next to us were Frenchmen who excelled themselves in whistling, hissing and shouting. I was completely beside myself with indignation and gave vent to my anger quite loudly. 'So this is the audience that boasts of good taste and pretends to dictate to the world what is beautiful and excellent in art! A lot of street urchins who haven't even enough manners to let people of another opinion listen in peace and quiet.' I went on speaking in that way so that Mrs. Wagner was frightened and whispered to me: 'Heavens, you are bold, you will get yourself into trouble.' However, I thought of nothing but my anger and my contempt for such an audience. Finally I faced my neighbors and said: 'Gentlemen, at least remember that the wife of the composer is sitting here next to you.' They were startled for a moment and quieted down. Then, however, they began afresh. Nevertheless, they did not succeed in bringing down the curtain and the performance was carried through to the end.

Wagner was now more inclined than ever to stop further scandal, but we others all voted for a third performance. It was to be given on a non-subscription night and we hoped that his opponents would stay away and only those who wanted to hear it would attend. Wagner had decided not to go, so as to escape the unnecessary excitement. His wife also did not attend the performance. I had taken a box so as to bring Olga and little Marie who lived with us. I hoped they would enjoy it undisturbed.

Unfortunately, however, that was not to be. The disturbers were there en masse to carry on their work, arriving for the very beginning, which was unusual for them. The singers were really heroic; they often had to stop for fifteen minutes or more, to let the storm which raged in the audience blow over. They stood quietly, looking into the audience, unshaken, and as soon as it became quiet, sang and went on to the end. Of course the outburst spoiled all enjoyment of the fine individual accomplishments and beautiful scenic effects.

Little Olga was just as indignant as I. She admired Wagner greatly and was moved to the depths of her young soul by this music. It affected her in so wonderful a way that I felt anew the inner truth of it. Olga took part in the fight with true courage, leaning over the edge of the box to call with all her might: 'À la porte, à la porte!' and pointing to the elegant hissing men. Two men in the adjoining box seemed charmed with her eagerness and said several times: 'Elle est charmante!'

It was two o'clock in the morning when we joined friends in the foyer and went to the Wagners, who would, we were sure, wait for an account of the performance. We were not mistaken. They were sitting comfortably at supper, Wagner smoking a pipe. He received the news of the repeated and even more bitter fight with smiling complacency. He joked with Olga, telling her he had heard that she had hissed him. However, I felt by his trembling, when I shook hands with him, that the disagreeable occurrence had excited him. Even though such behavior was a reflection on the public that was guilty of it, there was another hope gone and the dreary path of life, which would not smooth itself, again lay desolate, weary and hopeless before him.

Meysenbug 1937: 303–9

PRINCESS PAULINE METTERNICH (1836–1921)

> Pauline Metternich was the granddaughter of the
> Austrian chancellor and wife of one of his sons by a
> second marriage, Richard von Metternich-Winneburg
> (1829–95), the Austrian ambassador in Paris from 1859
> to 1871. She, too, has left an account of the first night
> of *Tannhäuser*.

The day of the performance drew near, and in most quarters was
awaited with considerable misgivings. Everyone said that protests
would be raised against the horrible 'music of the future,' and that
stormy scenes would take place in the Opera-House. At all the
clubs the men were up in arms because Wagner would not have a
ballet, except for a few dancing poses in the Venusberg scene. The
subscribers to the club boxes at the Opera are accustomed to see
a ballet introduced at half-past nine sharp in every opera (at any
rate, such was the practice in those days). How, indeed, a ballet
could be introduced in the middle of 'Tannhäuser' was more than
any of us could fathom, and Wagner declared that he would not
meet the wishes of those subscribers, because he could not. In this
he was perfectly right, but his obstinacy was to cost him dear. On
the evening of the 13th of March, 1861, I drove with my husband
to the Opera-House, which was then situated in the Rue Lepelletier.
In front of the entrance there was a barricade of carriages, as
was always the case on important first nights. With countless
acquaintances we made for the great staircase. The crowd was
enormous, and I was pelted with a thousand questions, such as,
'Well! Is your Wagner going to be a success?' 'They say he's unbearable,' retorted another. 'Princess,' said someone else, 'prepare to
hear your protégé hissed.' 'Why do you try to force this fellow
down our throats? He declares war upon all melody,' and so forth.

On my entering the great box between the pillars – *loge entre
les colonnes* – opposite the stage, all eyes in the house were turned
towards me, and everyone took stock of me, to see whether I was
excited or not. I put a bold front on the matter, and sat down,
outwardly calm, but inwardly I was in a whirl. I had a presentiment
that things would go wrong, for before a single note was played
people began trying to whistle on keys. In short, an atmosphere of

violent hostility prevailed, and from the start there seemed to be a determination to give 'Tannhäuser' the *coup de grâce*. This was painfully obvious. Then there appeared the most tedious of all conductors – the humdrum and lethargic Haindl.[1] A shrill hiss ran through the house. Haindl, who belonged to the category of conductors who merely beat time, raised his long fiddle-bow (for in France the *bâton* is never used and seems to be unknown). Then began the magnificent overture. When it was finished and had met with a fair measure of applause a gentleman in the box next to me said aloud: 'It's not so bad as I expected.' Later he might have been one of the most enthusiastic visitors to Bayreuth. After this, things went smoothly on the whole. The Venusberg was endured in a rather sulky silence, but when in the first act the little shepherd's song was heard there was loud laughter, and cries came from the gallery, such as: 'When you're quite finished with your reed-pipe tune, you idiot!' and the most hideous cat-calls added to the uproar. So they rang the changes on hissing, laughing, bawling, and contemptuous silence, until the Pilgrims' Chorus. Even Elizabeth's beautiful entrance: 'Thee, dear hall, I greet once more!' met with no favourable response from the audience. Only when the march was played was there warm, nay, enthusiastic applause, and at its conclusion a large part of the audience turned to the box in which I was sitting and gave me an ovation with true Gallic verve, as if *I* had composed the Pilgrims' Chorus!

After this, however, all the glory was over, and not a hand was raised except to put a key or a whistle to the mouth! It was a fiasco of the first water. I could not possibly say whether Niemann[2] was good or bad – I think he was bad: whether Marie Sasse sang or someone in the wings sang for her; in a word, I had lost all faculty for criticism, so great were my dismay and vexation at the failure. The famous dramatic critic, Jules Janin, wrote next day a charming article under the title 'The Fan.'[3] In this article, which

1. Georges François Hainl (1807–73) conducted the first performance of *L'Africaine* in 1865. As noted above, the conductor of *Tannhäuser* was Dietsch.
2. Albert Niemann (1831–1917) was given a year's leave of absence to study the role of Tannhäuser. His strained relations with Wagner notwithstanding, he went on to become arguably the leading Wagner tenor of his day.
3. Janin's reference to Princess Metternich's broken fan first appeared as part of a longer review in the *Journal des débats* on 15 April 1861 and was reprinted

created much stir, he expressed his regret at my disappointment, and, in order to make the affair interesting, recounted how, bathed in tears, I had broken my beautiful and costly fan. The article began: 'It is broken, the beautiful fan.' But the fan was not broken – there is no truth in the pretty story. I held out till the end of the performance, though I suffered real agonies through it all. As we were driving home, I said to my husband: 'Wagner was right; his music won't go down with the Parisians!'

A few more attempts were made to play 'Tannhäuser,' but these performances met with the same opposition, and there was no end to the hissing and bawling. In the club boxes the spectators behaved like men possessed, and before the curtain went up the hubbub always started in the house. Wagner therefore decided to withdraw his opera, and the directors gladly acquiesced in his decision.[1] Thus, after a brief but painful illness 'Tannhäuser' gave up the ghost. Wagner, however, was now in an awkward predicament. He had counted upon the royalties to defray the expenses of his stay in Paris, and it turned out that he was short of funds. Happy-go-lucky, as artists usually are, he had lived far beyond his means, so that debts of all kinds had sprung up like mushrooms here, there, and everywhere. The poor man was at his wits' end, and did not know where to turn. A friend told us in confidence of the distressing situation, and we decided to make a collection among his acquaintances and not too numerous admirers. My husband headed the subscription-list with 5,000 francs, and we succeeded in raising 25,000 francs within twenty-four hours. The debts were paid; Wagner still had a few thousand francs left for his travelling expenses, and left Paris in a very downcast frame of mind.

Metternich 1921: 148–53; see also Servières 1895

---

as a self-contained piece in the *Almanach de la littérature du théâtre et des beaux-arts* (Paris 1862), 88.

1. Writing in 1895 and drawing on information vouchsafed by the Opéra's director in 1861, Alphonse Royer (1803–75), and by the stage manager, Eugène Cormon (1810–1903), Hippolyte Fiérens-Gevaert (1870–1926) insisted that the order to abandon all further performances of *Tannhäuser* came from the Beaux-Arts and that it was only under duress that Wagner wrote to Royer to withdraw the score; see Fiérens-Gevaert 1895: 3; for Cormon's account of the production, see Cormon 1895.

GIACOMO MEYERBEER

In *Mein Leben*, Wagner repeatedly gives the impression
that opposition to *Tannhäuser* was orchestrated by
Meyerbeer, a view repeated by Chamberlain, who
claimed that the scandal was the direct result of
Wagner's remarks about Meyerbeer in 'Jews in Music'
and *Opera and Drama* (Chamberlain 1897: 76–7; see
also Glasenapp iii.285). Meyerbeer, who was in Berlin
at the time, recorded his reaction in his diary.

Today news arrived about the 1st performance of Tannhäuser,
which is said to have been a complete fiasco. The audience is said
to have laughed & sometimes even to have whistled at many
passages (in relation to both words & music). Princess Metternich & Countess Seebach,[1] to whose patronage the performance
of the work is ascribed, were treated to such contempt by the
audience that they left the theatre after the 2nd act. So unusual a
kind of displeasure for what is without doubt a most respectable &
talented work seems to me the result of a cabal, not of proper
judgement, and in my own view may even benefit the work at
future performances.

Staatsbibliothek Berlin, Preußischer Kulturbesitz

EDUARD DEVRIENT

In mid-April and early May Wagner paid two visits
to Karlsruhe in the hope of persuading Grand Duke
Friedrich (1826–1907) and his intendant, Eduard
Devrient, to stage *Tristan und Isolde*.

8 May 1861. Visited Wagner at his hotel. As he says himself, he
has earned absolutely nothing in recent years and got through a
vast amount of money in Paris, all of it belonging to his friends

---

1. Marie von Seebach was the wife of the Saxon ambassador in Paris, Albin Leo
von Seebach (1811–84), who was instrumental in persuading the Saxon court
to grant Wagner a full amnesty. It was Baroness von Seebach who notoriously
considered it 'a risky business' to take her daughter to *Tannhäuser*: see Wagner's
letter to Mathilde Wesendonck of [12 February 1861]; SL 506.

and which he ought now to be seriously thinking of repaying. This poor man sat there in his green velvet dressing gown, lined in purple satin, with Turkish trousers of the same material and a broad brown velvet beret perched askew on his head, making him look particularly comical atop his sharp-featured advocate's face. I left him in no illusion as to the slender hopes that he places in exceptional financial sacrifices on the part of the Grand Duke, both for the production of *Tristan* and, even more, for the honorarium that he is seeking, nay, demanding, so that he can lead a carefree existence in a home of his own, writing his music and doing just as he pleases – naturally, of course, in velvet and satin and the luxurious creature comforts that I know from Zurich. He vacillates between acquiescing in his fate and dreaming up the most fanciful plans and ideas. Finally he said, somewhat ominously, that if all else fails, he will settle in Karlsruhe, where he can live comfortably and inexpensively and travel between Paris and Germany. It would then be a pleasure for him to take an occasional interest in the work of the local theatre and in individual projects. What a hailstorm of trouble and unpleasantness I see looming and threatening me in my old age!

Devrient 1964: ii.382

WENDELIN WEISSHEIMER (1838–1910)

In August 1861 Wagner attended the inaugural festival of the Allgemeiner Deutscher Musikverein in Weimar, an event attended, among others, by Liszt, Bülow, Cornelius, Tausig and the young Wendelin Weißheimer. Weißheimer had first met Wagner in Zurich in July 1858 and in the early sixties was one of his closest associates. Their friendship foundered on Wagner's refusal to endorse his opera, *Theodor Körner*. His detailed account of Wagner is particularly valuable in that it presents a balanced picture. Here he describes Wagner's reception in Weimar, a demonstrative welcome accorded to a composer who, following the débâcle of the Paris *Tannhäuser*, was now hailed as a champion of German art and a victim of the perfidious French.

I was barely twenty yards from the house when I had the most extraordinary surprise: first the head and then the rest of the body of a man appeared above the pine shrubs at the foot of the steps and came bounding up towards me. I peered into his face and was most agreeably surprised to recognize none other than Richard Wagner. He had come unexpectedly to see Liszt, his first visit to his German fatherland that had been closed to him for more than eleven years but that was now open to him once again. It was said that the previous year, at a congress in Baden-Baden, Napoleon III had cornered King Johann of Saxony and persuaded him to restore Germany's great son to his fatherland.

And so he was here – and free! No officious spy was able to dog his every step and arrest him. In 'the case of Wagner', reason had finally prevailed, albeit far too late.

I recovered from my surprise and greeted him most warmly. He recognized me at once and asked whether Liszt was at home. I told him that no one was in: they were all at the rehearsal for the concert. After reflecting for a moment, I asked him whether he would like to go with me: it would be a delightful reunion with Liszt and the others. He immediately said yes, came back down the steps with me and followed me through the town. In my imagination I could already picture the forthcoming scene. We arrived at the hall where the rehearsal was taking place and where I asked him to wait for a moment and let me go in first. Smiling, he stopped. I dashed up the steps into the hall and went straight to Liszt: 'Wagner's here!' Liszt immediately turned to the orchestra: 'Wait! Before we go on with the rehearsal, let's give him a proper fanfare!' Everyone looked expectantly towards the door through which I had disappeared once again. The next moment Wagner appeared in the doorway. The most incredible scenes of jubilation broke out at the sight of him. The orchestra gave him the flourish of their lives, Liszt threw himself at Wagner and both men remained in each other's arms for some time. In many a friendly eye shone tears of joy and emotion. A dense group had gathered around the two men as they stood there kissing and hugging each other, with everyone struggling to obtain a kiss or at least a handshake from the great composer. It seemed to go on for ever.

Weißheimer 1898: 71–3

ÉMILE OLLIVIER

On leaving Weimar on 9 August, Wagner attached
himself to Émile and Blandine Ollivier and travelled
with them to Nuremberg and Bad Reichenhall, where
they met Cosima. Wagner then continued his journey
on his own to Vienna. Here Ollivier records his impressions in his diary.

9 August 1861. We leave Weimar for Munich and Reichenhal [sic].
We are going to visit Cosima, Wagner is travelling with us. Until
now he has been charming, full of poetry, grace, insights. Someone
complained in his presence about the difficulty of arriving at the
top. He replied that to present a work in public is to assert one's
superiority. Before accepting this claim and submitting, the public
resists. You have to fight and conquer them. It is not right to
complain at such a struggle. When you achieve your results, it is
such that it is worth every moment to win them over by violent
efforts. – You're right, I told him: in everything, *violenti rapiunt*.

14 August 1861. Wagner has left us, unfortunately having first
given us an all too plain demonstration of his egoistical and domi-
neering ways and his unbridled self-preoccupation. He had no
scruples in taking possession of a room with two beds, while
Cosima slept on a sofa. He travelled first-class throughout the
journey, even though a German proverb says that it is the act of a
madman to do so, as there is so little difference between first and
second class. Unlike France, where express trains have only first-
class compartments, the express trains here have both. And everywhere he chose only the most expensive items.

Ollivier 1961: ii.29–30

WENDELIN WEISSHEIMER

Wagner returned to Paris to work on the poem of *Die
Meistersinger* – a deliberate attempt to exorcize the
demon of French philistinism by writing this hymn to
German art at the very heart of the enemy camp. He
arrived in Mainz on 4 February and the next day

declaimed the poem at the home of his new publisher,
Franz Schott (1811–74).

We had already taken our seats in the salon as Wagner continued
to pace up and down, now and again looking anxiously at the
door and then at his watch. Finally he declared: 'We'll have to
wait a little while longer, Cornelius isn't here yet!' 'But he's in
Vienna,' I retorted, to which Wagner replied: 'No, any moment
now he will walk in through the door!' Almost at once there was
a knock, and Cornelius entered the salon. He had travelled from
Vienna to Mainz in mid-winter in order to be present when the
text of *Die Meistersinger* was read for the first time.[1] He ought to
have arrived an hour earlier, but as the Rhine was thick with ice
and the pontoon bridge had been swept away, he had had to wait
in Castel for the steamer that was ferrying passengers between the
two banks. 'That's what I call loyalty!' exclaimed Wagner, beaming
with joy, taking Cornelius in his arms and kissing him tempestu-
ously, while the rest of us, initially pinned to our seats by our
astonishment, now leapt up to greet our dear friend, whom we
assumed was elsewhere but who had now appeared in our midst
as though by magic. After greeting and kissing each of us in turn,
he sat down and Wagner finally began his reading, a reading that
I am sure that none of those who was present will ever forget. His
ability to modulate his voice was such that it was soon no longer
necessary for him to indicate the names of his characters. Everyone
knew at once whether it was Eva, Walther, Sachs or Pogner that
was speaking. Especially with David and Beckmesser, there was
something about his voice that made any confusion impossible.
Even in the passage in which the Mastersingers all talk at once,
each of the characters was so clearly distinguished that we already
thought we could hear a proper ensemble casting its spell on
its listeners, who responded with storms of applause. On several
occasions he had to stop and wait for these latter to subside before
he could continue with his feat of rhetorical virtuosity (for such it
was in the truest sense of the term). I scarcely need add how
enchantingly he read such passages as 'Wie duftet doch der Flieder'

1. A preliminary reading had taken place in Paris at the end of January, and the
Schotts had already been regaled with a reading of the prose draft on 3 December
1861.

in the second act and Sachs's allusion to Tristan and Isolde in the third, or how heartfelt was the sound of Eva's words in the unique quintet. At the end of this unforgettable performance, each of those present in the room was aware that he or she had attended the birth of a powerful and pioneering work of art, and its happy owner, Franz Schott, a man of few words, smiled contentedly to himself.

Weißheimer 1898: 88–90

EDUARD HANSLICK

> Wagner repeated this *tour de force* in Vienna on 23
> November. Among those present on this occasion was
> Eduard Hanslick, who, legend has it, recognized himself
> in the figure of Beckmesser and thereafter became
> Wagner's implacable enemy. His own version of this
> memorable evening casts doubt on this Wagnerian
> myth.

Among Wagner's oldest acquaintances was Heinrich Laube, the director of the Burgtheater. He invited Wagner to have lunch with me and a small gathering of friends. I was able to tell Wagner much that was new about the remarkable tale of *Tannhäuser* in Vienna. I had heard the opera in Dresden in 1846 and since then had been tireless in my attempts to commend it to the Court Opera, but it was not until 1859 that it was finally performed there. Two years earlier a suburban director had given the work in a wooden theatre used only during the summer months (the Thalia Theatre) and, in spite of the modest resources at his disposal, the work had enjoyed a notable success.[1] Now the director of the Court Opera, Julius Cornet, submitted six or seven requests to the lord steward's office, asking for permission to perform the opera. On each occasion his request was turned down with reference to the 'immoral libretto'. Only after *Lohengrin* had proved such a great success, did the authorities relent and allow *Tannhäuser* to go ahead, albeit with a number of most curious changes to the text.

1. The Thalia Theatre was run by Johann Hoffmann. The production opened on 28 August 1857.

The censor's office felt encouraged by the reactionary mood of the
fifties to revert to its old tricks, which, unduly sanguine as we
were, we had assumed were a thing of the past. The word 'Rome'
could not be used in the opera. How absurd it sounded when, in
the third act, Wolfram asked Tannhäuser, 'Were you not there?'
and the latter answered, 'Speak not of there!' There was another
amusing incident at the first performance. In Vienna we had got
to know the parody of *Tannhäuser* before the opera proper.[1]
Evening upon evening, audiences flocked to the Carltheater where
this priceless travesty delighted its listeners, with Nestroy as the
Landgrave and Treuman[2] as Tannhäuser. One of the funniest scenes
involved the comic actor Wilhelm Knaack as the Shepherd Boy.
He sat on a leafless tree, singing or, rather, bleating his May Song
and playing the ritornello not on an oboe[3] but on a bassoon. The
effect was indescribable. When the Shepherd Boy struck up his
May Song at the first performance of the real *Tannhäuser*, an
uncontrollable ripple of mirth passed through the entire house, as
everyone thought inevitably of Knaack and his cheeky bassoon.
The excellent tenor from Stuttgart, Adolf Grimminger, who was
singing the part of Tannhäuser, paced mutely to and fro across the
stage, growing increasingly uneasy and embarrassed and surrep-
titiously eyeing himself up and down in the belief that the cause
of the general merriment was some ridiculous lapse in his costume.

Wagner listened to all this with interest, but was otherwise very
offhand with me. Laube told me the reason. Wagner had *heard* –
he never read any reviews, of course – that I had been far less
warm in my support for *Lohengrin* than for *Tannhäuser*. This was
true. There is no denying the great technical and musical progress
in Wagner's later operas, but in *Tannhäuser* he was still in the
first flower of his youth. Only in the finest numbers from *Die
Meistersinger* does one find the same melodic freshness and
immediacy that distinguish *Tannhäuser*. The opening dialogue
between Tannhäuser and Venus (before the banal Hymn to Venus),

1. Nestroy's *Zukunftsposse mit vergangener Musik und gegenwärtigen
Gruppirungen*, with music by Karl Binder (1816–60), opened at the Carltheater
on 31 October 1857.
2. *Recte* Karl Treumann (1823–77), one of the leading figures in Nestroy's
company and also active as a librettist in his own right.
3. *Recte* English horn.

the Bacchanal in the Hörselberg (in the later version of the opera), the male-voice septet at the end of Act One, the second-act finale, the account of the pilgrimage – these are pieces whose musical charm and powerful dramatic expression I no longer find in *Lohengrin*, at least not to the same extent. What one finds in *Lohengrin*, above all, is that most admirable of Wagner's qualities: his ability to put his listener in the requisite mood within only a handful of bars. Listen to the opening of the orchestral prelude, to Elsa's entrance and the approach of the swan. The first act in general is a brilliant example of dramatic mood-painting. By contrast, I find the scenes between Ortrud and Telramund hollow and wearisome in their affected hysteria, Elsa's much-admired 'Es giebt ein Glück' is trivial and the popular Bridesmaids' Chorus likewise. On the whole, and especially next to *Tannhäuser*, the music of *Lohengrin* is mawkish, spineless and often affected; it is like the white magnesium light into which it is not possible to gaze for long without hurting one's eyes. It is this whitely flickering and unsteady light that dazzles unmusical and sentimental souls. *Lohengrin* is the favourite opera of all sensitive ladies. I find *Tannhäuser* more powerful, manly and natural, and in a good performance – with someone like Niemann! – can still hear it with pleasure, whereas *Lohengrin* soon wearies and bores me. [. . .]

Wagner used his stay in Vienna during the winter of 1862/3 to conduct several major orchestral concerts at the Theater an der Wien, the programmes of which included novelties from *Die Meistersinger* and *Die Walküre*. Dr Josef Standhartner, an enthusiastic Wagnerian, but at the same time kind and tolerant, invited me to a soirée at which Wagner read the complete text of *Die Meistersinger*. It was difficult for me to imagine how one could set the long list of 'modes'[1] reeled off by David. 'Ah, it flows along so easily when sung', said Wagner, 'that you won't even notice.' Leaving aside this and other examples of tasteless diction, I thought that the choice of subject matter was extremely felicitous and that it promised much, especially for a composer like Wagner. I reported on this reading in the *Presse*: 'After the sulphurous glow of the *Ring* comes an appealing genre scene of German municipal life,

1. There is no real English equivalent of Wagner's *Weisen*, which derives from the Middle High German *wîse* and refers to an existing template of metre *and* music.

now comic, now touching, based on a simple premiss, and motivated by the joy and suffering of simple folk. With *Die Meistersinger*, Wagner will do more for the German theatre than with the
Ring; while the latter awaits a future of which it can only dream,
the opera-less present waits for the latter. Wagner has simultaneously opened up two opposing routes. It cannot be a matter
of indifference to German art which of these Wagner will choose
and whether he will prefer to appear before his nation as a mastersinger or as a Nibelung.'

Hanslick 1894: ii.3–8; see also ML 703–4 and *Musikalisches Wochenblatt*, viii (6
July 1877), 388–9

WENDELIN WEISSHEIMER

Meanwhile, Wagner had settled in Biebrich, across the
Rhine from Mainz, where he hoped to work on the
music of *Die Meistersinger*. Here Weißheimer describes
his method of composition.

Sitting at the piano, he worked on the introduction to *Die Meistersinger* in the form of a very detailed sketch that looked like a piano
score but already included all the doublings and inner voices as he
intended to elaborate them for orchestra. He said: 'The more
detailed the sketch, the easier and more assured the instrumentation.' 'Young people very often commit the mistake of working
too hurriedly.' 'In fact, if you want to be really accurate, you
should give each wind instrument a system of its own.' 'Having
two woodwind instruments together on a single system is often a
considerable drawback when it comes to elaborating the part-
writing.' In order for his sketch to be as accurate as possible, he
would invariably consult the piano while preparing it: what
mattered for him was the *actual* sound, not the sound as he had
conceived it in his head. That is why he did not commit to paper
any chord or modulation until he had properly tested it and was
convinced that it sounded good. In other words, he needed to be
near a piano whenever he was working on a draft. The best way
of achieving this was to have the piano lid closed and projecting
over the keys, so that he could easily write on it while striking

individual chords with his left hand or even trying them out with both hands until he was clear about the phrase in question, which he immediately set down on paper, without having to get up and go over to a desk. This measured approach naturally meant that he did not make particularly rapid progress. But what was written down was now fixed, often so fixed, indeed, that he rarely had to change it. And when he moved on to the instrumentation, this went all the more easily and quickly. He told me that he was able to complete around six pages in full score every day, without any special effort.

Following the introduction, which, in spite of its contrapuntal and polyphonic complexities, he was able to get down on paper within only five days, he began work on the first act, attacking it strictly in sequence. The brief exchange between Eva, Magdalena and the knight simply oozed from his pen (and how delightfully!), whereas David proved more problematical. To list and deal with so many modes was no easy matter, but his bubbling good humour helped him through. He was right royally amused by the dancing apprentices and it was a treat to see him perform their comic round in his room, leaping grotesquely and singing their words in the most accomplished falsetto:

> Das Blumenkränzlein aus Seiden fein
> Wird das dem Herrn Ritter beschieden sein?

Outwardly calm though he seemed, he was inwardly terribly excitable while working on a piece. If he was elaborating anything that he had already sketched, my presence did not trouble him in the slightest; but if he was in the process of writing something new, he had to be left alone. Twice I interrupted him in the act of creation – on both occasions through no fault of my own, since he had summoned me in writing from Mainz for a particular time. When I arrived, I knocked at his locked door, but he did not answer and so I assumed he had already gone to the hotel for lunch. I was about to go in search of him there when I heard a noise inside. I knocked again. Finally he opened the door, his features completely altered, almost disturbed. 'I'm busy,' he cried and scurried away, retiring to his bedroom, where he remained hidden until he was quite calm again. I said how sorry I was that I had disturbed him at such a critical moment – he had run away as though he had committed some terrible crime. He laughed and showed me the pages on his piano, saying: 'Here you can see my terrible crime!' I looked at it: it was Pogner's address, which he had sketched out on a single folio. Once he had calmed down, he was happy for people to come, for then he would push back the lid of the piano and play what he had just written and see what impression it made on them. Delightful and alluring as such occasions were, I decided to be more careful in future. When he wrote to me again soon afterwards, asking me to come at a given hour, and the door was not opened to my knocking, I immediately retraced my steps with the intention of waiting for him elsewhere. I had scarcely descended to the street when the balcony door was thrown open above me and he shouted out in utter frenzy: 'Don't interrupt me now – I'm on heat!' An hour later he arrived at the 'Europäischer Hof'. He must still have been somewhat agitated, as he bolted his food almost unchewed, even though he had been warned not to eat so quickly. After the meal, which was normally taken between two and four, he would do no more work but would go for a walk, when he was always extremely talkative.

Weißheimer 1898: 97–100; see also Grey 1992: 102, 113

> Among Wagner's visitors to Biebrich in July 1862 were August Röckel (recently released from prison for his part in the Dresden Uprising), Röckel's wife and Hans and Cosima von Bülow. Together with Weißheimer, they undertook an excursion on the Rhine.

We planned to accompany the Röckels as far as St Goar. When St Goarshausen was called, we assumed that St Goar would be next and so we remained in our seats, only to discover that the two towns lay opposite each other and that a small boat had lain to on either side of our ship in order to ferry passengers to the right or left. In short, we had missed St Goar. Wagner was much put out by this, not least because the countryside now grew flatter. And so I suggested that we should go on to the Siebengebirge, which is said to be among the finest jewels in the area. There was no alternative, and so my suggestion was accepted. We got out at Remagen and had lunch at an extremely busy inn. From the adjoining room we occasionally heard snatches of a male-voice choir from Bonn, and when Wagner heard that they intended to sing for him, he lost no time in dragging us all off for a walk. It seemed as though the whole world and his dog were going to the famous Church of St Apollinaris that day,[1] and both sides of the road were, of course, lined with crowds of cripples and habitual beggars of a kind inseparable from every religious festival. I accompanied Frau von Bülow, while Wagner and her husband went on ahead. On both sides Frau von Bülow eagerly distributed alms, and when her purse was empty, she asked me for mine. This placed me in a ticklish situation, as I knew that Hans von Bülow had quite different views on the subject from his lady wife and that, if I were to accede to her request, both of us would be placed in an unpleasant position – he in repaying what his wife had demanded and I in my refusal to accept it. And so I preferred to do all I could to discourage Frau von Bülow from any further acts of charity. Of course she became quite cross with me and asked with some irritation: 'So you won't give me your porte-monnaie?' 'For any other purpose, I would do so with pleasure,' I said calmly, 'but for this, to my intense regret, no!' She now hurried away up the fairly steep path, hoping to catch up with the others. Once or twice I heard her calling out breathlessly: 'Hans! Hans!' But Hans did not hear and even quickened his steps somewhat, turning off into the church with Wagner as soon as they reached the top. Frau von Bülow, too, disappeared inside.

I followed slowly after them, telling myself: 'Now you're really in for it!' I had just reached the top of the hill when Hans von Bülow emerged from the other side of the church and came quickly over to shake my hand, saying: 'I can't tell you how grateful I am, thank you!' We descended by a different route, in the course of which I set about attempting to restore Frau von Bülow's former spirits.

Once back at the foot of the hill, we took a small boat across to Honnef, where we climbed the Drachenfels. Wagner had thrown his light summer coat over his arm, and we soon reached the summit, talking and joking as we went. We looked around and

1. Apollinaris is believed to have been the first bishop of Ravenna. His name day is 23 July (which in 1862 fell on a Thursday). The present church is a neo-Gothic pile designed by Ernst Zwirner (1802–61), dating from 1839–43.

then, as evening was beginning to fall, the rest of the party decided to make its way back and find accommodation for the night, while I myself preferred to stay up there for the night, as I liked it so much. And so the others set off without me. I arranged to meet the Bülows and Wagner at the railway station at Mehlem on the opposite bank at noon the next day.

Early the next morning I was surprised to receive a visit from a messenger bringing with him a note from Wagner saying that he had lost his little purse containing one hundred thalers. It had probably fallen out of the top pocket of his coat while he was carrying it over his arm. He asked me to keep an eye open on my way down; the purse must be somewhere along the path. I set off at once, but found nothing. I made enquiries and discovered that the path had been used mainly by workmen much earlier that morning on their way to some quarries an hour's walk away. Little consoling though this news was, I none the less decided to send a man to the quarries with instructions to bring any money that may have been found to the station at Mehlem at midday. I found long faces waiting for me at the station when I arrived there. 'Not found anything?' 'No!' I told them about the quarries beyond the mountains – and the temperature sank to zero. We had a snack in the station restaurant to fortify our spirits; the train would not leave for another three-quarters of an hour. During the meal I happened to glance out of the window and saw a young girl, some sixteen years old, running towards the station building. Without drawing attention to myself, I got up and went outside, detaining her with the words: 'Are you bringing the money?' 'Yes,' said the poorly but neatly dressed girl, 'my father found it at four o'clock this morning while on his way to the quarry. Here it is!' O working-class decency!!

I ushered the pretty young child into another room and, summoning the landlady, asked her for a plate and for the flowers on the sideboard. When they arrived, we placed the hundred-thaler note on the plate and decorated it with the flowers. Then I said to the girl: 'Now, go into the next room where you see the gentleman sitting with his back to the window. Curtsey to him and, as you hand over the plate, say: "Herr Wagner, I salute you!" '

I hope she did as she was told. I heard nothing, as I remained outside, peering in through the door, but I saw Wagner make such a face when the country wench strode up to him 'like a creature from the heights of heaven' that it is a crying shame that there was no Raphael on hand to immortalize his expression for posterity. Nor do I know whether he gave the pretty child a kiss, though I consider it likely, as she had certainly earned one – but I do know that, on removing the hundred-thaler note from its poetical surroundings, he immediately ran over to the till, got some change and handed over twenty thalers to the good little girl, who skipped away contentedly. Wagner then called out to the landlady: 'Quick! Let's have two bottles of your best champagne!' And we celebrated in style.

Weißheimer 1898: 135–9

VASILY ANDREYEVICH DOLGORUKII (1804–68)

Vasily Andreyevich Dolgorukii took over as head of the Third Section in June 1856. As such, he was responsible for the surveillance of foreigners in St Petersburg, where Wagner arrived on 12 February (OS) to conduct a series of concerts.

12 February 1863. The composer Wagner is arriving only today, and accommodation has been arranged for him on Nevsky Prospekt, in Prince Meshchersky's house opposite Gostinny Dvor, in the Dutchman Kunst's *chambres garnies*.

Although he took part in the disturbances in Germany in 1848,[1] these days Wagner seems to have settled down: last summer he lived very modestly in Biebrich on the Rhine.

15 February 1863. The composer Wagner has settled in at Prince Meshchersky's house, on the corner of Nevsky Prospekt and Mikhailovsky Street, in rooms managed by the merchant Kunst, where there is a *table d'hôte* every day for tenants and their acquaintances and where visiting foreign merchants usually stay. The accommodation for Wagner was arranged by the Russian

1. *Recte* 1849.

Musical Society, with whose representative, Rubinstein,[1] Wagner is on good terms.

Many local musical personalities have been gathering round him, and he has been overwhelmed with visits. Measures have been taken so that there is sufficient surveillance, but this entails great difficulties because of the location of his apartment.

20 February 1863. Last night, at the Hall of the Nobility, at the end of the concert, and according to the programme, the composer Wagner brought on a male and female choir to perform the national anthem, 'God Save the Tsar', which was received rather coldly by the audience, however. Some even turned and walked out on hearing the first bars: they were all young men with beards. [. . .][2]

15 April 1863. The famous composer of music Wagner has departed and left the country. Theatre musicians say that on the eve of his departure Grand Duchess Elena Pavlovna sent Wagner as a present the contract on the property on the Rhine which Wagner had been negotiating to secure. For this property it seems that the Grand Duchess paid 10 million florins.[3] Wagner really was living in Biebrich on the Rhine last year in a delightful house built in the garden, and was intending to buy it.

Russian State Archives, Moscow, F. 109, Op. 3, D. 2266, L. 1–7

NIKOLAY DMITRIEVICH KASHKIN (1839–1920)

> Kashkin moved to Moscow from his native Voronezh in 1860 and three years later began teaching for the Russian Musical Society. Between 1866 and 1906 he taught the piano and the theory and history of music at the Moscow Conservatory. He was an early champion of Tchaikovsky.

1. One of the foremost pianists of the nineteenth century, Anton Rubinstein (1829–94) founded the Russian Musical Society in 1859 and the St Petersburg Conservatory three years later. He was its director until 1867.
2. The omitted section refers to another performance of the national anthem and is unrelated to Wagner.
3. Wagner did not return to Biebrich but settled in Vienna. The Grand Duchess gave him 1,000 roubles.

At the end of 1862, the oldest Russian musical organization, the Petersburg Philharmonic Society, decided to invite Wagner to come and conduct, and so entered into an agreement with the Imperial Theatres Directorate, which made available the orchestra and auditorium of the then Bolshoi Theatre for the proposed concerts.[1] The huge success of the Petersburg concerts encouraged the Directorate to propose that Wagner repeat them in Moscow, with the box-office receipts to be divided equally between the Directorate and himself, which Wagner readily agreed to, since he was very short of money.

The Moscow office of the Imperial Theatres Directorate was then run by the brother of the composer of the national anthem, 'God Save the Tsar', Leonid Lvov, who was a fairly decent amateur musician, but someone who recognized only operas by Italian and German classical composers, and he had a completely negative attitude to Wagner. The invitation for Wagner to visit Moscow was not in fact arranged on his initiative, but on that of the Petersburg Directorate, which was hoping for the financial success of an undertaking which had brought them a good income.

Amongst the Moscow musicians of that time, Nikolay Rubinstein was the most important. He valued Wagner's musical talent very highly and had managed to organize the performance of some of his works during the first three years of the existence of the concert series of the Moscow branch of the Russian Musical Society, of which he was director. The performances were so successful that most of them had to be repeated. Rubinstein's closest assistant in organizing the concerts was Karl Albrecht, who was an enthusiastic admirer of Wagner's music, and had assiduously studied all his scores. Eduard Langer, who had studied music at the Leipzig Conservatory and who had heard some of Wagner's operas, including *Lohengrin*, while abroad, was no less of an enthusiast. The present author also belonged to this circle of Wagner devotees. Our circle was the centre for Wagnerians in Moscow, who were at that time very few in number. Although Wagner's name was well known, due principally to Serov's articles, almost no one knew any of his music, apart from what was played at the Musical Society.

1. The concerts took place in the Hall of the Nobility.

Wagner finally arrived in Moscow during Lent in 1863, and he stayed, as far as I can remember, at the Hotel Billo. As soon as he arrived in Moscow, by the way, he went to visit Nikolay Rubinstein, both as a famous musician and as representative of the Russian Musical Society. Wagner's first rehearsal was set up for the next day in the Bolshoi Theatre, and Rubinstein and I attended it. Karl Albrecht was actually playing in the orchestra of the Bolshoi Theatre at that time. Before the rehearsal began, when Wagner had just arrived, there was an emotional meeting with his old acquaintance the cellist Carl von Lutzau, who had played twenty-five years before in the Riga orchestra under his baton; they met like old friends and Wagner was clearly glad to see him. The programmes for the forthcoming concerts consisted only of works by Beethoven and by Wagner himself. The rehearsal began with Beethoven's Fifth Symphony, and Wagner amazed everyone at the beginning by standing in front of the orchestra. Before that time, conductors in Russia, as in the rest of Europe, used to stand in the first row of the orchestra facing the audience, but Wagner stood in front of the orchestra, turning his back to the auditorium, and it seemed so natural and sensible that everyone has done the same ever since.

The whole of the Fifth Symphony was played through almost without correction, for the orchestra was electrified by the presence of a European celebrity and played extremely carefully. Apart from that, Wagner's gestures were so well thought through that the players immediately understood his intentions. It should be pointed out, however, that Wagner's manner of conducting was extremely idiosyncratic, and he often did not beat time at all, but traced, for example, a large crescendo with a slow raising of his right hand over the course of several bars, while lightly indicating the tempo with the wrist of his left hand. The orchestra of the Bolshoi Theatre was then very uneven in its composition, and if more than half of the musicians were good, there were also some who were quite weak on the back desks of the strings or the second parts in the wind sections. Whatever the composition of the orchestra, though, everyone played their hearts out. They also played the overture to *Tannhäuser* at this rehearsal, and Wagner made some changes in pencil on the printed score, which had been taken out of the library of the Russian Musical Society. The overture was already familiar to the orchestra as they had played it before when Rubinstein had conducted it, and so, apart from the small changes made by the composer, it went smoothly and extremely well.

From the first movement of the Beethoven symphony it was already possible to discern a characteristic feature of Wagner's conducting, which consisted in his making a small variation in the tempo; this variation was barely noticeable, and I never heard anything like it either before or later. The orchestra had to give its full attention to ensure that the flexibility of the musical line did not interfere with the impeccable refinement of their playing. This manner of conducting gave the first movement of the symphony a kind of declamatory expressiveness. Conductors use a similar device these days, but apply it quite differently, changing the character of the tempo sharply, while with Wagner it was limited to a light, barely noticeable variation, which did nothing to destroy the unity of the general tempo of the work. It was a kind of tempo rubato really, which could be heard when Anton Rubinstein played Beethoven's sonatas, for example. The variation in tempo was much more pronounced in the *Tannhäuser* Overture, but nevertheless not as marked as it usually is these days. Wagner himself did not appear to know about the French horn effect which Arthur Nikisch would later use at the end of the overture, or at least he did not use it.

The Ode to the Evening Star was also included in the programme. The half-Russified Italian Finocchi, who was a member of the Bolshoi Theatre, was supposed to sing it, but refused to do so at the rehearsal because he was ill, although he hoped to be able to sing at the concert the next day. Then Wagner said that he should go through it anyway with the orchestra, and so he sang the whole romance himself, in a pretty decent recitative, but he did not have a terribly pleasant voice. It is curious to note that Wagner was always a little bit flat when he sang, so even the most musical ear clearly does not guarantee that one will be able to sing in tune. No one from the Imperial Theatres Directorate attended the rehearsal, and when it finished Rubinstein introduced Wagner to the best players in the orchestra and also to the present author. [. . .]

Our circle was embarrassed by the way in which Wagner was treated by the theatre management, which ignored him completely after discussing business arrangements. This amazed us all the more since Verdi had come to Moscow a few months previously, having put on his new opera, *La forza del destino*, in Petersburg. He came to Moscow to see the city and its sights, and did not manage to get to know any Moscow musicians during the few days of his stay, or perhaps he had no desire to. The theatre management received Verdi with extraordinary pomp and held a banquet in his honour, which was attended by all the most prominent music lovers from high society, as well as the theatre's senior management, but no musicians were invited. To counter this, Rubinstein decided to organize a dinner in Wagner's honour which he wanted primarily to be attended by musicians, and so he invited the members of the orchestra before anybody else, and most of them were keen to attend. The musicians in the Bolshoi Theatre orchestra received a much lower salary than they do now, and there was no freelance work to be had, apart from the Musical Society concerts, so the dinner had to be organized very cheaply so these poor people could afford it. The occasion took place in the dining room of the Hotel Labadi, on the Lubyanka, to the right of Lubyanka Square, in a building which belonged to an insurance company.[1] The time of the dinner was set early, and there were about forty people present, most of whom were members of the orchestra, but Prince V. F. Odoevsky was present, and so was Prince N. P. Trubetskoy, one of the directors of the Musical Society. The dinner was very straightforward, and there was only cheap red wine to drink, apart from vodka and beer. Rubinstein had ordered a couple of bottles of better wine at his own expense, including a bottle of expensive Rhine wine, especially for Wagner, but it turned out that Wagner preferred French red wine to German wine, so the Rhine wine was drunk by Prince Odoevsky. After the first courses, Prince Odoevsky gave a rather long welcoming speech in French, to which Wagner responded also in French, but with a strong German accent. Then there were other speeches, most of which were in German, and Wagner replied to them sometimes very wittily, but he did not say anything remarkable really. At the end of the dinner Prince Odoevsky left, as did Rubinstein, who had some business to attend to, but most of the other guests stayed for a long time afterwards, and

---

1. More recently it was the location of the headquarters of the KGB.

1 Wagner's stepfather, Ludwig Geyer (1779–1821). Self-portrait, 1813(?), showing Geyer wearing the sort of beret that Wagner himself affected from the 1860s onwards. 2 Wagner's mother, Johanna Rosine Geyer-Wagner née Pätz (1774–1848). Drawing by Auguste Böhm, 1839. 3 A sketch by Ernst Benedikt Kietz (1815–92) depicting a scene from Wagner's childhood and presented to his godson, Richard Avenarius (1843–96), in 1844: 'This for my little godson Richard Avenarius as a gift from his godfather in the absence of any other help. A scene from the life of his mother and of his uncle and godfather Richard Wagner. Paris, 19 Nov. 1844'. 4 Wagner. Pencil drawing by Ernst Benedikt Kietz, 1840–42.

5 Wagner. Photograph by Atelier Pierre Petit & Trinquart, 1860. The earliest known photograph of Wagner, taken in Paris in early March 1860 when he was forty-six.

6 Minna Wagner (1809–66). Photograph taken during the 1850s. 7 Mathilde Wesendonck (1828–1902). Oil painting by Johann Conrad Dorner (1809–66), 1850s. 8 Judith Gautier (1845–1917). Photograph by Nadar, 1875. 9 Cosima (1837–1930) and Richard Wagner. Photograph by Fritz Luckhardt, Vienna, 9 May 1872.

10 The first page of the first complete draft of Act One of 'Die Walküre' WWV 86B II (28 June 1854). The lettering in the top left-hand corner is believed to refer to Mathilde Wesendonck: 'G[esegnet] s[ei] M[athilde]' = 'Blessed be Mathilde'. 11 Letter to Pauline Viardot (1821–1910), 16 March 1869, justifying the republication of 'Jews in Music' and objecting to the tendency to distinguish between 'man' and 'artist'; see Spencer 1994.

12 Wagner acknowledging applause from the royal box at the first performance of 'Die Meistersinger von Nürnberg', 21 June 1868. Caricature by Josef Resch (1819–1901). 13 Wagner rehearsing on stage at the Bayreuth Festspielhaus. Sketch (now lost) by Adolf von Menzel (1815–1905), 8 August 1875. 14 King Ludwig II of Bavaria (1845–86). Photograph by Joseph Albert, 1864.

15 The exterior of the Bayreuth Festspielhaus. Photograph taken during the 1890s. 16 The auditorium of the Bayreuth Festspielhaus during a performance of 'Das Rheingold' in 1876. Drawing by Ludwig Bechstein (1843–1914).

17–18 Wagner conducting in London in 1877. Two drawings (now lost) by Henry Holiday (1839–1927). 19 The three Rhinepersons in the 1876 'Ring': (L. TO R.) Minna Lammert (1852–1921), Lilli Lehmann (1848–1929) and Marie Lehmann (1851–1931).

20 An evening at Wahnfried, 1876. Engraving by Ludwig Bechstein showing
(L. TO R.) Lilli Lehmann (1848–1929), Joseph Rubinstein (1847–84), Hans
Richter (1843–1916), Wagner, Amalie Materna (1844–1918), Franz Betz
(1835–1900), August Wilhelmj (1845–1908), Albert Niemann (1831–1917)
and Fritz Brandt (1846–1927).   21 Wagner and Siegfried (1869–1930).
Photograph by Biondi e Figlio, Naples, 1 June 1880.   22 Wagner. Oil painting
by Auguste Renoir (1841–1919), 15 January 1882.

the dinner then became something of a musicians' junket. Wagner, probably remembering old times and his previous life in musical circles, became so merry that he even started boasting of his gymnastical prowess, having jumped over a card table. Naturally he was helped in all this by the wine, in the consumption of which Wagner was not one of the most restrained. The party then began to become rather chaotic, and Pyotr Jürgenson, who was present at the dinner, suggested that Wagner might like to go over to his flat, remarking on how terribly stuffy it was in the dining room. I was at that time sharing the flat with Jürgenson, and so we all three set off to our flat above Jürgenson's shop. Wagner was in an incredibly good mood, but was not speaking very coherently, and, having drunk a bottle or two of soda water, sat down on the couch. A couple of hours later, after refreshing himself again with soda water, Wagner went home accompanied by Jürgenson, since he would have found it difficult to get there by himself, not knowing any Russian. Wagner later sent his photograph to everyone at the dinner, each individually signed.

Kashkin 1913: 372–8

BERTHA GOLDWAG

On 12 May 1863 Wagner moved into new rooms at 221 Wienstraße, Penzing, which he furnished with the proceeds of his Russian concerts. In this he was assisted by Bertha Goldwag, whose reminiscences were recorded by Ludwig Karpath (1866–1936) in 1906.

'When he moved to Penzing, where, as you know, he lived for some time in a villa, I had to decorate the whole apartment for him. Except for a single room, there were no difficulties, as all the rooms were furnished in the usual way, albeit elegantly. Only a single room, as I say, about the size of a closet, was decorated with extravagant splendour in keeping with Wagner's most detailed instructions. The walls were lined in silk, with relievo garlands all the way round. From the ceiling hung a wonderful lamp with a gentle beam. The whole of the floor was covered in heavy and exceptionally soft rugs in which your feet literally sank. The fur-

nishings of this boudoir – as I should like to call this room –
consisted of a small sofa, a number of armchairs and a small table.
All the seats had expensive covers and cushions, which he generally
used to support his elbows. I made them all myself. No one was
allowed to enter this room. Wagner always remained there alone,
and always during the morning. *Without my having to ask him*,
he once said that he felt particularly at ease in such a room, as the
wonderful colours inspired him to work. Furnishing this room was
entirely my own work. I stood on a ladder, fitted the garlands and
turned my hand to everything. Wagner was invariably so delighted
with my work that I subsequently had to attend to all his needs.
It is completely untrue that I ever made "satin drawers" for him.
He wore satin trousers, but they were normal trousers with a
matching jacket. I also knew the reason for this fancy, if it can be
called a fancy when someone wears satin rather than linen trousers.
The main reason was that Wagner always needed plenty of warmth
to feel comfortable. All the clothes that I made for him had to be
lined and wadded, as Wagner was always complaining that he was
cold. Of course, the Master went in for a certain luxury, I made
him lots of clothes and dressing gowns. That he wanted to have
colourful slippers to go with his colourful clothes is entirely natural.
But even in the case of his slippers, the main thing was that they
should be lined as heavily as possible. The cobbler *Helia* in the
Wollzeile, from whom I ordered his boots, told me that it was
impossible to get so much fur and wadding in a leather shoe.
Wagner loved everything soft. When I was with him in Munich,
he complained that the king's furniture was all so stiff and hard,
and he felt a different person when he sat in the armchairs in his
own apartment, which were all softly upholstered, so that you
sank right into them. The ease with which Wagner felt the cold is
shown by the fact that *even his outdoor clothes were all lined with
the heaviest satin.* As for the many cushions and the covers that
were *intended simply as throws*, I would merely refer you to today's
fashion. The more cushions you see lying on a couch today, the
more attractive is it thought to be. And while earlier generations
wrapped themselves in long linen dressing gowns, you nowadays
see men wearing almost exclusively silk dressing gowns, often
richly trimmed, such as you can see in the windows of the larger

men's outfitters. And what do these people do who now prance
around in these silk dressing gowns?'

'You often visited Wagner in Penzing. Did you ever see him
wearing any of these satin or silk outfits?' 'Never. Neither I myself
nor anyone else. I can tell you that for certain. I should add that
Wagner relied on my discretion and for this reason alone would
never have agreed to see any other milliner, or whatever you want
to call me.[1] At that time I still lived with my parents, curiously
enough in the very house where you find me now.[2] The neighbours
often admired my work, but nobody knew who had ordered it.
One day Wagner came to my rooms to enquire after various items
that he had ordered. It was already dusk, he came and went without
the neighbours noticing. A dressmaker who lived nearby and who
wanted to lure away so excellent a customer once drove after me
in a carriage, but Wagner refused to see her. I discovered this from
Wagner himself. "No, you soul of discretion," he added, "no one
else will displace you!" I always had to be on time, and when I
once arrived fifteen minutes late, I was not admitted. It was some
distance away, the communications were bad, no municipal railway
or tram as there is now, but only a rickety old omnibus that did
not even take me to the door. But I have to say that Wagner never
kept me waiting. Sometimes his friends Cornelius and Taussig [sic]
were there, generally around midday. Wagner ate very simply and
was kind enough to allow me to join him if I was still working on
the alterations that sometimes had to be made to his clothes. *He
was boundlessly affable.* On one occasion – his fiftieth birthday –
a male voice choir performed a serenade. A long procession of
singers arrived with lamps, and Wagner addressed them from the
balcony. He was presented with a silver drinking horn on a cushion.
They drank the best wine from this horn, and I too had to drink.
Wagner specifically wanted me to, honouring me in everyone's
presence in this way. For all his friendliness, Wagner was by no
means frivolous, but always checked my invoices and even discovered errors that I then had to correct.

1. As Karpath notes, the Austrian term *Putzmacherin* has no real equivalent in
other languages. The word 'milliner' is used here in its older sense of a vendor
of fancy goods.
2. 9 Matthäusgasse, close to what is now the Radetzkyplatz in Vienna's third
district. Penzing was on the other side of the city, to the west.

'His household was looked after by Frau Verena *Weidmann*, later
Frau Stocker, and a manservant, Franz, both of whom remained in
Wagner's service after he left Vienna.[1] They were both honest
people, who were loyal to Wagner till their dying day. It was from
them that I learnt that, shortly after Wagner had suddenly left
Vienna in 1864, two gentlemen had appeared at the villa and
demanded to see Wagner's study at all costs. The servants were
reluctant to admit them, but they identified themselves as emissaries
of King Ludwig and explained that they had the latter's instructions
to take away with them a handful of objects that had absolutely
no material value but that Wagner had constantly used. Only then
were they admitted. In fact, all they took were pencils, pens and
similar stuff. Wagner's clandestine departure caused me no little
embarrassment. Although I gave credit to all my best customers,
the bills that Wagner owed me amounted to thousands and now I
did not know how I was to get the money. Frau Vreneli and Franz,
who had also been left without any money, consoled me by saying
that their master would send word as soon as possible and that I
should not lose hope. I went to see the lawyer, Dr von List [*sic*],[2]
in the Schottenhof, to whom the two servants directed me, and he
told me repeatedly that I should not worry, but that I would receive
the money in the shortest possible time. And so it proved. I think
I was one of the first, perhaps even the very first, of Wagner's
creditors to be paid. I had already assumed that this would be the
end of my work for Wagner when I suddenly received instructions
from Munich to travel there immediately. As you know, Wagner
was living in the Briennerstraße. I travelled twice to Munich *in
order to furnish Wagner's rooms there along the lines that were
already familiar to me.* Here, too, I decorated a closet just as I
earlier described it and to this end remained in Wagner's house for
some considerable time.

'I had brought goods with me from Vienna to the value of
around ten thousand florins. At Wagner's bidding, I had to travel
incognito, and in Salzburg, where I had to pass through customs,

1. Verena ('Vreneli') Weidmann (1832–1906) had been in Wagner's employment
since 1859. She married Jakob Stocker (1827–1909) in January 1867. Franz
Mrázek died in 1874 (see CT, 6 August 1874).
2. Eduard von Liszt (1817–79) was the composer's uncle. He later became
Imperial Attorney General; see Eger 1975.

I told them that all the silk shirts, dressing gowns, covers and so on were for a countess in Berlin. My bills were always paid without a hitch. When Wagner moved to Switzerland, I once travelled to Triebschen, where I *saw to the furnishings for a third time*.'

Karpath 1907: 24–9; see also Vetter 1992: 126–8

GUSTAV SCHÖNAICH (1840–1906)

Wagner's doctor in Vienna was Josef Standhartner (1818–92). Here Standhartner's stepson, Gustav Schönaich, recalls a meeting between Wagner and Brahms (1833–97) on 6 February 1864. Also present were Cornelius, Tausig and the Porges brothers, Heinrich (1837–1900) and Friedrich.

We all met that evening at his Penzing villa. The whole company was in the best of moods and Wagner proved particularly attentive to his younger colleague, who was his junior by thirty years.[1] He immediately invited Brahms to play something and the latter responded with a number of pieces by Sebastian Bach, including the Organ Toccata in F major, a work he was fond of playing at that time.[2] At Wagner's express wish, he then played his Variations on a theme of Handel, which Wagner had already heard us praise. His playing that evening bore all the hallmarks of genius, displaying, as it did, that magnificent plasticity that emerged most often when Brahms was performing among musicians or in a private circle that he found sympathetic, qualities that always seemed less pronounced in the presence of a larger audience, when he was invariably filled with unease. None of us who was present on that occasion will ever forget the unfeigned warmth with which Wagner, who always found it impossible to praise a work that had nothing to say to him, commended the young composer and how convincingly he discussed every detail of the piece. 'You see', he said at the end, 'what can still be achieved in the

1. *Recte* twenty.
2. BWV 540.

old forms when someone comes along who knows how to handle them.'

Schönaich 1897; for an account of the later relationship between Wagner and Brahms, see Swafford 1998: 264–9

ELIZA WILLE (1809–93)

Eliza Wille was a novelist who lived with her husband François (1811–96) at Mariafeld near Zurich. Wagner was a regular visitor to their home during the 1850s, and in March 1864, on the run from his creditors in Zurich, he sought refuge with her during her husband's absence in Constantinople.

The weather was stormy and cold despite the approaching spring. Mariafeld was somewhat isolated, and I was sorry that Wagner had to stay here without the stimulating company of the head of the household. Nor was his stay with us enlivened by a single outward incident that I would describe as in any way noteworthy. I had provided our distinguished visitor with exactly the sort of accommodation and facilities that he had requested in his letter. He wanted to work, completely undisturbed, and I had even given him his own servants. Many a visitor from Zurich, lured by curiosity and interest when it was heard that the famous man was staying in Mariafeld, was turned away; Wagner was not in the mood to deal with such interruptions. He wrote and received many letters and asked me to take no notice of him, but to allow him to eat alone in his room, as long as this did not unduly disrupt my household arrangements. It was a pleasure to do my friend's bidding in whatever ways I was able. He did not want to go into Zurich; his work gave him no pleasure, but he went for long walks on his own. I can still see him on our garden terrace in his brown velvet robe with his black beret on his head, pacing to and fro, like some patrician from a picture by Albrecht Dürer.

The peace and quiet that he needed after the terrible experiences that he had had he was to find with us; the demands of a nature like his were not to be denied. His nervous irritability and the powerful workings of his imagination made the difficulties of that

period a sheer torment for him. I understood this and avoided all
that might upset him: there was – I said, and it was my firm
conviction – no man of any importance who had not survived the
struggle with opposing forces of often the most trivial kind and
who had not finally achieved his goal. Wagner answered with a
dismissive smile, but he sensed what I meant and was not displeased. He was in the state of mind in which a son seeks out his
mother if he is fortunate enough still to have one. Even the
strongest man sometimes needs a heart that treats discontent, complaints and unjustified and barely suppressed anger as though they
were a passing distraction. When I spoke of the greatness that was
his in happiness and unhappiness alike and of the immeasurable
riches bestowed on him, so that all the unpleasantness that he had
suffered was of no more significance than the passing clouds, he
did not spurn such consolation. [. . .]

On the days when Wagner felt like joining us the sun seemed to
enter our lives. All who knew him know how warm-hearted and
kind he could be. He paid the friendliest heed to sons and mother
alike. He knew that the 'good lady', as he called me, prized her
sons more highly than the whole divine splendour of Greek youth
and certainly more than the Norse Siegfried. Wagner was also a
delightful tease and raconteur. He had enjoyed himself in Vienna,
which he called the only musical city in Germany.

His rooms in Penzing he had furnished in a way that was both
tasteful and pleasing to him. He told me about the two servants,
one male, the other female, who had seen to his household needs,
and of the large dog, a magnificent, faithful animal that he now
missed.

But his good moods soon passed. Letters arrived that depressed
him. He withdrew to the solitude of his room, and whenever he
found me alone, he would break into a flood of words that rarely
boded well for the future. [. . .]

One day I found the dear man so out of sorts that I did not
know whether to speak or remain silent, yet it was he who had
come to me, he who was waiting for me to ask him something.
How sad it was, I thought, that life's secure and solid bonds in the
form of family, siblings, the friends of his youth and even the wife
whom he had had for years had all now vanished from the life of
this wonderful man. When, years earlier, he had read to us the

preface of *Opera and Drama*, his wife had been with us and she, too, had heard the harsh words that he had spoken on the subject of an unhappy marriage contracted in one's youth under wretched circumstances.[1] She said at the time: 'Well, I've enough letters to prove who was the driving force. It wasn't me!'

Wagner had replied with a laugh: 'You poor woman, who had to live with a monster of a genius!'

I now felt that Wagner had indeed loved this woman in his youth, though she was nowhere near his equal. He was now thinking of her lonely life in Dresden. The responsibility of sending her what she needed was weighing on him, as were other worries caused by his financial entanglements. He had spoken to me about this very worry only the day before.

I said nothing, and so he took out a letter: 'The problem that I told you about yesterday has been solved. In Paris, whenever outdoor concerts are given, they are decent enough to send the composer a royalty on the works that are played in this way!'

Then, suddenly flaring up: 'Everything might have been fine between me and my wife! It was just that I spoilt her utterly and gave in to her in everything. She did not *feel* that a man like me can't live with his wings clipped. What did *she* know of the divine right of passion, a right that I proclaim when the valkyrie, denied the grace of the gods, dies in the flames of the funeral pyre. With love's ultimate sacrifice comes the dusk of the gods!'[2]

With each passing day it became clearer that something exceptional must happen, a bolt from the blue: by self-help and patience alone, this mighty artist could not break free from the rock to which hostile gods had bound him.

It is easy to say all this. But at the time it was not easy to bear, as, moved by deep fellow feeling, I sought to sing songs of solace to the bound figure, songs like those once sung by the helpless Oceanides.

1. Eliza Wille is confusing the preface to *Opera and Drama* with the coeval *Communication to my Friends*, in which Wagner regrets the 'feverish haste' of his marriage and speaks of the 'trials of a poverty-stricken home': GS iv.256; PW i.297.

2. It is difficult to know how much credence to place in this anecdote. Wagner's glorification of love – the 'Feuerbach ending' of the *Ring* – dates from 1852 but had been superseded in 1856 by a Schopenhauerian–Buddhist peroration; see Spencer 1981.

I had collected together everything I could find in my husband's library and placed it in Wagner's room: works on Napoleon, Frederick the Great, even works by German mystics that meant a lot to Wagner at a time when he rejected Feuerbach and Strauß as dry academics.

Blissfully uninhibited, I told him everything I knew; but there was nothing I could say to cheer him.

I can still see him sitting in the armchair that stands now, as it did then, beside my window, listening impatiently as I spoke to him one evening of the glorious future that undoubtedly lay before him. The sun had just set in its majesty, earth and sky were aglow.

Wagner said: 'Why speak of the future when my manuscripts are locked away in the cupboard? Who is to perform the work of art that I alone can produce with the help of benevolent demons, so that the whole world knows that *this* is how it is, *this* is how the Master envisaged and intended it?'

In his agitation, he was pacing up and down the room. Suddenly he stopped in front of me and said: 'Mine is a different kind of organism, I have sensitive nerves, I must have beauty, radiance and light. The world owes me a living! I can't live the miserable life of an organist like your Master Bach! Is it such an outrageous demand to say that I deserve the little bit of luxury that I can bear? I, who can give pleasure to thousands?'

So saying, he raised his head as though in defiance. Then he sat down in the chair by the window again and stared into space. What did he care for the glorious view and the peace of Nature? It was not all joy while Wagner was staying at Mariafeld. [. . .]

I shall pass over a period that Wagner, in one of his letters, described as a Calvary that he had to surmount in order to feel worthy of his own later happiness.

The disagreeable aspects of his situation had made themselves felt through insults that added to his sombre mood. I have too much respect for the lofty gifts of the spirit and the achievements of men of genius not to understand their weaknesses, too.

Letters came and went. Only gradually did a ray of light penetrate the blackness of his mood.

One day, after he had been working solidly all morning, he said: 'My dear friend, your resignation isn't for me. I too could speak

of experiences that you hail as the victory of the invisible forces in
our souls over a seductive world. I know what you mean when
you say that you like the burgher's parlour in which I have set my
Hans Sachs. I think I have also shown another side to him: he
stands outside in the meadow on Midsummer Day, while town
and populace acclaim him because *he* is the mastersinger. The
world will be amazed when it hears the notes and chords that I
strike in honour of my mastersinger! I feel an inner strength and
earnestness of purpose! *My* Hans Sachs is authentically *German*,
as German as the good-natured burgher who sings the song of the
Wittenberg Nightingale in honour of your Luther.[1] You should
respect my mastersinger.'

Wille 1908: 95–108

WENDELIN WEISSHEIMER

> Wagner left Mariafeld on 28 April and the next day
> arrived in Stuttgart, where he stayed at the Marquardt
> Hotel. Weißheimer joined him there on the 30th.

What a sad reunion, to find the great genius helpless and in such
despair! How I shrank when I heard him utter the words: 'I've
reached the end – I can't go on – I'll have to disappear from the
face of the earth, unless you can stop me!' In consternation, I asked
him what had brought about this sudden change, as I had assumed
that he was being well looked after and hard at work, but he said
much the same as he had told Frau Wille, and, to my horror, it
slowly dawned on me that his journey had all the appearance of a
flight – in those days, the law still allowed a creditor to have
a debtor imprisoned.[2] Such a scandal had to be avoided at all costs,
and even though Wagner never said as much, I was not in the least
surprised when he spoke of his choice of a quiet and secluded refuge
where he could hide away until some other solution presented
itself. When he asked me with tears in his eyes whether I would

1. Luther's poem *Die Wittembergisch Nachtigall* (1523) is a 700-line allegory
that praises the nightingale (Luther) at the expense of the lion (the Pope). Wagner
set the opening lines in his 'Wach auf' chorus in Act Three of *Die Meistersinger*.
2. This law was repealed in the German Confederation in 1868.

accompany him – in other words, disappear with him – I agreed
without hesitation. In such a situation he could not be left on his
own and, indeed, could not have managed on his own, as he was
completely without means. I was firmly resolved, therefore, to go
with him and when I said yes, he flung his arms round my neck in
his happiness. We quickly agreed on the choice of some secluded
spot in the Rauhe Alb,[1] where I could finish the vocal score of the
first act of *Die Meistersinger* as soon as possible in order to persuade his publisher, Franz Schott, to continue paying him. Our
departure was fixed for two days hence or, at the latest, Tuesday,
as there was a performance of Mozart's *Don Giovanni* at the
Court Theatre that he was very keen to hear the next day, Sunday
1 May.

We spent the Saturday evening at the home of the local conductor, Karl Eckert, who was no less devoted to Wagner than his
beautiful and kind other half, a woman who, Wagner told me, had
previously been married to a Viennese banker, but who had come
to Stuttgart with Eckert when the latter resigned his post as conductor and intendant in Vienna and moved here. In his previous
capacity, Eckert had paved the way for *Lohengrin*'s triumphant
entry into Vienna. His wife Käthi had followed him to Stuttgart,
having previously divested herself of her banker who, however,
had generously sent her an annual allowance of 4,000 florins. Frau
Eckert was a real Viennese, somewhat corpulent, but full of life
and, as I have said, extremely kind by nature, whereas her husband
was rather gaunt. His health was already giving a certain cause for
concern.[2] Yet his eyes still had a fiery glint in them and he ruled
his court orchestra with astonishing security – and calmness. The
two men fell to talking about the forthcoming performance of *Don
Giovanni* and about the entrance of the stone guest just before the
end, a scene that Wagner described as the greatest in the whole
world of opera, explaining that in Dresden he had reproduced the
sound of the Commendatore's six steps by having someone under
the stage striking forcefully from beneath with a crowbar, which
added to the impact of this terrifying scene in a quite exceptional
way. In order to ensure that the steps coincided with the blows, he

1. A range of mountains between Stuttgart and Ulm.
2. Karl Eckert (1820–79) had been Kapellmeister in Vienna from 1853 to 1860
and held a similar position in Stuttgart from 1860 to 1867.

beat a weighty *alla breve*, recalling that he had once seen an *alla breve* sign at the beginning of the overture (in other words, the same music) in older editions of the score.[1] Mozart must have imagined the tempo here somewhat faster than it is normally taken. Eckert saw what Wagner meant and announced that he would attempt this at the following day's performance of *Don Giovanni* – but for safety's sake he would first let the orchestra know what he was planning. [. . .]

The performance itself was a success. I shall pass over its various points of interest and mention only Angelo Neumann's strikingly long legs, which, if I may be allowed to mix my metaphors, stuck out like sore thumbs in a pair of frightful white tights and amused Wagner hugely.[2] Together with Eckert and the young Johann Joseph Abert,[3] we returned to the hotel, where Wagner lavished the most unqualified praise on Eckert's conducting. With Abert he seemed to be on a not particularly friendly footing and teased him about his behaviour at the time of the *Tannhäuser* affair in Paris. It was impossible to say whether there was any truth in these allegations, but Abert denied that there was, and I expect that they were attributable to spiteful insinuations on the part of his enemies. At one point, the conversation turned to French opera and Wagner cited *La muette de Portici* as a model of its kind, a work in each of whose five brief and highly effective acts, there burnt an inextinguishable fire.[4] Gounod's *Faust* struck him as somewhat sentimentalized, and he said that 'if Meyerbeer had written this opera, it would undoubtedly have had more ideas in

1. Although the time signature in Mozart's autograph score (now in the Bibliothèque Nationale) is indeed *alla breve*, this was emended to a common-time signature in all the early full scores and vocal scores. The *alla breve* marking was not restored until Bernhard Gugler's critical edition of 1868.
2. Angelo Neumann (1838–1910) sang the role of Don Giovanni; see his reminiscences below.
3. Johann Joseph Abert (1832–1915) was the father of the German musicologist Hermann Abert (1871–1927) and Eckert's successor in Stuttgart from 1867 to 1888. He first met Wagner in Paris during the winter of 1860/1 and submitted a not entirely favourable review of *Tannhäuser* to the *Staatsanzeiger für Württemberg* (27 March 1861); see Abert 1916: 53–6.
4. First staged at the Paris Opéra in 1828, Auber's *La muette de Portici* remained one of Wagner's favourite operas; see GS ix.42–60; PW v.35–55; and Bauer 1998: 54–6.

it'.[1] Although opinions may differ on this point, there will be no one who does not share Wagner's high opinion of Auber's *La muette*, and I am happy to inform the world of this now.

We had fixed our departure for the Rauhe Alb for Tuesday 3 May, and so Wagner spent the Monday making a few calls in the town and also went with me to see the court actor, Dr Grunert, who was to take over the running of the Leipzig Stadttheater on 1 September.[2] He effusively recommended my opera *Theodor Körner*, which Grunert immediately agreed to put on. Since his agreement had been given so quickly, Wagner was reluctant to pass straight on to the main purpose of our visit, which was to ask Grunert to make me his conductor in Leipzig. As we were leaving, he said to me, entirely appropriately, that to get his way on two such important points at once had seemed to him too much, but that the post would no doubt be offered to me as a matter of course following the performance of the opera. As we were passing along the street in front of the Königsbau, he added: 'A year before my *Rienzi*, no one in Dresden would have thought of making me music director, still less of appointing me Kapellmeister, and to judge by all that I know about the plot of your opera, *Theodor Körner* will be your *Rienzi*.'[3]

We soon found ourselves back outside our hotel – Wagner clearly had no inkling of the incredible stroke of good fortune that was awaiting him, for I now had to order the carriage that was supposed to take us next morning to Untertürkheim, from where we were to continue our journey by train. Having returned to his first-floor room (facing the direction of the Court Theatre), he began packing his large trunk, again sinking into the depths of gloom as he set about his task. It was around evening when the waiter brought in a visitor's card bearing the inscription: 'Von Pfister-meister, Secrétaire aulique de S. M. le roi de Bavière.' Wagner was feeling so disheartened and assumed that, whatever it was, it boded

1. Although Wagner claims in *Mein Leben* (639) that nothing would have induced him to hear Gounod's *Faust*, he in fact attended a performance in Wiesbaden on 9 February 1862.
2. In the event, Karl Grunert (1810–69) remained in Stuttgart, and Theodor von Witte took over in Leipzig.
3. Weißheimer's 'patriotic opera' *Theodor Körner* was first staged in Munich on 28 May 1872.

no good, with the result that he could not initially bring himself to receive Herr von Pfistermeister, and it was only when the latter insisted that he had come on the supreme orders of King Ludwig II and begged most insistently for an audience that Wagner agreed to admit him. In order not to disturb him during what was bound to be an extremely important meeting, I made my excuses and left. The meeting went on and on – a good sign! When the gentleman in question finally took his leave and I was able to return to the room, Wagner, who was completely overcome by his sudden change of fortune, showed me a valuable diamond ring of the king's and, on the table, a photograph of His Majesty shining with a wonderful sheen. 'That *this* should have happened to me – and that it should have happened *now*!' And, beside himself with happiness, he threw himself around my neck, weeping uncontrollably.

Weißheimer 1898: 260–6

v (1864–72)

1864   4 *May* Wagner meets the newly installed King Ludwig II
of Bavaria. Ludwig pays off his debts and places at his
disposal the Villa Pellet on Lake Starnberg, where Wagner
spends the whole summer, with the exception of two
visits to Vienna to sort out his affairs. Cosima von Bülow
arrives on 29 June and offers herself to him, an offer he
accepts *faute de mieux*
16 July Completes essay 'On State and Religion' for
Ludwig, an attempt to minimize the extent of his earlier
involvement in revolutionary politics
August Writes *Huldigungsmarsch* for King Ludwig
7 October Receives official contract to complete *Ring*
15 October Moves into house at 21 Briennerstraße in
Munich provided by Ludwig
At Wagner's insistence, Bülow is appointed 'performer to
the king' and moves to Munich with his family, 20
November
26 November Ludwig decides to build festival theatre in
Munich for performances of *Ring*
22 December Wagner resumes work on Act Two of
Siegfried
29 December Semper commissioned to design new
theatre

> Following Denmark's annexation of Schleswig, Saxon and
> Hanoverian troops enter Holstein, followed in February by
> Austro-Prussian troops. The Danish forces are defeated at
> Düppel and German troops invade Denmark, April. Under
> the terms of the Peace of Vienna, Denmark cedes Schleswig,
> Holstein and Lauenburg to Austria and Prussia, 30 October
> Wedekind and Richard Strauss born
> Meyerbeer (72) and Lassalle (39) die

Offenbach, *La belle Hélène*
Bruckner, Mass in D minor

1865   Increasing hostility to Wagner both at court and in Munich
in general
23 March Submits report on a school of music to be
established in Munich
10 April Birth of Isolde, Wagner's daughter by Cosima
von Bülow
10 June Première of *Tristan und Isolde* under Hans von
Bülow
17 July At Ludwig's bidding, Wagner begins to dictate his
autobiography
21 July Death of Ludwig Schnorr von Carolsfeld
27–30 August Stays as guest of King Ludwig in hunting
lodge on the Hochkopf and writes prose draft of *Parzival*
14–27 September Writes 'What is German?', a
nationalistic essay intended to prepare the ideological
ground for *Die Meistersinger von Nürnberg*
Public disquiet at Wagner's interference in Bavarian politics
continues to grow and Ludwig is invited by his prime
minister to decide between 'the love of his loyal people
and his friendship for Richard Wagner'
10 December Wagner is asked to leave Munich
23 December Takes out lease on villa near Geneva

Nielsen, Glazunov, Dukas and Sibelius born
Proudhon dies (56)
Meyerbeer, *L'Africaine*

1866   Wagner spends most of January looking for a place to
settle in the south of France
25 January Minna dies, but he does not attend the funeral.
Returns to Geneva, 29 January. Cosima joins him on 8
March
23 March Completes full score of Act One of *Die
Meistersinger*
15 April Moves to Tribschen on Lake Lucerne, where he
is joined by Cosima and her children on 12 May
Ludwig toys with the idea of abdicating and turns up

unannounced at Tribschen on Wagner's birthday, 22 May.
Wagner sees it as Bavaria's role to 'save Germany'. Ludwig
is deceived by Wagner and Cosima into signing a public
declaration that they are not having an affair, 11 June
Continues work on *Die Meistersinger*

> Austria declares war on Prussia, with Bavaria siding with the
> former. Austria defeated at Königgrätz, 3 July. Bavaria
> defeated at Kissingen, 10 July. Prussia's position is
> strengthened
> Busoni and Satie born
> Smetana, *The Bartered Bride*
> Ambroise Thomas, *Mignon*
> Dostoevsky, *Crime and Punishment*

1867   *17 February* Eva, Cosima's second daughter by Wagner,
is born
Visits Munich in March and April to discuss political
situation and proposed school of music
11 June Tension between Wagner and Ludwig over
production of *Lohengrin*
22 June Completes full score of Act Two of *Die
Meistersinger*
9–10 October Liszt visits Wagner at Tribschen in an
attempt to sort out Wagner's private life
Writes 'German Art and German Politics' for Fröbel's
Süddeutsche Presse
24 October Completes full score of Act Three of *Die
Meistersinger*
28 October–4 November Visits Paris
19 December Ludwig bans further publication of 'German
Art and German Politics'

> North German Confederation formed under Prussia. Austria
> and Hungary form Dual Monarchy
> Paris World Fair introduces Japanese art to the West
> Toscanini born
> Baudelaire dies (46)
> Marx, *Das Kapital*, vol. I
> Verdi, *Don Carlos*
> Gounod, *Roméo et Juliette*

Bizet, *La jolie fille de Perth*
Zola, *Thérèse Raquin*

1868　Plans to build a festival theatre in Munich come to nothing
Issues *German Art and German Politics* in book form
Plans republication of *Opera and Drama* and complete
writings in six volumes
Writes memoir of Schnorr von Carolsfeld, 3 May, and of
Rossini, 7 December
21 June Première of *Die Meistersinger von Nürnberg*
under Bülow
August Sketches scenario for play about Luther
Breaks off relations with Röckel and Laube
14 September–6 October Cosima and Wagner visit Italy
together. She decides to seek a divorce, while he informs
Ludwig of their decision
8 November Visits Leipzig and meets Nietzsche
16 November Cosima and her daughters Isolde and Eva
move in with Wagner at Tribschen

　　Freedom of press in France
　　Rossini dies (76)
　　Boito, *Mefistofele*
　　Ambroise Thomas, *Hamlet*
　　Dostoevsky, *The Idiot*

1869　Cosima begins to keep a diary which, by the date of
Wagner's death, runs to nearly one million words
Nietzsche appointed to Chair of Philology at Basel:
between now and April 1872 he visits Tribschen twenty-
three times
Wagner completes second full score of Act Two of *Siegfried*
on 23 February and begins first complete draft of Act
Three on 1 March
March Republishes 'Jews in Music', this time under his
own name
7 May The Royal Academy of Arts in Berlin appoints
Wagner a foreign member
6 June Siegfried born
17 June Bülow agrees to a divorce

16–25 July Visit by Judith Gautier, Catulle Mendès and
Villiers de l'Isle-Adam
22 September Delayed première of *Das Rheingold*,
following inadequacies in the staging, the defection of
Richter (conductor) and Betz (Wotan) and a renewed rift
with the king
2 October Begins first complete draft of
Götterdämmerung, while delaying completion of
Siegfried in order to prevent Ludwig from performing it
31 October Begins essay *On Conducting*
25 December Reads prose draft of *Parzival* to Nietzsche
('renewed feelings of awe', according to CT)

> Suez Canal opens
> First Vatican Council
> Bakunin founds Social Democratic Alliance
> Berlioz dies (65)
> John Stuart Mill, *The Subjection of Women*
> Flaubert, *L'éducation sentimentale*
> Verlaine, *Fêtes galantes*

1870   *5 March* Wagner considers Bayreuth as site for festival
26 June Die Walküre performed in Munich against
Wagner's wishes but to great acclaim
19 July France declares war on Prussia. The occasion
coincides with a visit to Tribschen by Gautier, Mendès,
Villiers, Saint-Saëns, Duparc and Joly
20 July–11 September Writes 'Beethoven' essay to mark
centenary of composer's death
25 August Cosima and Wagner married in Protestant
Church at Lucerne
November Wagner writes *A Capitulation*, a gleeful
pastiche of Offenbach, celebrating France's defeat in the
Franco-Prussian War
December First volume of privately printed
autobiography appears and is sent to a handful of
intimates
25 December First performance of *Siegfried Idyll*

> *18 July* Dogma of Papal Infallibility declared
> Rome becomes the capital of Italy

2 *September* Napoleon capitulates at Sedan
19 *September* Siege of Paris begins
23 *November* Alliance between North German Confederation
and Bavaria
Schliemann begins excavations at Troy
Lenin born
Dickens dies (58)
Delibes, *Coppélia*
Disraeli, *Lothair*

1871   Writes stridently nationalistic poem 'To the German Army
Outside Paris'
5 *February* Completes full score of Act Three of *Siegfried*
14 *April* Kaisermarsch premièred in Berlin
16 *April* Wagner and Cosima visit Bayreuth and decide to
build new theatre there, as the existing one is unsuited
to their needs
28 *April* Delivers lecture *On the Destiny of Opera* to the
Academy of Arts in Berlin
3 *May* Meets Bismarck
5 *May* Conducts concert at Berlin Opera in presence of
court
12 *May* Announces first Bayreuth Festival for 1873
Writes foreword to edition of collected writings (22 May),
a memoir of Auber (31 October) and a nationalistic
report on the 'circumstances and vicissitudes that attended
the realization of the stage festival drama *Der Ring des
Nibelungen*' (7 December)
Visits Bayreuth to discuss arrangements with local
authorities
20 *December* Conducts concert in Mannheim in support
of local Wagner Society (the first of its kind)

   18 *January* Wilhelm I of Prussia proclaimed German Emperor
   at Versailles
   28 *January* Paris capitulates
   18 *March*–28 *May* Paris Commune
   July Bismarck suppresses Roman Catholic office at Ministry
   of Religion (*Kulturkampf*)
   Proust and Valéry born
   Auber (89) and Tausig (29) die
   Darwin, *The Descent of Man*

Whistler, *The Artist's Mother*
Verdi, *Aida*

1872   *8 January* Site for festival theatre chosen below
Bürgerreuth at Bayreuth
1 February Wagner acquires plot of land for Wahnfried
and sets up committee to run the festival
Society of Patrons of the Bayreuth Festival established
Late April The Wagners leave Tribschen and move to
Bayreuth

LUDWIG II OF BAVARIA (1845–86)

It is unclear when Ludwig first became familiar with
Wagner's work (the earliest surviving evidence dates
from 1861) but there is no doubt that Wagner's
Romantic operas filled an emotional void in his life,
developing into such an obsession that by 1863 barely
a day or night passed without his thinking and dreaming
of the composer and his works. He had already resolved
to write to Wagner on 28 December 1863 and, following his accession on 10 March the following year,
he wasted little time in summoning Wagner to Munich.
The following entries are taken from his private diary.

4 May 1864. After two o'clock, rapture, fairest hope fulfilled, the
man I have longed for came: 'Richard Wagner!'[1] spoke until quarter
to four about decline of art, alas! About his career, works!
'Tristan & Isolde', 'Lohengrin', 'Tannhäuser', Meistersinger v.
Nürnberg', 'Ring des Nibelungen'! Music ecstasy! – Sublime
delight! Sun's radiant light! To cherish Him and perish, to grasp
Him, ne'er unclasp Him, to hold Him, joy untold! What wondrous
fate is this! O rapture and, oh, bliss![2]

9 May 1864. O day of joy! Overture to Tannhäuser, joyful, woven
through with joy. Two o'clock. Sublime hour 'Richard Wagner!' –
spoke of his delight at now being able to live for his art, undisturbed and in peace! – His circumstances; the influence that he
must acquire over the theatre, the essay that will proclaim his
intellectual growth, his works, plans, Parcival, who, after a long &
futile search & the most earnest striving, will find the Castle of
the Holy Grail (his soul emerges purified! –). Buddha, Indian
legend, metempsychosis, memory (music) of the past! – Overture

1. These two words are written in large letters across the whole of the double-
page spread.
2. Ludwig is echoing the language of *Tristan und Isolde*, the poem of which had
been published in January 1859.

to Lohengrin, spoke of 'Tristan & Isolde'! Ring of the Nibelung, Brünnhilde, holiest bride! – Of redemption, compassion, love! – spoke until after half past three. Great joy (recitation, Bülow) – Oh, like a dream, I scarcely dare [illegible word]! – The hallowed secret of the essence of the Grail, Lohengrin's departure, he journeys forth by sea! – Love's longing aroused, ardent embrace, Lohengrin, Elsa! – Joy! I cannot speak! – O noble spirit! Sacrosanct are the gifts invested in you! – Sun of life, may you ever shine on him who yearns for you!

29 July 1864. Two o'clock Wagner! Herr v. Bülow, Klindworth, played, sang from 'Die Walküre', 'Tristan & Isolde', Overture to 'Der fliegende Holländer', Faust Overture, – Beethoven's C sharp minor Symphony,[1] dined with me at half past four, spoke of the sad state of affairs (art), Paris, the depravity of the masses, performances of these sublime works! Ah, beautiful, sublime hours! – thank me, O my friends, I am nothing, HE everything.

7 October 1864. The Sublime Light came to see me – moved, plans to complete the 'Ring des Nibelungen'! – Joy inconceivable!

14 December 1864. Wagner to see me this evening: spoke of the sadness, the depravity of artists and the nation, Semper, large theatre, national monument, India, Tristan, Victors.[2]

Evers 1986: 99–100

> Ludwig immediately settled Wagner's most pressing debts of 4,000 florins and a month later presented him with a further 16,000 florins in cash. In the course of their nineteen-year association, Wagner received from the king a total of 562,914 marks, entirely from the civil list (see Eger 1992). The nature of their relationship soon aroused comment, as Friedrich Pecht recalled.

1. Presumably the Fifth Symphony in C minor op. 67.
2. Wagner had first toyed with the idea of a Buddhist opera, *The Victors*, as early as 1856. It was a theme that continued to obsess him until the end of his life: see Suneson 1985 and WWV 89.

FRIEDRICH PECHT

With the outbreak of the Schleswig-Holstein conflict in the winter
of 1864, the situation in Germany finally took a decisive turn and
one, moreover, that we patriots welcomed with enthusiasm. But
the old German lack of political understanding found expression
in the fact that there was virtually no one in southern Germany
who was willing to see Prussia claim these provinces for herself,
even though she had won them by right of conquest. Instead, most
people wanted them to retain their independence and to remain
simply yet another small state. Soon after that King Maximilian
died,[1] and the justifiable grief felt for so benevolent a prince was
made all the greater by the fact that his successor's extreme youth
was bound to fill every thinking person with considerable concern
at a time of such adversity. As we know only too well, his first
independent action was to summon to his side my old friend
Richard Wagner, whom I had seen only once since 1848 – an
encounter in Karlsruhe, when I had been struck for the first time
by a number of curious aspects to his personality. Now that he
entered upon what, for him, was an entirely new field, I was of
some value to him – at least initially – as a tolerably well-informed
and reliable friend, as a result of which he placed great trust in
me. The young king's infatuation with the tone-poet was at first
almost childlike and he treated him in every way as an advisor and
friend, while Wagner in turn displayed the most fatherly tenderness
towards him, but at the same time already imagined himself as
joint ruler of the whole kingdom of Bavaria. In this way I got to
see many letters and notes that the king sent Wagner and that even
then struck me far less for their intellectual content than for their
effusiveness. That this effusiveness would not be mitigated by the
king's dealings with the composer who, genius though he may have
been, was still incredibly excitable, was obvious, more especially
because he was disposed to despise the whole human race, with
very few exceptions, and to treat it simply as material to be
exploited by the elect. As a result, Wagner's influence on the young
king was most emphatically not beneficial, not least because it

1. King Maximilian II of Bavaria died suddenly on 10 March 1864 and was
succeeded by his eighteen-year-old son.

simply encouraged his tendency to become engrossed in his own fantastical world of dreams. After all, Wagner himself was only too willing to believe that the world existed only for the sake of his music and to hold everything else in contempt. Such natural egoism on the part of genius was hardly likely to exert a beneficial influence on anyone like the young king, whose own egoism could only get worse in consequence. Since Wagner also had a large pile of debts and considerable needs, he had no choice but to make excessive demands on the king's exchequer, thereby bringing down on his head the mute hostility of all the officials at court.

It was not long, therefore, before the wildest rumours reached the general public concerning his exploitation of his noble patron. Not only the worthy philistine but court circles, too, would have found it entirely natural if the king had spent ten times as much on a pretty mistress, but on a great artist – well, that was intolerable![1] [. . .]

There can be no doubt that, of all the artists of genius whom I have known, Wagner was by far the most gifted and richly talented. In the first place, none of them possessed his indomitable courage and tremendous will-power. Yet he was the most good-natured and benevolent master towards his servants and, in spite of his feverish impatience, invariably showed them forbearance, doing everything in his power to see to their needs. For his musicians and singers, he was quite literally an inspiration, and they would do anything for him. As a result, there was nothing more interesting than to watch him conduct a rehearsal; then the little man with the enormous head, long body and short legs resembled a volcano spewing out fire and sweeping all before him. His talent, like his courage, never forsook him, even when difficulties and dangers towered far above him. Just as Semper was won over to the cause of the Dresden Uprising by being told to build better barricades than the ones that, in his view, were badly designed, so Wagner rang the tocsin so effectively that many were maddened by nervous excitement, while he once admitted to us at a later date that he had never liked Dresden as much as he did during this hellish

1. It was not long before Wagner became known as Lolus Montez, an allusion to Lola Montez (1820–61), whom Ludwig I took as his mistress and created Countess of Landsfeld.

music of alarm bells. Indeed, his true element was the most violent
excitement.

Pecht 1894: ii.134–42

ADOLF FRIEDRICH VON SCHACK (1815–94)

> Adolf von Schack settled in Munich in 1855 and became
> one of the city's leading patrons of the arts. Active as
> a poet and playwright, he also translated and wrote
> on Arab literature. Both Wagner and Cosima thought
> highly of his work. During the 1860s, he was Wagner's
> neighbour in the Briennerstraße in Munich.

For some considerable time Wagner lived in a house abutting on
to my own, with the result that it seemed only natural for him to
visit my gallery on a fairly frequent basis. In this way I got to know
him and on several occasions had pleasant conversations with him.
Above all, he liked looking at Genelli's paintings and even went so
far as to study their every detail. During his youth he had known
this artist in Leipzig and he told me that he had always admired
him greatly; and his compositions had had a significant influence
on his own art.[1] A further topic of conversation between Wagner
and me was Firdausi.[2] He told me that he had repeatedly read the
latter's poem in my own adaptation and was toying with the idea
of using one of the episodes from the great Persian epic as the
basis of a music drama – this was what he always called his operas.[3]
He vacillated between the tale of Rustam and Asfandiyár and the
death of Siyáwush. It is a matter of deep regret that the Master
never realized this aim. If he had staged one of these episodes, he
would have drawn readers' attention to this great work more than

1. Giovanni Bonaventura Genelli (1798–1868) worked in the neoclassical
tradition. His watercolour *Dionysus Among the Muses* later hung in Wagner's
drawing-room at Tribschen. Wagner's attitude to the visual arts has been
inadequately explored, but see Hall 1992 and Comini 1997.
2. The Persian poet Abul Kasim Mansur Firdausi (*c.*950–1020) is the author of
the epic *Shahnama*, which tells the legendary history of the ancient kings and heroes
of Persia.
3. But see Wagner's article 'On the term "music drama"' of November 1872: GS
ix.302–8; PW v.299–304.

has been the case so far, a work, moreover, which, having dressed it in German guise, I may legitimately describe as one of the most glorious ever written. Wagner also told me that he had often had the idea of taking as the basis of one of his compositions one of the Indian legends that I had adapted in my *Voices from the Ganges*.[1] I do not know which of these legends he had his eye on; but I hear that even in his final year of life he was still preoccupied with this idea and that the text that he was planning was to be called 'The Penitents'. This title could equally well apply, of course, to several of the legends in *Voices from the Ganges*.

Schack 1888: ii.24–5

ÉDOUARD SCHURÉ (1841–1929)

Among the many sympathizers with Wagner's cause who came to Munich for the first performance of *Tristan und Isolde* on 10 June 1865 was the young French writer Édouard Schuré. Inspired by what he heard, he approached the composer in person.

My heart beat wildly as I crossed beneath the Propyläen and entered the Briennerstraße. It was here that Wagner lived in an elegant villa half-hidden by a grove of trees and surrounded by a garden. I opened the iron gate, rang the door bell and was admitted by a mulatto servant, who ushered me into a small salon decorated with dark wall-hangings, luxurious rugs, paintings and statuettes barely visible in the mysterious half light. At that very moment, a curtain parted, and the Master appeared. His powerful hand gripped mine, and I found myself face to face with the composer of *Tristan und Isolde*. He looked tired, and his smile consisted of no more than a slight contraction of his lips. His words tumbled out, coming in fits and starts. After we had exchanged the usual compliments, his first words were: 'Your letter gave me immense

1. Schack's *Stimmen vom Ganges* appeared in 1857. Wagner read it almost at once. The subject matter of *The Victors* was drawn from Eugène Burnouf's *Introduction à l'histoire du buddhisme indien* (Paris 1844), which Wagner read during the winter of 1855/6.

pleasure. I showed it to the king and told him, "You see, everything is not lost!" '

'What?' I exclaimed. 'How could everything be lost after the miracle of these performances? The press is against you, but the public is with you . . .'

'Don't you believe it!' he broke in at once. 'They understand nothing. When a Frenchman shows his enthusiasm, good, then there's no stopping him. But the Germans aren't the same. If, by chance, they are moved, they start to ask if their feelings accord with their philosophy and they go off and consult Hegel's *Logic* or Kant's *Critique of Pure Reason*, or else they write ten volumes to prove that they were not moved and could not have been. Ah! this public, this press, these critics, you see, it's unbelievably wretched. It doesn't exist.'

'So you're not satisfied?'

'Satisfied?' He sprang up, his eyes flashing. 'Satisfied! Yes, when I have *my* theatre, only then will people understand me. For the present, I feel only exasperation, and you find me in a state of extreme irritation.'

He threw himself on the divan, with his head back. He seemed to be genuinely in pain; a yellowish colour and an expression of fatigue suffused his features. But his trembling lips and feverish volubility bespoke a tireless energy and a will that was always ready to reassert itself. The light from the window fell directly on his head and I was finally able to examine it in detail.

Wagner was then fifty-two years old. It was impossible to see this magician's head, evocative and subjugatory, and not retain an indelible impression of it. What a life of bitter struggles and tumultuous emotions could be read in these troubled, furrowed features, in this sunken mouth whose thin lips were both sensuous and sardonic and in this pointed chin that signalled an indomitable will! And in this mask that concealed a demonic drive, this vast beetling brow that told of power and audacity. Yes, this ravaged face bore the traces of passions and sufferings capable of wearing down the lives of many men. But one also felt that this immense brain that laboured constantly beneath this brow had tamed life's baser matter and reduced it to substance for the intellect. In these blue eyes, dimmed with listlessness or flashing with desire, eyes that always seemed to see an immutable goal, there was one con-

stant vision that dominated all others and lent them what I can
only call an eternal virginity: it was a vision of an ideal, the pride
and divine dream of genius!

To observe Wagner's head was to see one after the other, and in
a single face, both Faust and Mephistopheles, the former viewed
from the front, the latter in profile. There were other times when
he resembled a fallen angel, brooding on heaven and saying: 'It
does not exist, but I shall create it.'

In a word, this man impressed me less by his prodigious abilities
and astonishing contrasts than by their formidable concentration
and this marvellous unity of thought and will that was for ever
directed at a single goal.

His manner was no less surprising than his physical appearance,
changing, as it did, between reserve and absolute coldness on the
one hand and, on the other, a familiarity and unceremoniousness
that could hardly have been more complete. There was no trace of
the poseur about him, not a vestige of affected solemnity, no sense
of deliberation or calculation. As soon as he appeared, he burst
forth like a floodtide that nothing can stem. One was left dazzled
by his exuberance and protean nature, a nature, moreover, that
was passionate, private, extreme in everything and yet marvellously
balanced by his all-consuming intellect. The frankness and extreme
daring of a character whose qualities and faults were plain for all
to see had the effect of a spell on some, but served only to repulse
others. His conversation was a constant spectacle as every thought
found a corresponding action. On this vast brow, ideas and sentiments succeeded each other like flashes of lightning, no two of
which were the same. He bore within him all his great heroes.
Within minutes one could see in the expression on his face the
Dutchman's black despair, Tannhäuser's unbridled desire, Lohengrin's unapproachable pride, Hagen's glacial irony and Alberich's
rage. Oh, what a strange whirl of emotions one felt on peering
into this brain. It was, as the poet says, *la bufera infernal che mai
non resta*.[1] And dominating all these characters, there were two
that revealed themselves almost always simultaneously, like the
two poles of his nature: Wotan and Siegfried! Yes, on the deepest
level of his thinking, Wagner resembled Wotan, this German

1. Dante, 'Inferno', Canto V, l.31.

Jupiter, this Scandinavian Odin whom he created in his own image, a strange god, a philosopher and pessimist, for ever troubled by the end of the world, for ever wandering and brooding on the enigma of all things. But in his impulsiveness he resembled Siegfried more than anyone else, the strong and ingenuous hero, who knows neither fear nor scruples, forging a sword for himself and setting out to conquer the world. The miracle is that these two different characters were merged as one. The result was the constant union between profound reflection and ebullient spontaneity. With him, excessive thinking had not dulled his vital spark, and whatever life's vicissitudes, he never ceased to philosophize, combining a calculating, metaphysical intellect with the joy and eternal youth of a truly creative temperament.

His high spirits overflowed into a joyous froth of acts of sheer buffoonery and eccentric jokes, but the least contradiction provoked unprecedented anger. Then he was like a caged lion, roaring like a wild animal, pacing the room, his voice growing hoarse and the words coming out like cries, his words striking at random. He then seemed like an unleashed force of nature, a volcano erupting. But, withal, there were outbursts of ardent sympathy, expressions of touching pity, excessive tenderness for the men he saw suffering, for animals and even for plants. This man of violence could not bear to see a caged bird; a cut flower made him blanch and when he found a sick dog in the street, he had it brought home. Everything about him was larger than life.

Schuré 1933: xxxviii–xlii

JULIUS FRÖBEL (1805–93)

The son of the educational reformer, Julius Fröbel first met Wagner while working as a journalist in Dresden in the 1840s. Following the abortive uprising in Vienna in 1848, he fled to America and did not return to Europe until 1857. By the 1860s he was back in Vienna, where he renewed contact with Wagner. In 1867, at Wagner's instigation, he was appointed the first editor of the *Süddeutsche Presse*, the official Bavarian

journal designed, in Wagner's words, to support 'the
same noble and salutary tendencies' in politics as those
championed by the composer himself (letter to Lorenz
von Düfflipp, 27 July 1867; Petzet 1970: 787). The
following entry is taken from Fröbel's diary.

27 October 1865. In recent weeks – since 16 August, when we
went to Lilienfeld – a number of important links have been forged
with Munich. Friedrich Pecht wrote and asked whether I would
accept a post as editor of a major newspaper to be set up by the
king – one into which the *Bayerische Zeitung* is to be transformed.
The idea is Richard Wagner's, and it was he who suggested me to
the king. The king immediately took to the idea. I have said yes in
principle and, in a second letter to Pecht, explained that I need a
position like this to stop me from returning to America, as we have
often thought of doing in recent months. Later Wagner himself
sent me two memoranda that he has given the king. In one of them
I am described as the only person capable of implementing this
idea. And then Wagner himself came here a few days ago to discuss
the matter in person. The idea is for me to negotiate directly
with the king over the running of the newspaper. Wagner has
latched on to the young king's idealism and natural feelings for all
that is great and sought to build a bridge between art and national
politics. Wagner is much taken with the idea that his relationship
with the king, which appears to be very close, places great and
lofty obligations on him. In this he is right. But he sees the affair
in an entirely poetical, almost theatrical, light. He also told me
about a curious incident with a mysterious old woman from the
people, who came to him one evening and told him that she had
to speak to him about the young king and his calling.[1] She
had already advised Ludwig I and Max II, but neither of them had
followed her advice. But the young king, she went on, was destined
for greatness, it was written in the stars. 'Do you believe in the
stars?' she had asked Wagner in a loud and solemn voice. 'It is
written in the stars that this young king has been singled out for
great deeds. I want my king to have peace of mind, and you, Herr
Wagner, must protect him and guard him against the machinations
of evil men who seek to destroy him just as they destroyed his

1. Frau Dangl; see Newman iii.359–60.

father and grandfather.' Wagner became extraordinarily agitated when he told me about this encounter, which appears to have left a deep impression on him.

Röckl ii.216–17

LUDWIG II OF BAVARIA

Between 11 and 18 November 1865 Wagner spent a
week as the king's guest at Hohenschwangau.

11 November 1865. 'HE' approached, my noble friend came. The sun shone once more, even Nature rejoiced to see Him, He came at half past two! – Sacred hours, He is happy! Joy at the thought, (Parcival, Castle of the Grail) – spoke about His works, His terrible fate, the blind masses; parable, people (worshippers in the ancient temple), ministers, priests with their customs & ceremonies), the king (God). Spoke about Herr v. Bülow, admirable character, loyal to Him; the festival theatre of the future; the significance of Our love (not understood by the common people; His spirit certain of creating the most perfect works) – What undreamt-of delights may yet lie ahead of Us!? – Is it a dream? Am I on earth!? Now everything must be decided, every action made clear! Spoke until a quarter past four. [. . .]

12 November 1865. Wind players on the towers proclaiming the day, Lohengrin's hallowed sounds, a glorious day, at half past twelve, the Unique and Incomparable One came, spoke about the delights of the coming winter, (excerpts from the Ring of the Nibelung),[1] training, the current state of music & the depths to which it has sunk, Cornelius, series of lectures on Tannhäuser, the stupidity of the masses, so happy with me! Seeds in the German nation, O what a godlike guest – on the false and feigned appreciation of art on the part of the Grand Dukes of Baden & Saxe-Weimar; ah, how remote from what is pure & true! – Everything approaching fulfilment, – revealed to me the

1. This plan came to nothing following Wagner's enforced departure from Munich on 10 December.

shameful intrigue![1] A curse on these false friends, they will be seen through, a new & impartial friend is at hand!

Evers 1986: 101–2

CHLODWIG VON HOHENLOHE-SCHILLINGSFÜRST (1819–1901)

Chlodwig von Hohenlohe began his career as a Prussian civil servant, but on the death of his uncle in 1845 became Prince of Schillingsfürst and, as such, an hereditary member of the Bavarian Upper House. His liberal views and anti-Jesuit attitude endeared him to Wagner, who recommended him to Ludwig as prime minister following Ludwig von der Pfordten's resignation in December 1866. Hohenlohe was appointed minister of the royal house and of foreign affairs and president of the council of ministers on 31 December 1866. He remained in office for three years.

12 March 1867. Wagner having called on me the day before yesterday, but having subsequently excused himself on account of illness, I wrote to him to-day, asking him to come to me this evening. He came at half-past-six. At first he was somewhat embarrassed, spoke of indifferent things and excused himself, saying that he really had no right to come to me at all. I put him in a more comfortable frame of mind by saying that we had two points in common – we were both hated by the same party and we were united in equal veneration for the King. Thereupon he became more communicative, spoke about the way in which the King had been treated and so tormented that he had twice written to him that he would abdicate; and told me, amid protestations of not wishing to take credit to himself, that it was *he* who had recommended me to the King as Minister. Then he came to the task of Bavaria as a German State, whose population united the versatility of Franconia with the imagination of Swabia and the native strength of Bavaria; said that the King was just the man to rule

1. As early as 11 October, Wagner had noted the words 'breach with Pfistermeister' in his diary (BB 144). Opposition to him was mounting at court and rumours of his relationship with Cosima were circulating freely.

this German State and to realise the ideal of the German spirit (*Deutschtum*); went on to speak of his artistic aims, of his experiences in this country, of his plans for the establishment of a school of art, of the obstacles that had been put in his way, and came finally to the Cabinet. Among other things he spoke of the necessity of my remaining in the Ministry. To which I replied that this did not depend upon myself; that I could not guarantee that attempts would not be made to undermine the King's confidence in me, and that I was the less sure of retaining this, since the King, following the tradition of the Royal House, did not treat with me direct, but only through the Cabinet. He then said that this could not continue so; whereupon I drew his attention to the danger of engaging in a conflict with the Cabinet, a danger of which he must be well aware. He mentioned my political programme, into a few details of which I entered.

Finally he expressed the hope that the King would never lose confidence in me.

Hohenlohe-Schillingsfürst: 198–9

> Wagner completed *Die Meistersinger von Nürnberg* on 24 October 1867. He initially wanted it to be staged in Nuremberg itself as part of a wider programme of political reform involving institutions that would be 'German and non-Jewish in character',[1] but in the event he threw his weight behind a production in Munich. The following account of one of the rehearsals was submitted to the Vienna *Neue Freie Presse* on 21 June 1868 and was reprinted by Ludwig Nohl (1831–85) the following year.

Normally there are noisy scenes outside the Court Theatre of an evening, with pedestrians and carriages hastening towards the entrance, for the performances begin at half past six. But now the pedestrians pass calmly by. The Munich Court Theatre is closed at present and only odd members of the chorus and orchestra cluster in groups around the stage door, all engaged in the liveliest conversation. The clocks in the nearby towers are just striking six

1. Letter to Hans von Bülow, 20 February 1866; see Rose 1992: 102–18 and Spencer 1993.

as an open carriage crosses the Residenzplatz. As soon as its presence is noticed, the groups disperse; the cab stops outside the stage
door and a lady and two gentlemen alight. All three are engaged
in lively conversation, gesticulating wildly with their hands before
disappearing a moment later inside the dark and narrow pas-
sageway. Other people crowd in after them, and we too follow the
sombre group, exchanging the mild evening glow for the light of
the gaslamps. The pedestrians remain outside, gazing inquisitively
in through the door and hoping to see or hear what is going on
inside the building. A passing stranger stops and asks what is
happening. A newsmonger gives himself airs and explains that they
are rehearsing *Die Meistersinger* by Richard Wagner.

We have entered the vast expanse of the auditorium. High above
the stalls hangs the gas chandelier, which today gives out only a
weak light. The small and slightly built man has already taken up
his position and is standing at the conductor's desk – it is Hans
von Bülow. The very fact that he never sits to conduct distinguishes
him from his predecessor Lachner.[1] He has fine, sharply etched
features, a domed forehead and large eyes permanently shielded
by the inevitable pince-nez; above and beneath his small mouth is
a thin beard that does not merit regular attention but often serves
as a distraction for his unoccupied left hand. Bülow taps his
battuta. 'Gentlemen, if you please, let us begin!' he calls out to the
full orchestra in his thin, hoarse voice. The band has been
reinforced with some extra wind players and now numbers eighty.
The music starts. Bülow uses his whole body to indicate the
nuances he wants and gets so terribly worked up that one trembles
for the violins and lamps around him.

The other man who arrived with Bülow is standing on stage. It
is *Richard Wagner.* In a state of continuous excitement that makes
one nervous, he accompanies every note with a corresponding
movement that the singers imitate as closely as they can; only
someone who has seen the composer working and gesticulating in
this way can have any idea of the multitude of nuances that he
himself has thought up. Virtually every step, every shaking of the

1. Franz Lachner (1803–90) had known Schubert and Beethoven in his youth.
He settled in Munich in 1836 and soon found himself playing a leading role in
the city's musical life, a role abruptly curtailed by Wagner's arrival in Munich
in 1864. He was also a prolific composer.

head, every hand movement, every opening of a door is 'musically illustrated', and there is in *Die Meistersinger*, in particular, such a mass of music to go with the singers' dumb show that we should regard it as a miracle if a production of the opera that was not rehearsed under the composer's direction managed to include all the gestures intended to accompany this music. Only when Fräulein Mallinger is singing[1] does Wagner occasionally suspend his instructions and listen with visible pleasure, trotting to and fro, with one hand in his trouser pocket, or sitting on a chair next to the prompt box, nodding in satisfaction and smiling all over his face. But if there is something in the orchestra that he does not like, as happens not infrequently, he leaps up as if bitten by a snake and claps his hands. Bülow breaks off and Wagner calls down into the orchestra: '*Piano*, gentlemen, *piano*! It must be quiet, quiet, quiet, as though it comes from another world!' And the orchestra begins again. 'Even more *piano*!' Wagner calls out and makes the appropriate gesture with his hands. 'So, so, so – good, good, good, – very nice.'[2]

And so it goes on all evening. Herr Bülow duly breaks off and time and again repeats a passage, often only for his own information and even if Wagner reassures him: 'You know that already, we've already discussed this in private!' Anyone who witnesses this and knows the demands placed on the wind players in particular will understand the scene that took place at a recent rehearsal that had already lasted five hours and that had been preceded by daily rehearsals lasting just as long, when the first horn player[3] roundly declared that he could not play any more, causing Herr von Bülow to become not a little angry. There has just been a short break. Wagner thinks that the trombones are drowning the singer and so he immediately makes a correction, only to find that he does not like it, and after various failed experiments, he delivers himself of a lecture and tells the trombones that it will have to stay as it is.

Nohl 1869: 357–62

1. Mathilde Mallinger (1847–1920) made her début in Munich as Norma in 1866 before taking on Wagnerian roles.
2. Nohl notes that this intervention was directed at the passage in Act Three just before Eva launches the Quintet.
3. The player in question is believed to have been Franz Strauss (1822–1905), the father of the composer.

FRIEDRICH NIETZSCHE (1844–1900)

The twenty-four-year-old Nietzsche was introduced to
Wagner at the Leipzig home of Heinrich Brockhaus on
8 November 1868. He described the meeting in a letter
written the following day to Erwin Rohde (1845–98).

We enter Brockhaus's comfortably furnished drawing room: there
is no one else present apart from the immediate family, Richard
and the two of us.[1] I am introduced to Richard and tell him briefly
how much I respect him: he wants to know exactly how I got to
know his music, complains terribly about every performance of his
operas, with the exception of the famous Munich productions, and
makes fun of the conductors who call out good-naturedly to their
orchestras: 'Gentlemen, it's now getting passionate.' 'My good
fellows, let's have a little more passion!' W. likes to imitate the
Leipzig dialect.

Let me tell you briefly what the evening had to offer: truly,
delights of such peculiar piquancy that even now I am still not
quite my old self and can do nothing better than talk to you, my
dear friend, and tell you this 'wondrous tale'. Before and after
dinner Wagner played all the important passages from *Die Meistersinger*, imitating all the characters with total self-abandon. He is,
indeed, an incredibly lively and impassioned man, who speaks very
quickly, is very witty and certainly livens up a very private party
of this kind. In between I had quite a long conversation with him
about Schopenhauer; ah, you will understand what a pleasure it
was for me to hear him speak of Schopenhauer with such indescribable warmth, saying what he owed to him and how he was the
only philosopher to have understood the nature of music; he then
asked how today's professors regard him, laughed a good deal at
the Philosophy Congress in Prague and spoke of the 'servants of
philosophy'. Afterwards he read to us from his autobiography,
which he is now writing, an utterly delightful scene from his student
days in Leipzig, which I still cannot recall without laughing; I must
say that he writes with extraordinary skill and intelligence. At the
end, as we were both getting ready to leave, he shook my hand

1. The meeting was arranged by the Sanskrit scholar Ernst Windisch
(1844–1918).

very warmly and was kind enough to invite me to visit him and discuss music and philosophy. He also asked me to introduce his sister and his other relations to his music, which I have solemnly undertaken to do.

Nietzsche 1986: ii.340–41

> Following his appointment to the Chair of Classical Philology at Basel University in February 1870, Nietzsche found himself fortuitously in Wagner's proximity and became a frequent and welcome visitor to Tribschen, where Wagner had been living since April 1866, revealing a willingness to be exploited of which Wagner and Cosima took shameless advantage. Here, in a passage from a letter to Rohde of 3 September 1869, he sums up his early feelings of fulfilment.

Like you, I too have my Italy, except that I can escape there only on Saturdays and Sundays. It is called Tribschen and has already become a second home for me. In recent weeks I have been there four times in rapid succession, and a letter passes between us at least once a week. My dearest friend, what I learn and see there, what I see and understand, is indescribable. Schopenhauer and Goethe, Aeschylus and Pindar are still alive, believe me.

Nietzsche 1986: iii.52; for a full account of the subsequent course of the relationship between Wagner and Nietzsche, see Love 1963, Janz 1978 and Hollinrake 1982

JUDITH GAUTIER (1845–1917)

> Meanwhile, other visitors were descending on Tribschen, some more welcome than others. Here the French *wagnérienne* Judith Gautier describes one of the drawbacks of Wagner's notoriety.

I arrived alone at Tribschen soon after the two o'clock dinner, a little fearful of having come, perhaps, too soon. The clear sky made the lake very blue and the fresh green of the banks mirrored itself as usual in the tranquil water. I disembarked at the point of the promontory by the foot of the garden, under the little shed which sheltered the wooden steps.

As there was neither door, nor doorkeeper, nor bell, I arrived without giving any signal, and, walking slowly, fearing to find my hosts still at table, I took the least direct route to the house, through a charming, very shady path which follows the edge of the lake. It grows steep very quickly, and the slope which, covered with bushes, topples down to the water, has the appearance of a picturesque little precipice, and nothing could be more lovely to see than the stains of azure made by the lake through the interlacing of the branches. The children have named this corner, where they are forbidden to go alone, for fear of the descents, 'The Park of Brigands,' and they tell long tales about the adventures which come to pass there after nightfall. At the moment when I came out from the shelter of the trees, the eldest of the little girls saw me and came running, signalling to me not to speak or make any noise. When she reached me, she drew me, without a word, through clumps of trees where I nearly lost my hat, toward a sort of little summer-house of verdure, very near the house, where the coffee had been served. The Master was there, seated on a cane easy-chair, smoking a cigar; Cosima, standing, peeped through the interstices of the bushes, and made me a sign to keep silent: but Wagner, looking at me fiercely, said in a low tone, 'What, did you bring all these people?'

'What people?'

Cosima called me, by a gesture, near to her, and from there I could see why my hosts were keeping so quietly out of sight. A coach full of tourists had stopped before the steps of the house. A personage clothed entirely in brown holland, against which appeared the black cord of a lorgnette, was interviewing the servant. I thought at first sight that it was a question of some tiresome acquaintance whom they were endeavouring to get rid of as politely as possible; but I soon comprehended that these were foreign tourists, entire strangers, who, with an incredible assurance, insisted upon visiting Richard Wagner. This excursion was doubtless fitted in between the ascension of the Righi and the promenade to the Lion of Lucerne. They insisted with unparalleled impertinence, feigning not to comprehend the assertions of the servant, prolonging the discussion wilfully, while, in the little grove nearby, one dared not breathe, for fear of being discovered. At length Jacob persuaded these intruders that the Master was absent. The carriage was started again amid the creaking of old iron, and the vehicle, crowded with green umbrellas, blue veils, and red shawls, went back down the hill.

'At last we are free!' cried the Master, rising.

'How,' said I, 'could you believe that I would bring such a rabble here?'

'You arrived at the same time,' said he; 'but I ought not to have suspected you.'

'Nor to have given me that terrible look.'

'The look was for the tourists,' said he, laughing. 'I am simply beset by the audacity of these strangers,' added he. 'This scene is very often repeated. The worst of it is that Jacob is against me. He finds all these people very distinguished, and cannot understand why I refuse to see them.'

Gautier 1910: 43–6

CATULLE MENDÈS (1841–1909)

> Judith Gautier arrived in Lucerne on 16 July in the company of her husband Catulle Mendès and the Symbolist poet Philippe-Auguste Villiers de l'Isle-Adam (1838–89). Cosima's initial reaction was that she was 'so lacking in manners that I find it downright embarrassing, yet at the same time good-natured and terribly full of enthusiasm' (CT, 16 July 1869). Here Mendès recalls Wagner.

While waiting for lunch, which was always served at two o'clock exactly, we talked in the large, brightly lit salon which, with its four open windows and sfumato setting, was filled with the mountain air. Sometimes we would be seated, but he – never! No, I recall seeing him seated only once, except at the piano or at table. Walking the length and breadth of the salon, moving the chairs, changing the position of the armchairs, looking in all his pockets for his snuffbox, which was invariably missing, or for his spectacles, which were sometimes found hooked to the pendants of the candelabra, but which were never on his nose, grabbing his velvet beret, which hung over his left eye, making him look for all the world like some black-crested bird, kneading it between his tense fingers, stuffing it into his waistcoat, pulling it out again, replacing it on his head and talking, talking, talking. He often talked of Paris. He had not yet become unjust towards our country. He loved the city of his hopes and sufferings. With the tenderness and anxiousness of the exile, he asked after the districts where he had lodged and which he suspected might have changed as a result of the recent rebuilding programme. I saw his eyes fill with tears on account of a house he recalled, on the corner of a street, that had now been demolished. Then he would be carried away: sublime images, puns, barbarous turns of phrase, an endless flood, always disjointed, never repeating himself, words that were proud or tender, violent or comic. And, now laughing until you thought he would split his sides, now growing tearfully tender, now rising to the heights of prophetic ecstasy, he omitted nothing from his extraordinary improvisation: the dramas he dreamt of, *Parsifal*, the king of Bavaria, who was no 'naughty boy', the tricks played on him by Jewish conductors, the subscribers who had booed *Tannhäuser*, Mme de Metternich, Rossini ('the most voluptuously gifted of musicians'), these wretched publishers, the reply he intended to send to the Augsburg *Allgemeine*,[1] the theatre that he would build on a hill near a town and to which peoples of every nation would come, Sebastian Bach, Monsieur Auber, who had been very kind to him, his plans to write a play called *Luther's Wedding*,[2] and a score of anecdotes besides: tales of his political life in Dresden, the beautiful dreams of his childhood, his escapades, of sitting in the back row of the stalls to see the great Weber conducting, Mme Schröder-Devrient, the tenderest and most grateful memory of his whole existence – this admirable and dear, dear woman! he said with a sob – and the death of Schnorr, who had created the role of Tristan; and as he spoke the word 'Tristan', one felt a tremendous, all-consuming sense of exaltation at the febrile

1. Wagner submitted a 'Correction' to the Augsburg *Allgemeine Zeitung* on 16 September 1869; SS xii.304–8. Mendès is clearly conflating his reminiscences of July 1869 with those of 13–17 September 1869 and a later visit of 19–30 July 1870.
2. See BB 182–5 and WWV 99.

eternity of the *Liebestod*, a state of frenetic nirvana! And all the while, we sat there, dazed and bemused, laughing with him, weeping with him, sharing his feelings of joy, seeing his visions and submitting to the terror and charm of his imperious words like sun-flecked motes of dust at the tempest's mercy.

Mendès 1886: 13–17; see also Villiers 1887

JUDITH GAUTIER

Gautier describes the Tribschen interior.

We look about us with respectful curiosity, at the interior of the temple, of which the quiet and pervading richness forms a strong contrast to the simple gray of the exterior.

The drawing-room is rather large; it occupies an entire angle of the house, and has windows on two sides. It is bathed in warm and restful shadows between its walls covered with yellow leather traced with arabesques of gold. A thick carpet muffles the footsteps. The velvet draperies of the windows fall in heavy folds and mass themselves upon the floor. A fine portrait of Beethoven holds sway at the end of the grand piano, and faces a mirror which reflects it. Upon two other panels Goethe and Schiller hang facing each other.[1] From the ceiling depends a big bronze lamp.

A large divan of purple damask stands against the wall, and soft easy-chairs and cabinets are grouped here and there. 'Will you come to see my gallery?' asks Wagner, with a smile which mocks the ambitious title. A wide arch connects the drawing-room with a long, narrow room hung in violet velvet, against which the whiteness of small marble statues[2] stands out in soft relief.

They are the heroes of the Master's works: Tannhäuser touching

---

1. The portrait of Beethoven was a copy by Robert Krauße (1834–1903) of the famous oil painting by Ferdinand Georg Waldmüller (1793–1865). The oil portrait of Goethe was a copy, by Franz von Lenbach (1836–1904), of a contemporary copper engraving, while the portrait of Schiller was after Johann Friedrich August Tischbein (1750–1812). The salon also contained oil portraits of Ludwig II and Ludwig Geyer. Genelli's watercolour hung in a corner; see Fehr ii.258.
2. By Caspar Zumbusch (1830–1915).

the strings of his lyre, and singing the passionate song to the glory of Venus. Lohengrin, like an archangel, drawing his sword for the defence of innocence. Tristan, the knight, who believes that he drinks from the goblet of death, and drains instead the cup where sparkles the philtre of love. Walther von der Vogelweide, and the last-born, the youthful and impetuous Siegfried, holding between his fingers the fatal ring.

There are also some tapestries, the gift of King Ludwig of Bavaria, which portray scenes from the Nibelungen. In a niche a gilded Buddha,[1] Chinese incense-burners, chiselled cups – all sorts of rare and precious things. In one corner there are two round table cabinets with covers of glass, which protect a collection of magnificent butterflies with great gold and purple wings.

'This collection of butterflies came from the Paris Exposition,' announces the Master, laughing, 'and from amid all that great mass of things which owe their existence to the prodigious labours of mankind this is the one thing that an artist finds most to his taste.' [. . .]

At the end of the drawing-room at Tribschen, to the left in coming from the garden, a heavy portière, raised by a cord, allowed one a glimpse of a very small room, which I could not approach without great emotion. It was the sanctuary, the Holy of Holies, the work-room of Richard Wagner! Sombre draperies, a restrained half-light, two walls covered with book-shelves, filled with splendid works: music, poetry, philosophy; a piano of a special design (almost an altar), furnished with drawers and a plane like a table; a single picture, the portrait of Ludwig II., the royal friend, the ministering spirit: 'The man who,' said Wagner, 'seems to have been sent to me from heaven!'

Gautier 1910: 21–3, 35–6

> By 18 July, Wagner and Cosima had revised their views
> of the Mendès couple: 'R. regards her and her husband
> as a real enrichment of our lives, and they are certainly
> an extraordinary, noble couple' (CT, 18 July 1869). On
> 22/3 July Wagner organized an excursion to Brunnen.

1. A gift from Marie d'Agoult that Wagner had reclaimed from Natalie Planer at the end of 1868.

'I wish to say to you,' announced the Master, one day as we arrived, 'that you are invited by me to make an excursion into a very interesting corner of Switzerland – the country of William Tell. The trip is all planned, and everything is arranged.'

Again we were rather embarrassed, and endeavoured to protest. But Madam Cosima made signs to me, and, coming nearer, said in a low voice:

'Do not refuse: he would be angry. And let him manage it all; let him take the lead, if you do not wish to grieve him.'

'The weather is beautiful,' continued Wagner. 'We ought not to wait. If it is convenient to you, let us start to-morrow.'

'Joyfully, Master.'

'Then that is agreed upon. We shall begin the journey by coach, and will call for you at the Hôtel du Lac.'

'At what hour?'

'Ah! as to that, it must be early in the morning in order to avoid the great heat. Be ready at half-past five.'

'Half-past five. We shall be ready.'

The next day, before day in fact, two carriages stopped before the Hôtel du Lac. Wagner was alone in one: Madam Cosima and her daughter Senta[1] occupied the other.

We descended hurriedly, all ready to go, if still a little sleepy. Villiers, very much flurried, instead of going directly to the carriage, tried to get into the little shop of Monsieur Frey, close at hand; but the amiable hairdresser was not yet awake, and his disappointed client was forced to go without being curled. He went with me in Wagner's carriage, which took the lead, and the expedition started on its way.

What roads we travelled, what landscapes unfolded before us during that radiant and never-to-be forgotten morning, I should be quite unable to relate, for I avow that I saw nothing! When one has gazed at the sun, for a long time one sees nothing more than a flame which comes between the eyes and all other things. So it was with me; the face of the Master masked all Nature, so that I saw only that. I remember very well that the slanting rays of the

1. Judith persistently calls Daniela von Bülow (1860–1940) Senta, though her confusion is pardonable, given the fact that the Wagners addressed her variously as Loulou, Lulu, Lusch and Luschchen.

rising sun enveloped Wagner, and cast a light on his under-lip; this light sparkled at every inflexion, and his words seemed like stars.

I questioned him with regard to Mendelssohn: the works of Mendelssohn had a great charm for me, which endured in spite of my Wagnerian exclusiveness, a fact of which I was a little ashamed.

'Mendelssohn is a great landscape-painter,' said he to me, 'and his palette has a richness that is unequalled. No one else transposes the external beauty of things into music as he does. The Cave of Fingal, among others, is an admirable picture. He is able, conscientious, and clever. Yet, in spite of all these gifts, he fails to move us to the depths of the soul: it is as if he painted only the appearance of sentiment, and not the sentiment itself.'

Before noon we expected to reach an inn, where we should try to get luncheon, or rather, the German dinner. At that point the coaches were to be abandoned, and the journey would be continued by steamboat.

For a long time we skirted the edge of a lake, very blue between its green banks – that is all I remember about it; then stopped in front of a commonplace little house by the side of the road. Where this was I do not know. A recent study of Baedeker makes me suppose that it was at a place called Brunnen.

On the other side of the road was the lake, and the landing-place for the boats was almost in front of the house.

There was nothing to indicate that it was an inn, but the Master knew the people,[1] and while we went upstairs to a room on the first floor, furnished only with a round table, some chairs, and an old piano, he conferred with the proprietor and arranged the *menu*. He returned to us triumphant, and cried:

'We shall have "un druide" of ancient Gaul!' The meaning of this terrible pun did not strike us at first, but we laughed immoderately when we found that it was a question of 'une truite' (a trout)!

Two windows of the little room that we were in faced the lake, a third, a side window, was open and overlooked the court, where a blacksmith was at work. Wagner listened to the ringing stroke of the hammer on the anvil. Suddenly he opened the piano

1. Wagner had been coming to this inn – *Zum Goldenen Adler* – since 1851. It was run throughout this period by Xaver Auf der Maur (1822–1904) and his sister Agathe; see Fehr i.112.

and began to play the *motif* of Siegfried forging the sword. At the measure where the blade is struck he stopped, and it was the blacksmith who, striking the iron with an astonishing precision, unconsciously completed the theme.

'You see,' said the Master, 'how well I have calculated the time, and how exactly the blow falls.'

But '*le druide*' made his entrance, and we proceeded to render him the honours that he merited. Wagner was an admirable organiser. Just as the coffee was finished and the cigarettes smoked, we heard the whistle of the steamboat, and had only to cross the road and go aboard. What is there to tell about this voyage, except that there are some moments in life when all nature is illuminated by the light that you carry within yourself; when the air seems more limpid, the sky more luminous, the water more transparent; when all vibrates harmoniously throughout the scene which envelops your joy.

Certain it is that there was never for me such a blue lake between such fresh hills, and yet I did not see them. The face of the Master, his beaming eyes, where blended the most beautiful shades of sapphire – that was what I saw, and I said to Madam Cosima, who thought quite as I did, – 'Now, at last, I comprehend that happiness of paradise, so extolled by believers, the seeing of the Gods face to face!'

Gautier 1910: 58–63

VALENTINA SEROVA (1846–1927)

The Mendès' visit overlapped with that of the Russian composer Alexander Nikolayevich Serov (1820–71) and his wife, who had first made Wagner's acquaintance in Vienna in 1864. Here Valentina Serova describes their first visit to Tribschen on 8 July 1869.

The little boat bobbed gently up and down on the smooth surface of the emerald lake. The beauty of the surrounding shores was plain to see as the young Swiss man steered the boat with an easy grace. He was regaling us with fantastic tales of the master of the Tribschen headland, but little did he suspect that this magician was his passengers' friend. Serov kept turning impatiently in his seat to try and make out the landing stage for the villa of the elusive 'Bavarian exile', as the boatman called him. 'On land there are terrible dogs to stop you getting close,' he was saying, 'while sheer cliffs prevent you approaching from the lake. The cliffs are not high, but they are still hard to climb.'

'We've got to pull in to shore somewhere,' Serov exclaimed anxiously. 'That's impossible! They don't allow strangers and certainly not foreigners,' the Swiss man persisted.

'Take us in to the landing stage,' Serov ordered.

'You'll see how right I am. You won't be allowed into the villa.'

What looked like a small bay appeared in the distance. Serov disembarked but came back shortly to inform us that Wagner was working until lunchtime and would see no one. He had not even come out to greet him but had invited the whole family instead to lunch the following day. 'How very different from our way of doing things,' we both thought. 'A Russian could not have endured that! He would have broken off his work quite naturally, for a moment or two, in order to embrace a friend.' But Wagner, the punctilious German, would not abandon his score until the predetermined time.

The invitation to lunch was a sign of higher favour because at the time he was leading a very secluded life. The following day we were that much bolder in our approach to the inhospitable cliffs, and our boatman had changed from being a guide plying us with information to someone curious to know more about our visit. We tied up at the shore. Wagner's grey-haired old valet led Serov off to meet him, while I was shown the way to Cosima Bülow's rooms and a maid took our son[1] off to join the children. After a while we were summoned to lunch. The table had been laid formally under old Johann's supervision[2] in a long narrow room decorated

1. Valentin Alexandrovich Serov (1865–1911) became one of Russia's leading portraitists and landscape painters.
2. The Tribschen household comprised Wagner, Cosima, Blandine (1863–1941), Daniela, Isolde (1865–1919), Eva (1867–1942) and (since 6 June) Siegfried, their governess, a nanny, a housekeeper (Verena Weidmann), a man servant (Jakob Stocker), two stable lads, a parlourmaid and a French cook, together with a Newfoundland (Ruß), a terrier (Koß), a horse (Fritz), two peacocks (Wotan and Fricka), two golden pheasants, a cat and an assortment of sheep and hens; see Fehr ii.231.

with large pictures of heroes from Wagner's operas. It was indeed natural that, on entering Wagner's abode, the visitor should feel himself caught up at once in the fantastic world of Germanic legend.

Wagner was in a good mood and told Johann to serve a vintage hock. 'And mind it's a vintage, do you hear! He's forever complaining about our housekeeping,' Wagner explained to us, 'and he hates giving our guests good wine.'

Johann replied modestly that not all guests deserved a good wine.

'Well, my old Johann, we understand each other. So, fetch a fiery, sparkling wine, and be quick about it!' Wagner kept on trying to persuade Serov to come and live in Germany for the sake of both his health and his vocation. (While trying to complete *The Power of the Fiend*,[1] Serov almost yielded to his entreaties.) After lunch we went off to see the children. We found our son sitting fearlessly astride an enormous Newfoundland dog. Alongside him stood Wagner's daughter Eva, a dark-eyed, golden-haired girl of the same age.[2] Her bright little voice broke into peals of laughter as she kept egging the dog on: 'Ruß!' (the dog's name) 'Come on, come on then, Ruß!'

Wagner took Eva by the hand and headed off in the direction of the lake. The little girl hung back, protesting miserably: 'Don't want to bathe, Eva don't want to bathe!' She thought she was being taken for a swim, but Wagner calmed her down: 'Come on, let's go and visit the little Russian!' he said. Then we took all the children off for a walk. Tosha, our son, set off astride Ruß, Isolde and Eva ran after him with their dolls, and baby Siegfried, resting in his nurse's arms, gave little shrieks of delight. Wagner laughed as he told us how Ruß would stand guard fiercely at the entrance to the grounds and had on more than one occasion frightened some inquisitive Englishwomen who had come up to the railings; they had turned tail when this black Cerberus had barked at them.

1. *Vrazh'ya sila*, an opera in five acts to a libretto by the composer and Alexander Ostrovsky (1823–86), completed by Nikolay Feopemptovich Solovyov (1846–1916) and Valentina Serova and premièred at the Mariinsky Theatre in St Petersburg on 1 May 1871, three months after the composer's death.
2. Presumably an error for Isolde.

'Oh, my faithful watchdog!' Wagner exclaimed, stroking the dog's shaggy neck. Ruß dashed off down the avenue and set his tiny rider down by a cage of golden pheasants. We went into the summer house and there Wagner suddenly started to talk in the most intimate terms of how unbearable his domestic situation had become and how, until such time as Cosima could become his wife, he was vulnerable to all kinds of mischief. They were simply waiting for the divorce to free them from this oppressive state of affairs.[1] Bülow was spoken of in nothing but the most refined and delicate terms, Wagner even referring to him as a most noble being. This scene in the summer house remained for ever in our memories. It was a long time before we forgot the look Cosima gave Wagner when he leaned over to her and said with particular affection: 'There are even better times ahead!' [. . .]

A few days later Cosima paid us a visit and asked us over to Tribschen to meet some French visitors newly arrived from Paris. They had decided to feed the children before the guests arrived, so she wanted us to bring our son along much earlier than his normal lunchtime. We were all ready to set off at the appointed hour and had started down the hill when suddenly our son disappeared. We searched and searched, but he was nowhere to be found! We ran all over Lucerne asking after him, but no one had seen him. Just then the shrill braying of a she-ass echoed through the town, and Serov and I explained as one: 'I bet Tosha is with the donkeys!' They were his dearest friends, and to ride on their backs was one of his most cherished desires. We were still some way from the donkey noises when we could hear our runaway's little voice. We were delighted to see him, but our faces fell when we realized Tosha was covered in dirt! We had to go back uphill and change his clothes. There was no chance now of arriving at the requested time and this made us very anxious. When we finally arrived at Wagner's, the children had already had their lunch and Wagner was clearly not pleased with us.

The day was not a success in any case. The strangers turned out to be two Frenchmen, who were followers of Wagner, and a lovely

1. The Bülows were not legally separated until 18 July 1870. Wagner and Cosima were married on 25 August 1870.

Frenchwoman who played the part of the ardent admirer.[1] If his articles were anything to go by, one of the Frenchmen was quite sincere in his devotion to Wagner, but we found his way of expressing his pleasure extremely distasteful. Inevitably, even Wagner himself grew tense: he was straightforward enough, but a certain stiffness would creep into his manner. We tended to notice this precisely at those times when Wagner wished, it seemed, to appear at his least constrained; he did not always succeed, and certainly not now when the kisses which the Parisian beauty would place on his hands and the fatuous exclamations of the men were becoming so tiresome.

They asked Wagner to play something on the piano (something that would never have occurred to us to do), and he played the wedding march from *Lohengrin*, evidently to be rid of his guests' importunate demands. Halfway through he got mixed up in the harmonies and growled: 'God only knows what harmony comes next!' Then, banging the keys with his fist, he got up and left the piano. After this little episode Wagner at last regained his natural tone and we were no longer bothered by the sweet nothings of the Frenchmen. Saying goodbye to Wagner, Serov expressed the desire to see him again when there were no strangers present, since it was his hope to have many more occasions to talk seriously with him.

The next day the following note arrived: 'Do come! We'll be alone, and you can be as sycophantic as you like!' We set off to see him happy and content. Everything in this house was becoming precious to us: the velvet beret which Wagner was forever losing and constantly asking his servants if they had seen; Ruß barking enthusiastically and leaping all round Tosha; Johann, formal but good-humoured, assuring us that his 'master' liked us; Siegfried's corpulent nurse; and even the sweet smell which pervaded the rooms and which must have emanated from a tree, a cypress perhaps. Wagner met us with a gentle jest at our appearance, but we took not the slightest notice. Cosima looked radiant as they

1. Judith Gautier recalled: 'We exchanged some rather cold salutations. It was evident that our presence displeased the newcomers as much as theirs disturbed us. They felt that we were more intimate than they in the household; they saw that we were received very cordially, that Russ and Cos did not bark, but gave evidence of pleasure in our arrival' (Gautier 1910: 91). The Wagners seem to have been blithely indifferent to their visitors' jealousy (CT, 24 July 1869).

told us how they had celebrated Richard's birthday. He had just finished sketching out the famous scene of Siegfried with his silver horn. She had secretly copied out the horn solo and had sent it to the young musician Richter in Munich. He had arrived in Lucerne early in the morning and, standing under the window, had played the merry tune on the horn. This had awoken the astonished maestro, who had been unable to tell whether he was really listening to his own music or whether he was dreaming, so recently had it taken shape.[1] After the initial greetings we departed once more into the realm of legend, myth and fable and the teachings of Greek philosophy. And then there was the usual finale: Johann with his lantern, the thin silhouette of the tall, slender woman, and our host waving his kerchief.

Since relatives would often visit Wagner on a Sunday, Serov asked if he could come and see him on Saturday evenings. Wagner replied jokingly: 'What are you doing to me? There I go writing against the Jews and you force me to celebrate the Sabbath!' On one of those unforgettable 'Sabbath' days he played us the scene of Erda's appearance which he had just finished. He played poorly, often striking the keys with his fists, and he declaimed in a hoarse voice. He evidently could not manage the difficult piano part: even so, his animated, highly charged delivery endowed his performance with a power such as I have never heard from singers on stage. It was understandable that the author's own interpretation, for all its glaring faults, would remain one that we would never forget. It was thrilling to see the way Wagner emphasized those passages which are significant yet which so often get lost in weak and untidy performances.

Being preoccupied with the composition of *Siegfried* at the time, Wagner was happiest, naturally enough, to steer the conversation, whenever he could, to this work. 'That strong young man, what a picture of health he is! The way he frees himself so instinctively from the sway of that fearful old ruler Wotan. The despot, for his part, is fascinated by the independence of the protest. "What do you look like then, old man?" Siegfried asks with boyish ardour. "And where did you lose your eye?" he gently chides the god-wanderer. In this confrontation the god sees standing before him

1. See CT, 22 May 1869.

one of his successors. Fate has decreed that dominion over the earth will pass to him, now that the dwellers in the sky have lost their powers and begun to fade away. Siegfried's childlike ways affect Wotan profoundly and, although he is certain of the imminent downfall of the gods, he still yearns to witness an act which is a genuine expression of free will and completely independent of divine intervention. The weary god regrets nothing as he concedes power to the burgeoning new generation, standing before him as a simple, artless lad. "Go your way, I cannot prevent you!" he says as Siegfried passes. The vanquished lord of the universe is shaken to the roots. Siegfried is to be the embodiment of everything that is best in our German nation: strength, simplicity and integrity. I don't mean Germany as it is today, of course; that seems to suffer from a permanent and chronic cold in the head.'

At this point Wagner broke off suddenly. Someone made so bold as to ask why Wotan could rejoice in Siegfried's protest, yet punish his daughter so cruelly for her disobedience. Wagner glanced fiercely at the questioner. 'Because', he replied, 'Brünnhilde herself is no more than Wotan's desire (his "Wunschkind"). When his desires begin to contradict his own will, in other words, when he has lost the power of free will, the violence of his anger is directed not against Brünnhilde but against himself. Brünnhilde may be the outward manifestation but its essence lies in Wotan's inner discord.'

'In that case, why must Siegfried be killed?' the questioner went on.

'Because evil always prevails over good. Alberich's powers are invincible: he is the spirit of evil who pursues his dark ends with a grim, unflinching determination. And he passes on this resolve to his son Hagen. One woman alone, Brünnhilde, is able to redeem the evil through her heroic action and to reconcile us at last to the crimes and intrigues of humanity. Those elements which lend dignity to our faults are concentrated in the arms of this loving woman.' With these words he turned gallantly to the women present. [. . .]

The weather in Switzerland had changed abruptly at this time. Although Serov had been ordered by his doctor to live up in the hills, the unbelievable rain and mists made us decide to move down and settle opposite Tribschen, where we would be able to take even more advantage, in those final days, of our precious evenings with Wagner. One day one of the servants in the hotel rushed into us in great agitation to announce 'The master and mistress of Villa Tribschen!' Cosima, looking elegant and wearing a fine matinée dress perfectly suited to the occasion, was coming up the stairs, leaning gracefully on Wagner's arm. He was wearing a grey overcoat which hung awkwardly on his spare little frame. The large black wide-brimmed hat he was wearing and the way he had set it slightly askew 'à la Wotan' gave to his alert features a sense of simple German *Biederkeit*. You can imagine what a marked contrast this formed to the tall, refined elegance of Cosima. We led our guests out on to the balcony. Serov was feeling unwell and was not in good spirits. Wagner was talking to him as if to a younger brother and was entreating him in the tender tones of a close friend to quit Russia, to abandon his stoicism and to start to live life as a European. What did he mean by this word 'stoicism'? Wagner believed that a life of hardship and troubles was an inescapable evil in Russia, one which almost always attended the lonely existence of the creative spirit, unless he had the backing of an institution. He imagined that Serov had chosen such difficult circumstances on principle, and for this reason he often expressed his amazement at Serov's stoicism.

While we had been talking, quite a crowd had gathered downstairs under the balcony to take a look at the famous composer. Wagner turned to us and smiled slyly: 'They look as though they'd like to see into the deepest recesses of our souls. Just look how shamelessly they examine our outward features!' After sitting with us for a while, Wagner and Cosima left for home and we offered to accompany them to their boat. Dear Wagner turned to me with these words: 'Why so depressed? Is it your husband's illness that's worrying you?' These past few days I had indeed been feeling terribly weighed down by Serov's gloom over his inability to finish *The Power of the Fiend*. Moreover, his illness had now taken a more menacing turn: he was suffering from more frequent chest spasms, and long walks were becoming more difficult, nay wellnigh impossible. These depressions did not occur often, however, and never lasted long. Wagner's visit happened to coincide with one of these ill-fated days. The sight of Serov's pale and sickly features troubled Wagner so much that he made every effort to be especially warm and tender in his affections. They walked arm in arm down the boulevard in Lucerne; a crowd of passing foreigners stood respectfully aside as the famous hermit of Lucerne went on his way. Cosima's arms were shaking as she grasped my hand and begged to walk a little faster down the boulevard, for fear of some unpleasant encounter or some other piece of mischief. Her own situation was so fraught with risk that she dared not show herself in public in the street.

Serova 1891: 67–71

JUDITH GAUTIER

Wagner initially agreed to the piecemeal staging of the *Ring* in Munich. (Legally, he had no choice in the matter.) But reports of inadequacies in the production of *Das Rheingold* assiduously retailed to him by Richter, Judith Gautier and others persuaded him to travel to Munich and attempt to rescue the situation. In the event, he was not allowed near the theatre and had to return to Tribschen without having achieved his aim. Here Judith Gautier describes his fatalistic response to the situation on the morning of 2 September 1869. She accompanied him from the rooms where he had been staying with Reinhard Schaefer (1827–84) in the Alte Pferdestraße to the station.

The Master looked very well, and the serenity of his humour seemed to have increased since the day before.

After we had started, I complimented him upon the strength of mind which sustained him in the face of this disaster, upon his magnanimous resignation, or perhaps, his Olympian scorn.

'Neither the one nor the other!' said he. 'I have found my force in the belief that nothing essential, nothing of that which is closest to me, is hurt by this contention. My work, after the impression which it has made upon all of you, who understand me so intimately, must be just what I wished for it, and it soars away intact and free, from amidst the tawdry rubbish with which they try to disguise it.

'There is still another thing; it is that human malignity is no longer able to reach or hurt me deeply across the warm affection and the devotion which surround me. This certainty has comforted me. You see that even here, as I go away, I leave friends. You also know with what anxious tenderness they watch for my arrival at home! Truly, when I think of the past and the despair into which such circumstances as these could have plunged me then, when I had to bear my pain alone, I am able to feel almost joyous.'

Gautier 1910: 201–3

> Ludwig, by contrast, was not 'almost joyous'. 'J'en ai assez,' he told Pfistermeister, refused to see Wagner and insisted that the production go ahead with another conductor. Wagner now began a brief flirtation with Bismarck in an attempt to break loose from his ties with Bavaria. Hence, in part, his agreement to conduct a concert in Berlin in the presence of the court on 5 May 1871. Five days earlier, on Sunday 30 April, he had conducted a concert at the Singakademie. Among the audience on both occasions was the American pianist Amy Fay.

AMY FAY (1844–1928)

18 May 1871. Wagner has just been in Berlin, and his arrival here has been the occasion of a grand musical excitement. He was received with the greatest enthusiasm, and there was no end of ovations in his honour. First, there was a great supper given to him, which was got up by Tausig and a few other distinguished musicians. Then, on Sunday, two weeks ago, was given a concert in the Sing-Akademie, where the seats were free. As the hall only holds about fifteen hundred people, you may imagine it was pretty difficult to get tickets. I didn't even attempt it, but luckily Weitzmann, my harmony teacher,[1] who is an old friend of Wagner's, sent me one.

The orchestra was immense. It was carefully selected from all the orchestras in Berlin, and Stern,[2] who directed it, had given

1. The German composer and writer on music Carl Friedrich Weitzmann (1808–80) was an early champion of Wagner.
2. Julius Stern (1820–83) founded the Stern Gesangverein in 1847 and the Berlin (later Stern) Conservatory in 1850.

himself infinite trouble in training it. Wagner is the most difficult person in the world to please, and is a wonderful conductor himself. He was highly discontented with the Gewandhaus Orchestra in Leipsic, which thinks itself the best in existence, so the Berlinese felt rather shaky. The hall was filled to overflowing, and finally, in marched Wagner and his wife, preceded and followed by various distinguished musicians. As he appeared the audience rose, the orchestra struck up three clanging chords, and everybody shouted *Hoch!* It gave one a strange thrill.

The concert was at twelve, and was preceded by a 'greeting' which was recited by Frau Jachmann Wagner, a niece of Wagner's, and an actress. She was a pretty woman, 'fair, fat, and forty,'[1] and an excellent speaker. As she concluded she burst into tears, and stepping down from the stage she presented Wagner with a laurel crown, and kissed him. Then the orchestra played Wagner's Faust Overture most superbly, and afterwards his Fest March from the Tannhäuser. The applause was unbounded. Wagner ascended the stage and made a little speech, in which he expressed his pleasure to the musicans and to Stern, and then turned and addressed the audience. He spoke very rapidly and in that childlike way that all great musicians seem to have, and as a proof of his satisfaction with the orchestra he requested them to play the Faust Overture under *his* direction. We were all on tiptoe to know how he would direct, and indeed it was wonderful to see him. He controlled the orchestra as if it were a single instrument and he were playing on it. He didn't beat the time simply, as most conductors do, but he had all sorts of little ways to indicate what he wished. It was very difficult for them to follow him, and they had to 'keep their little eye open,' as B. used to say. He held them down during the first part, so as to give the uncertainty and speculativeness of Faust's character. Then as Mephistopheles came in, he gradually let them loose with a terrible crescendo, and made you feel as if hell suddenly gaped at your feet. Then where Gretchen appeared, all was delicious melody and sweetness. And so it went on, like a succession of pictures. The effect was tremendous.

I had one of the best seats in the house, and could see Wagner

1. Sir Walter Scott, *St Ronan's Well* (1823), chap. 7. Wagner's step-niece was forty-four. The 'greeting' was written by Ernst Dohm (1819–83).

and his wife the whole time. He has an enormous forehead, and is the most nervous-looking man you can imagine, but has that grim setting of the mouth that betokens an iron will. When he conducts he is almost beside himself with excitement. That is one reason why he is so great as a conductor, for the orchestra catches his frenzy, and each man plays under a sudden inspiration. He really seems to be improvising on his orchestra.

Fay 1893: 102–4

VI (1872–83)

1872   24 *April* Wagner arrives in Bayreuth and is joined on the
30th by Cosima and their children. They stay at the Hotel
Fantaisie at Donndorf
12 May Conducts concert for the Vienna Wagner
Society
22 May Foundation stone of new theatre laid in Bayreuth,
after which Wagner conducts Beethoven's Ninth Symphony
Resumes work on *Mein Leben* and Act Three of
Götterdämmerung
14 September Completes essay *On Actors and Singers*
21 September Moves into temporary accommodation at
7 Dammallee until Wahnfried is ready
31 October Cosima formally accepted into the Protestant
Church
10 November–15 December The Wagners set off on a
tour of German theatres in search of singers for the *Ring*
Writes critical report on his experiences, 'A Glance at the
German Operatic Stage of Today'
First symptoms of heart disease
Finished copies of the second volume of his autobiography
arrive in time for Christmas

   25 June Jesuits expelled from Germany
   Meeting of Three Emperors in Berlin leads to *entente* between
   Germany, Russia and Austro-Hungary
   Scriabin and Vaughan Williams born
   Grillparzer (81), Mazzini (66) and Théophile Gautier (61)
   die
   Bizet, *Djamileh*
   Franck, *Les béatitudes*
   Nietzsche, *The Birth of Tragedy*
   Hardy, *Under the Greenwood Tree*

1873   Between 12 January and 8 February visits Dresden, Berlin,
       Hamburg and Schwerin, with concerts in Hamburg and
       Berlin. Writes essay on 'The Festival Theatre at Bayreuth'
       (1 May), which he submits to Bismarck on 24 June.
       Bismarck ignores his appeal
       21 *November* Wagner meets Düfflipp in an attempt to
       persuade Ludwig to help subsidize the Festival, which
       has now been postponed until 1875
       24 *December* Completes the full score of Act One of
       Götterdämmerung

       Financial crisis begins in Vienna in May and soon spreads to
       other European capitals
       Rachmaninov born
       Bulwer-Lytton dies (69)

1874   Ludwig initially refuses to guarantee the Festival's financial
       future but, following Wagner's renewed flirtation with
       Bismarck, offers him credit facilities of 100,000 thalers,
       20 February
       28 *April* The Wagners move into Wahnfried
       23 *May–6 June* Further tour of inspection of German
       theatres, this time in the company of Hans Richter
       26 *June* Completes full score of Act Two of
       Götterdämmerung
       Spends summer rehearsing with singers
       21 *November* Completes full score of Act Three of
       Götterdämmerung

       First Impressionist exhibition in Paris
       Schoenberg and Ives born
       Peter Cornelius dies (61)
       Mussorgsky, *Boris Godunov*
       Johann Strauß, *Die Fledermaus*
       Verdi, *Requiem*
       Smetana, *Ma vlast*
       Flaubert, *La tentation de Saint Antoine*
       Hardy, *Far from the Madding Crowd*

1875   Wagner conducts concerts in an attempt to raise funds for

Bayreuth: Vienna (1, 14 March, 6 May), Budapest (10
March), Berlin (24, 25 April)
1 July–14 August Rehearsals in Bayreuth
Spends November and half of December in Vienna
superintending rehearsals of *Tannhäuser* and *Lohengrin*
under Richter
Copies of the third volume of his autobiography are ready
by Christmas

> Ravel born
> Bizet (36) and Hans Christian Andersen (70) die
> Bizet, *Carmen*
> Goldmark, *Die Königin von Saba*
> Tchaikovsky, First Piano Concerto

1876   *17 March* Completes Centennial March for Philadelphia
Visits Vienna to conduct *Lohengrin* (2 March) and Berlin
to supervise rehearsals for local première of *Tristan und
Isolde* (20 March)
3 June Rehearsals begin in Bayreuth. First cycle of
performances begins on 13 August, third cycle ends on
30 August. The deficit amounts to 148,000 marks. During
the Festival, Wagner begins an affair with Judith Gautier
that is continued by correspondence until discovered and
abruptly curtailed by Cosima in February 1878
15 September–15 December The Wagners spend three
months in Italy, visiting Verona, Venice, Bologna, Naples,
Sorrento (where they see Nietzsche for the last time), Rome
(where they meet Joseph-Arthur Gobineau) and Florence

> Bell patents the telephone and Edison invents the phonograph
> Marie d'Agoult (70) and George Sand (71) die
> Brahms, First Symphony
> Delibes, *Sylvia*
> Morris, *Sigurd the Volsung*

1877   *23 February* Completes second prose draft of *Parzival*
(orthography changed to 'Parsifal', 14 March). Poem
completed, 19 April
7–29 May Together with Richter, gives eight concerts at
Albert Hall in an attempt to reduce the Festival deficit

After taking the waters at Bad Ems and visiting Tribschen,
Munich and Weimar, the Wagners return to Bayreuth, 28
July
Not for the first time, Wagner toys with the idea of
emigrating to America
15 September Informs delegates of Bayreuth patronage
scheme of his wish to found a school and perform all his
works from *Der fliegende Holländer* onwards. The
ideological background is spelt out in the *Bayreuther
Blätter* under its editor Hans von Wolzogen
Between 17 and 24 September begins composition of
Parsifal

> Rodin, *The Bronze Age*
> Tchaikovsky, *Swan Lake*
> Saint-Saëns, *Samson et Dalilah*
> Bruckner, Third Symphony
> Ibsen, *The Pillars of Society*

1878   First issue of *Bayreuther Blätter* published. Between now
and his death, Wagner contributes a series of essays on
his hopes for the regeneration of Germany
Under the terms of an agreement of 31 March with Ludwig
II, the king is entitled to perform all Wagner's works in
return for a 10 per cent royalty set against the earlier loan.
At the same time, Ludwig agrees to allow his Munich
forces to give the first performance of *Parsifal* in Bayreuth.
(The conductor Hermann Levi is part of the deal.) Wagner
continues to work simultaneously on the first and second
complete drafts of *Parsifal*, the prelude to Act One of
which is given a private performance at Wahnfried on 25
December

> Anti-Socialist legislation in Germany
> Nietzsche, *Human, All Too Human*

1879   *26 April* Completes second complete draft of *Parsifal* and
begins full score, 23 August
Continues to contribute to *Bayreuther Blätter*: 'Shall We
Hope?' (May), 'On Poetry and Composition' (June), 'On
Opera Poetry and Composition in Particular' (July), 'On

the Application of Music to the Drama' (October) and
his antivivisectionist 'Open Letter to Herr Ernst von
Weber' (October)
20 October Heinrich von Stein, a pupil of the positivistic,
anti-Semitic philosopher and economist Eugen Dühring,
arrives at Wahnfried as Siegfried's private tutor
31 December The family leaves for Italy

> Albert Einstein and Joseph Stalin born
> Tchaikovsky, *Eugene Onegin*
> Brahms, Violin Concerto
> Ibsen, *A Doll's House*

1880   The Wagners stay at the Villa Angri near Naples, where
their visitors include the Russian painter Paul von
Joukowsky and Engelbert Humperdinck. They remain
here until 8 August, then move on to Siena, where they
remain until 30 September. The month of October is
spent in Venice, after which the Wagners return to
Germany, stopping off in Munich (where Wagner sees
Ludwig II for the last time on 12 November) and arriving
back in Bayreuth on 17 November
Wagner makes little progress on *Parsifal* but continues
work on *Mein Leben*, ending it (provisionally) with his
meeting with Ludwig in 1864, and writes 'Religion and
Art' (July) and 'What Use is this Knowledge?' (October)

> Flaubert (58), Offenbach (61) and Mary Ann Evans (61) die
> Rimsky-Korsakov, *May Night*
> Zola, *Nana*

1881   Writes 'Know Thyself' (February) and 'Heroism and
Christianity' (September)
Completes full score of Act One of *Parsifal*, 25 April, and
that of Act Two, 20 October
Attends two cycles of the *Ring* in Berlin, 5–9 May and
25–9 May, the latter in the company of Joseph-Arthur
Gobineau, who spends four weeks as Wagner's guest in
Bayreuth
1 November The Wagners leave Bayreuth for Italy. They
stay at the Hôtel des Palmes in Palermo

13 March Assassination of Tsar Alexander II. Pogroms in
Russia
Bartók and Picasso born
Dostoevsky (59) and Mussorgsky (42) die
Offenbach, *Les contes d'Hoffmann*
Ibsen, *Ghosts*

1882 *13 January* Completes full score of Act Three of *Parsifal*
2 February Moves to Villa Gangi, where he stays until 20
March
The Wagners return to Germany via Acireale, Messina and
Venice, arriving back in Bayreuth on 1 May
Gobineau is Wagner's house guest for five weeks, 11
May–17 June
2 July Rehearsals for *Parsifal* begin and the production
opens on 26 July. At the last of the sixteen performances
on 29 August, Wagner takes over the baton from Levi
during the final transformation scene and conducts the work
to the end
14 September The Wagners leave for Italy and move into
rooms in the garden wing of the Palazzo Vendramin in
Venice
24 December Wagner conducts his C major Symphony of
1832 at a private performance in the Teatro La Fenice

Virginia Woolf, James Joyce, Kodály and Stravinsky born
Darwin (73), Garibaldi (74) and Gobineau (66) die
Nietzsche, *The Gay Science*
Rimsky-Korsakov, *The Snow Maiden*
Gounod, *La rédemption*
Ibsen, *An Enemy of the People*

1883 *11 February* Begins essay 'On the Feminine in the Human'
13 February Suffers fatal heart attack and dies in
Cosima's arms at around half past three. He is buried
privately in the garden at Wahnfried on 18 February

Webern, Varèse, Kafka and Mussolini born
Karl Marx (65) and Turgenev (65) die
Brahms, Third Symphony

EMIL HECKEL (1831–1908)

The Mannheim music dealer Emil Heckel was instrumental in setting up a network of Wagner Societies to
fund the Bayreuth Festival. Wagner had chosen Bayreuth as the site of his proposed Festival in 1870,
initially in the belief that the town's existing opera house
could be pressed into use. Its ornate Rococo interior
proved unsuited to his purposes, but his reception in
the town encouraged him to build a theatre of his own
there. The foundation stone was laid on his fifty-ninth
birthday, 22 May 1872, the ceremony marked by a
performance of Beethoven's Ninth Symphony in the
Margraves' Opera House. Here Heckel describes one of
the rehearsals.

At the beginning of the quartet, when Niemann[1] called down to
him from the so-called 'trumpeters' box' where the soloists were
stationed: 'Master, if you don't beat time for me here, I cannot
sing,' Wagner answered, 'I shall not beat time – for it would
make the rendering stiff. You must sing this passage with absolute
freedom. Such an eminent artist as yourself must be able to. That's
why I chose you and the others for the quartet. I paint it for you
in the air.' At the unison for the celli and double-basses he said:
'Gentlemen, you must know this by heart now. Look at me. There
is no beating time. I draw it for you in the air. It must speak like
a recitative.' The effect was marvellous.

To Professor Riedel's[2] question: 'Do we sing "Was die Mode frei

1. Although Wagner never forgave Niemann for his behaviour as Tannhäuser in
Paris in 1861, he could hardly ignore Germany's leading Wagner tenor and,
anxious to secure his services for the *Ring*, invited him to take part in the
performance of the Ninth Symphony with Marie Lehmann (1851–1931), Johanna
Jachmann-Wagner and Franz Betz (1835–1900).
2. Carl Riedel (1827–88) was the president of the Leipzig Wagner Society. A
composer in his own right, he acted as chorus master for the performance of
the Ninth Symphony.

getheilt"?' he answered: 'We sing "frech getheilt," '[1] and in his intonation there was an echo, as it were, of the ire with which
Beethoven himself may have effected that amendment. [. . .]

At the foundation-laying a splendid picture was presented by
Niemann's giant frame, when he suddenly sprang forward, and,
the living image of a Wagnerian hero, stretched out his hammer
for a mighty blow. The master pressed his hand in deep emotion.

After the ceremony was over, Wagner returned to the town with
Nietzsche, von Gersdorff,[2] and myself. He sat in earnest silence,
as Nietzsche has so well described it, 'with a look plunged deep
within.'[3] Well might all his life crowd back upon him at this hour,
his inner vision see both near and far with equal clearness. But as
every mood and thought condensed itself to action, in his works,
so now he felt impelled to vent his feelings in a telegraphic message
to 'his King,' who that morning had sent him a similar greeting
with the words: 'To-day more than ever I am with you in spirit.'[4]

On account of the heavy rain, the meeting adjourned to the old
Operahouse. Here Wagner himself took the word. In firm reliance
on his German people he spoke the 'Festival address'[5] so clearly,
calmly and persuasively, that his undaunted confidence found its
way into the heart of every hearer. The designation which I had
used in connection with the Mannheim concert, 'National theatre
at Bayreuth,' he disallowed in this speech, for 'Where is the Nation,
to erect itself this theatre?' Yet he described the building as hallowed by 'the German spirit that shouts to us across the centuries
its ever young Good-morrow.'

Heckel 1899: 35–8

1. Beethoven in fact set Schiller's 'Was die Mode streng getheilt', i.e., 'What
fashion strictly parted', rather than Wagner's 'What fashion brazenly parted'.
2. Baron Carl von Gersdorff (1844–1904) had been a friend of Nietzsche's since
his schooldays.
3. 'Richard Wagner in Bayreuth', Nietzsche 1983: 199.
4. *Königsbriefe* iii.3. The king's telegram was enclosed within the casket placed
beneath the foundation stone, together with a quatrain of Wagner's own
composition. If Wagner sent a telegram in reply, it has not survived.
5. GS ix.326–30; PW v.324–8.

ANTON SEIDL (1850–98)

Among the team of young musicians who worked in
the Nibelung Chancellery, copying parts and running
musical errands, was Anton Seidl, who was later to
conduct the *Ring* for Angelo Neumann's touring
company. He moved to New York in 1885, where he
proved one of the most influential and charismatic Wagnerians of the late nineteenth century. Here he recalls
his mentor's working habits.

I went to Bayreuth in the autumn of 1872. The six years during
which I lived in the house and near to Wagner will never be
forgotten by me; they determined my whole future. My mode of
thought, the manner in which thenceforward I conceived everything, the vigor with which, thereafter, I attacked everything, all
had their origin in that gracious and blessed house, where, with
the utmost simplicity and naturalness, all strove continually for the
loftiest and most ideal in life and art. The companionship of that
great, era-making man was so fascinating that all who had the
good fortune to be able to gaze upon him in the last few remaining
years of his life, agree that in him God created one of his greatest
men. When I came to Bayreuth the master was still engaged on the
composition of 'Die Gotterdammerung.' [*sic*] He had just finished
the sketch of the last scene of the third act.[1] On one of the first
evenings a few friends were gathered together, when Wagner,
carrying his composition in a portfolio under his arm, entered the
room, bowed with mock solemnity, and modesty to the company
and begged their kind indulgence and mild judgment on the new
work. Then with a comically serious face he seated himself at the
piano and the reading began. Enlivening episodes like this happened by the thousands and mark the natural, merry, scintillant
and witty manner of the master when in the midst of his friends and
disciples. On the occasion in question I enjoyed the first privilege
vouchsafed to mortal man to hear the mighty, cataclysmic sounds
of the funeral music and the broad, world-redeeming harmonies of
'Brunhilde's' [*sic*] last address in the 'Gotterdammerung.'

1. The first complete draft had in fact been finished on 10 April, the second
complete draft on 22 July 1872. Seidl arrived to take up his duties on 28
September 1872, when Cosima Wagner described him as 'the taciturn Magyar'.

It is impossible to speak with certainty about Wagner's manner of composing. He often laughed heartily when telling about some composer, whom he had visited, and found with a long pipe in his mouth engaged in completing a symphony, and who had complacently shown his composition, turning backward and forward among the pages and crying out while designating certain passages: 'Here there is quiet; now it grows angry; now it is becoming dramatic; here I let loose a thunderbolt; here we begin the down grade; and now quiet again,' the last word coming through a cloud of tobacco smoke. It is not necessary to say that Wagner could never compose in this manner. A glance into his scores will disclose the exalted seriousness with which he approached his task and the superearthly regions in which he soared when he created his ideal characters. By the time that he had written the poem of his drama (during the work on which, of course, much of the music was originated in his mind) he had already noted down a great number of the musical thoughts upon loose pieces of music paper. These notes he made in pencil and there must be a vast number of them in existence which are being anxiously saved for late posterity by Frau Cosima Wagner. She has gradually gone over all of them with ink, otherwise the majority of them would have become illegible. Only a few can boast of having received one of these little sketches as souvenirs or reward from the master in some moment of peculiarly good humor.

After a considerable space had intervened since the completion of the poem and he had given himself wholly up to its musical spirit, he was not to be seen in his family circle until 2 o'clock in the afternoon. From 5 o'clock in the morning until 2 in the afternoon he worked almost without interruption; sometimes even longer. After dinner he rested, either taking a walk in the open air or attending to his private correspondence. This lasted until 7 o'clock, when supper was eaten. Then the whole family met in the music-room to pass the time till 11 or 12 o'clock with music alternating with conversation and the reading of essays. These evenings form the subjects of the most vivid recollections of my life. In one of them it was often possible for me to learn more than all the conservatories or great musicians could offer. To hear the master on occasions like this talk about Bach, Beethoven, Mozart, Weber, Marschner, Spontini, or Auber and Rossini, explain their music, occasionally illustrating what he said at the pianoforte or by singing, dissect their styles, or appreciate them by the power of his own genius, was so instructive and so amazing to me that I saw everything in a strange, magical sort of light and my understanding of such masters, for instance, as Bach, Beethoven, and Weber, took a course whose existence I had never even suspected, but from which I will never swerve. That this course is the only correct one to follow in the interpretation of the works of these masters is proven by the success of Wagner and Von Bulow [*sic*] in the production of Beethoven's works with the entire cultured portion of the public. I followed it, too, in my concerts. This mode of interpretation is not an arbitrary or accidental distortion of the tempi, but the product of ripe, thorough, and minute study of the compositions. I am ready to advocate and defend all that I undertake in this respect.

I am convinced that Beethoven never made any metronome music and that consequently his symphonies are not to be played according to the metronome. We have too many proofs of his manner of conducting not to have firm ground for believing that although Beethoven put many more marks of expression in his music than Mozart, for instance, he nevertheless left the greater part of the question of interpretation with the conductor. [. . .] Whoever saw Wagner conduct the 'Eroica' in Vienna, in 1872,[1] will remember the half-hour's jubilation on the part of the public which this performance inspired. The same happened when he performed the C minor symphony in Berlin, in 1873,[2] with an orchestra composed of musicians who had been picked up all over and had never played together before. Here was a proof of his genius as a conductor. The performance made an impression which is indescribable. All were carried off their feet by the power and weightiness with which he infused this dramatic masterpiece of symphonic writing.

1. On 12 May 1872, when Wagner conducted a concert for the Vienna Wagner Society. The programme included the 'Eroica', Wotan's Farewell and the Magic Fire Music from *Die Walküre* and, by way of conclusion, the *Tannhäuser* Overture and new Venusberg music.
2. Possibly Seidl is confusing this with the concert in Hamburg on 21 January 1873. Wagner's only concert in Berlin in 1873 (like his later concerts in the city) featured an all-Wagner programme. Alternatively, Seidl may have been thinking of the performance at the Berlin Opera House on 5 May 1871.

As a conductor, technically and intellectually, Wagner can surely be given the highest place. He ruled the musicians completely with his gestures – yes, even sometimes with his eyes alone. He lifted them up into the fairy realms of his imagination, and confided tasks to them which they had never before thought of. He inflamed them with his fiery eyes; an energetic sweep of his baton would bring out a heavy chord from his orchestra such as had never before been heard from it; the oboe player suddenly found himself able to play the so-called cadence [sic] in the first movement in the C minor symphony with a seemingly infinite breath and a sobbing tenderness which made one think he was listening to an entirely new phrase. In one of the rehearsals before the 'Nibelungen' festival in Bayreuth, the oboe player declared that he could not conquer the technical difficulties offered by a passage in the first act of 'Siegfried,' but a word of encouragement and explanation of the proper mode of delivering the phrase cleared away all difficulties to the complete satisfaction of the master. The side-drummer in the Philadelphia Centennial March[1] gave out a triplet figure which occurs very often in a somewhat careless manner; a glance from Wagner and a sharp accentuation of the rhythm from his left hand brought the man to rights without an interruption of the orchestra. He could charm as ravishing a piano out of the brass instruments as out of a violin; and to extract a pianissimo simultaneously from all the instruments of the orchestra was the most wonderful feature of his conducting. He was able to initiate the musicians in the melos of a composition without superfluous words; a sententious comparison, a witty remark would throw more light on Wagner's intentions than whole books which have been written about the controverted passages. In fact he was an enemy of many words; deeds were his demonstrations. His attitude before an orchestra was like that of a general, firm, sure, energetic; he did not shrink up to dwarf's size at a piano, nor jump up like a bird of prey at a forte, but seemed always a piece of majesty conducting, or rather composing the music. Only the muscles of the face[,] the expression of the eyes, the angles of the mouth played the orchestral piece along with the musicians, and reflected the entire contents of the composition, and it was for this reason that the musicians learned

1. Given a read-through in the Festspielhaus on 2 July 1876.

his wishes so quickly. They were always in a state of enthusiasm and his witticisms thrown out in the pauses kept them continually in a state of good humor throughout the longest and most wearying rehe[a]rsals.

Seidl 1887

GUSTAV ADOLPH KIETZ

Although Ludwig had agreed to Wagner's choice of Bayreuth with an understandably bad grace, he was persuaded to contribute 25,000 thalers to the cost of Wagner's villa in the town, work on which proceeded only slowly, and it was not until April 1874 that Wagner was able to move in. Meanwhile, between 16 June and 8 July 1873, Kietz used the airy but still unglazed rooms as a studio in which to model a bust of Wagner. He describes the sittings in a letter to his wife.

The sittings are proceeding on a regular basis. Unfortunately, I rarely have Wagner to myself, since the children generally come with him, as does Ruß, their large dog, and, last but not least, Frau Cosima, too. All this makes my work more difficult, since he is always so animated. Once we're alone together, he generally throws back his head and sings from symphonies, quartets, operas and other tunes that I don't know. On more than one occasion, particularly when I've been engrossed in my work and then turned back to him to check a certain detail, I have discovered, to my horror, the most frightful grimace staring back at me, as he pulls his mouth wide open with both fingers and rolls his eyes – the sort of face that Leipzig street urchins make! On one such occasion, Frau Cosima came in and explained in dismay, 'But Richard!', to which Wagner replied, 'What's wrong then? It's to remind Kietz of home. After all, he's from Leipzig, too.'

Kietz 1906: 157

A carpenter by the name of Strunz who worked on Wahnfried later recalled Wagner's obsession with his grave to the rear of the house.

The grave had long since been finished when they moved into Wahnfried. While it was being dug, the Master would go to the site every day to see how the work was progressing. The path leading to the finished vault was his favourite walk. He would often climb down into the grave. If there was someone else there, he was a quite different person, serious, yet affable. Once I myself was with him in his grave. He talked to me about dying and death, though I no longer remember exactly what he said. I praised him, lifted him out and commented that he didn't have time to die, as he still had so much to do, so many great works to write. To which he said: 'Ah, I wish I was already in it!'

Schmidt and Hartmann 1909: 20

GUSTAV ADOLPH KIETZ

Kietz returned to Bayreuth for the preliminary rehearsals in July and August 1875 and wrote to his wife to report on their progress.

3 August 1875. We have now had the first orchestral rehearsal. Everyone assembled in the theatre yesterday afternoon shortly after four. Only a few tickets had been handed out to the general public. The orchestra consists of 115 players: 32 violins, with Wilhelmj as leader,[1] 12 violas, 12 cellos, 8 double basses, completely new tubas that created such a stir in Vienna,[2] 6 harps, &c., &c. Hans Richter began with the passage from Scene Two of *Das Rheingold*, where Wotan catches sight of the citadel of the gods. After it had been

1. August Wilhelmj (1845–1908) had known Wagner since the latter's days in Biebrich. (The family owned vineyards in the area, and Wilhelmj senior kept Wagner supplied with regular quantities of Rhine wine.) One of the leading violinists of his day, he moved to London in 1894 and taught at the Guildhall School of Music. The size of Wagner's orchestra may be compared with Dresden's 71 and the Paris Opéra's 77 in 1890; see Koury 1986.
2. i.e. at Wagner's concerts in Vienna in 1875. The instrument was used by Wagner to bridge the gap between horns and trombones. He appears to have begun work on *Das Rheingold* without any thought of such an instrument, but a visit to the workshop of Adolphe Sax (1814–94) in Paris in October 1853 alerted him to the existence of the saxhorn, so that when he started work on the full score, the trombones specified in the complete draft were replaced by Wagner tubas. Four are used in the *Ring* and played by an extra quartet of horn players.

rehearsed several times, Betz joined in, singing the part of Wotan quite gloriously. Wagner arrived at the theatre at around five. As he and his family entered, he was greeted by Betz singing: 'Vollendet das ewige Werk.'[1] At the end he was given three rousing cheers. Wagner was deeply moved and went down into the orchestra pit and warmly welcomed the players, who all listened to what he had to say with the greatest attention. One of the things he said was: 'There will no doubt be widely differing opinions about the great task ahead of us, but I believe that all those taking part will be fired by the thought that the work in question is a "work of art" of great import, not "a fraudulent sham".' He then crossed the gangplank on to the stage and went to sit at his small desk close to the pit, where the heavy score rested against a crate on top of which stood an oil lamp.

Hans Richter conducted. Wagner followed the score, but in his excitement kept waving his arms and legs around. Although the auditorium was very dark,[2] that great artist Adolf von Menzel[3] succeeded in capturing this scene in a most characteristic chalk drawing. The improvised conducting stand worried me in the extreme; how easily the table, crate and lamp could have been knocked over by Wagner's movements and how easily it could all have gone up in flames! During a break I went in search of Brand [sic][4] and asked him to fix the table to the floor before the music started up again. He did so at once, and I was now able to concentrate on enjoying the rehearsal.

Kietz 1907: 215–17

1. 'The everlasting work is ended': it is with these words that Wotan hails the completed Valhalla in Scene Two of *Das Rheingold*.
2. Wagner took the unprecedented step of darkening the auditorium during the performances. Hitherto it had been customary to leave the (gas) lighting turned up in order that patrons could read their copies of the libretto. In his review in the *Schlesische Presse* of 12 August 1876, Paul Lindau complained that plunging the auditorium into darkness caused severe eye strain.
3. Adolf von Menzel (1815–1905) was one of the foremost exponents of German realism. He produced two charcoal and pencil drawings in 1875, the originals of both of which are lost.
4. Carl Brandt (1828–81) worked on the Munich productions of *Das Rheingold* and *Die Walküre*. Wagner met him in May 1871 and invited him to work with him as technical director on his Bayreuth production. His premature death prevented him from fulfilling a similar function on *Parsifal*.

LILLI LEHMANN (1848–1929)

The great German soprano, who sang Woglinde, Helm-
wige and the Woodbird in the inaugural *Ring*, recalls
the musical soirées at Wahnfried during the 1875
rehearsals.

Wagner loved and revered Mozart.[1] How often I had to sing for
him arias from *Figaro*, which he always discussed with admiration
of Mozart. I sang several times for Frau Cosima, especially, Liszt's
Mignon, even before he, himself, appeared in Bayreuth. One day
when I was doing it again 'by request,' I saw Wagner enter and
listen to the end. Then, with his head thrown back, a bearing that
gave him the appearance of great self-consciousness, he strode
rather stiffly through the drawing-room with a bundle of music
under his arm, and turned, before leaving, to Frau Cosima. 'Really,
my dear,' he said, 'I did not know that your father had written such
pretty songs; I thought he had rendered service only in fingering for
piano playing. On the whole, the poem about the blooming lemon
trees always reminds me of a funeral messenger.' Whereupon he
imitated the gestures of a funeral attendant carrying lemons.[2] Frau
Cosima had to receive, with a laugh, what was not pleasant for
either her or me to hear.

But one had to excuse him, as it was not always easy for him,
when the attempt was made to 'educate' him, at the age of sixty-
two, if he, for instance, did not use his knife at table sufficiently
in the English fashion, whereby many a dinner came to a speedy
and unexpected end. But he was usually very affable and joked a
great deal with his children – his eldest daughter had just returned
from boarding school. If one or the other, however, appeared upon
the scene, he would ask her, rather sarcastically, what was the
word for lamp, cup, book, etc., in French, and tease her because
the use of French in his own house was very distasteful to him.
His antipathy to it went so far that, in 1876, he issued a formal

---

1. For a more qualified assessment, see Gruber 1991: 159–67.
2. The practice of carrying lemons at funerals is also mentioned by Büchner in
Woyzeck. (The practice had evidently died out by the early twentieth century,
as Berg altered this line when setting it in *Wozzeck*.) For a sympathetic account
of the relationship between Liszt and Wagner, see Kesting 1988: 9–48.

prohibition of it in his house, and expressed the wish to his guests that only German might be spoken at 'Wahnfried.'

Lehmann 1914: 211–12

SUSANNE WEINERT

The Wagner children's governess at Wahnfried was Susanne Weinert, who took up her duties in July 1875. Here she describes the Wagners' visit to Vienna in November, where Wagner had agreed to superintend performances of *Tannhäuser* and *Lohengrin* in return for the use of Court Opera singers in the *Ring* the following summer. The Wagners put up at the Imperial Hotel.

The hotel is a former archduke's palace and is quite wonderful! The broad, richly ornamented and carpeted stairs, the high stairwell painted with frescos, the large mirrors and magnificent flowers everywhere – it all makes a princely impression. At the top of the stairs, double doors opened before us and we passed through a series of rooms whose elegance left nothing to be desired.

8 November 1875.[1] Our things have been unpacked and I have put them away in the various cupboards.

My charges and I have separate bedrooms here, whereas at Wahnfried we share a single large room; but I have been given Siegfried to look after during the night. Everything is incredibly beautiful here: chandeliers, luxuriously upholstered furniture, heavy, full-length curtains; you would think you were in a lavishly furnished private residence, rather than in an hotel.

The curtains, upholstery, carpets and tablecloths are all in the same shade of colour and arranged with immaculate taste.

We occupy several rooms and all are equally beautiful: the splendid blue salon, the friendly dining room, the little girls' bed-

---

1. The dates in Susanne Weinert's diary do not necessarily relate to the events that took place on those days: she simply filled whatever space was available for her studied prose. After two nights at the Grand Hotel, the Wagners moved to the Imperial Hotel on 3 November.

room with crimson furnishings and the room occupied by Siegfried and me, which is furnished in a delicate shade of yellow.

10 November. What a beautiful city Vienna is! Today, after I had dressed the girls in their delightful blue-and-grey-checked dresses and Siegfried in a brown velvet suit trimmed with grey fur, we walked up and down the beautiful Ringstraße, enjoying the splendidly decorated shop windows. 'Those are Wagner's children with their governess,' I often heard people whispering, and many a friendly gaze was directed at the pretty little children. They are always so well-behaved when they are with me. Isolde and Eva like to hold on to my arm, but I normally take Siegfried's hand, and the girls walk on ahead of us.

It was unusually mild outside today, so we immediately went out again after lunch. [. . .]

15 November. How many visitors the great poet–composer and his wife receive every day! There is a constant coming and going, and I hear the liveliest conversations coming from the salon.[1]

17 November.[2] I am still transported by yesterday evening's wonderful performance of *Lohengrin*. The previous day my mistress had said to me: 'Fräulein, tomorrow evening you will hear *Lohengrin* with the children. Are you familiar with the opera?' When I replied that I was familiar with the subject matter, but that I had not yet had an opportunity to hear the piece, Herr Wagner added, 'Well, I'm sure you'll like Elsa and Lohengrin.'

After dinner, I did the girls' hair once again and dressed them in

---

1. Visitors included Countess Marie Dönhoff (1848–1929), Marie Hohenlohe and the artists Franz von Lenbach (1836–1904), Hans Makart (1840–84) and Gottfried Semper. Wagner was kept busy rehearsing *Tannhäuser* and *Lohengrin*, but he and his wife also found time to hear Verdi's *Requiem* ('about which it would certainly be best to say nothing'; CT, 2 November), Bizet's *Carmen* ('a new French work, interesting for the glaringness of the modern French manner'; CT, 3 November), Sardou's *Andrea* ('an excessively bad play'; CT, 8 November), Goldmark's *Die Königin von Saba* ('no gold, no marks, but plenty of Mosenthal'; CT, 10 November), one act of Meyerbeer's *L'Africaine*, a piano quartet by Brahms ('a red, crude-looking man, his opus very dry and stilted'; CT, 18 November), Adolf von Wilbrandt's *Arria und Messalina* ('a dismal piece of hack work, performed by actors without any talent'; CT, 26 November) and Gounod's *Roméo et Juliette* ('true nausea'; CT, 30 November).
2. The performance of *Lohengrin* took place on 15 December.

their charming little white dresses. Little Siegfried in his real black velvet suit with a broad white lace collar also looked very pretty. I threw myself into my evening dress and we all made our way to the salon, where my mistress was already waiting for us in a black satin dress that ended in an impressive train.

The Court Opera is not far from the Imperial Hotel and we were soon there. As we left the carriage, I was literally blinded by the dazzling light that flooded towards me. After the servant had taken our wraps, we made our way to our boxes. Herr and Frau Wagner occupied that of the Court Opera director, Herr Jauner, while the children and I sat in the adjacent one. What a magnificent scene unfolded before my eyes! Everywhere I looked I could see bejewelled people, expectant faces, shining eyes, obliging but also cold smiles!

The first sounds emerge from the orchestra. Now the curtain goes up, and look – on his proud throne sits King Henry the Fowler, surrounded by Saxon and Brabantine nobles and the people.

Oh, this wonderful opera that knows how to seek out the deepest recesses of the human heart with its magical sounds! The first act is over and applause such as I had never heard before filled the enormous room. Opera glasses were trained incessantly on the Master's box and, standing by the parapet, he bowed, smiling amiably. The lovely children attracted attention, too, for in my enthusiasm I had lifted dear Siegfried on to my knees in order for his intelligent child's face to be seen more clearly.

The enthusiasm was universal. During the act, Herr Wagner came into our box to speak to his children, whose cheeks were aglow and whose eyes shone. I could see with what passion he followed the opera; when a slower tempo was wanted, he gestured accordingly, but when the music was not moving swiftly and passionately enough for him, his whole body would start to move and, gesturing violently with his arms, he would mutter: 'What deplorable dawdling.'

In the third act, as the strains of the Bridal Chorus with its sweet melody, 'Treulich geführt', died away, the delight of the audience reached new heights. The enthusiasm was unstoppable and people started to shout 'Richard Wagner! Richard Wagner' loudly and incessantly. All eyes were turned to his box, from where he quickly

vanished, only to reappear on stage. There he stood, the very
picture of genius in his finely cut day suit, surrounded by laurel
wreaths and flowers bestowed on the prince of music by his
enthusiastic disciples. He began to speak – and time and again
the enthusiastic cry went up, 'Richard Wagner', before dying down
sufficiently to allow people to hear the heartfelt words which, his
voice trembling with emotion, he addressed to the Viennese,
thanking them for their friendly reception of his *Lohengrin* and
also thanking the artists, who had done everything in their power
to make the opera so moving, magnificent, beautiful and lovely.
Richard Wagner then left the stage and the second scene began.
When the moving scene begins where the swan reappears and
Lohengrin takes his leave of Elsa, I saw all the ladies reaching for
their handkerchiefs and I, too, was unable to stop myself crying.
Pressed into the corner, my handkerchief to my eyes, I was sobbing
quietly when I heard the door of the box open. The great Master
came in and asked me quietly: 'Well, Fräulein, what do you think
of *Lohengrin*?' I turned to him but was unable to answer him at
once. He went out again, smiling serenely to himself.

When we entered Wagner's box at the end, my mistress was just
wiping away her tears; it is said that she weeps every time she sees
Lohengrin, she is always so moved by it.

NA

ANGELO NEUMANN (1838–1910)

Angelo Neumann, whom we last saw sporting a pair of
white tights in Stuttgart in 1864, was a member of the
Vienna Court Opera ensemble from 1862 to 1876,
when he retired from singing to take up theatre management. His most significant Wagnerian feat was to
mastermind the touring production of the *Ring* that
visited the whole of Europe between 1882 and 1889.
He was able to observe Wagner from close quarters at
the rehearsals for *Tannhäuser* and *Lohengrin* in November and December 1875.

What an inspiring director he was! How well he understood the

art of spurring on his men, of getting his best work out of each
one, of making every gesture, each expression tell! These rehearsals
convinced me that Richard Wagner was not only the greatest
dramatist of all time, but also the greatest of directors, and a
marvellous actor as well.[1] Now at the end of these long thirty years
I can still distinctly recall certain incidents of his wonderful mimetic
powers. I never hear a performance of 'Tannhäuser' or of 'Lohengrin' without his image rising before me in certain scenes.

How wonderfully he took the part of Tannhäuser finding himself
at the crossways in the Thuringian forest after his release from the
enchantments of the Venusberg. Riveted to the spot, he stood like
a graven image, with arms upraised; then gradually, at the entrance
of the pilgrims, came to life with a tremendous shuddering start,
and finally, overcome with emotion, sank to the ground as the
chorus proceeded; to break out at the end in his great cry – 'Ach,
schwer drückt mich der Sünden Last!'

What stately dignity and what knightly fire he put into this rôle
as Tannhäuser listens to the song of Wolfram. Then in the great
final scene of the first act how he dominated, moved, and inspired
his company – assigning places, prescribing gestures, and arranging
expressions, till the tableau was perfect and the whole cortège,
Landgrave, knights, chorus, horses, and dogs took their places with
utmost artistic precision. These were moments to make an indelible
impression on my mind.

His plan for the entrance of the guests has been the model for
all later performances. It was his idea that the Landgrave and
Elizabeth should stand with their backs to the audience, receiving
their guests as the pages ushered them in. Previously to this they
had taken their places upon the throne, and the pages had simply
preceded the guests and announced them *en masse*. The incident
of the widow bringing her two daughters was customary, to be
sure; but it was Wagner who first showed us how, after the official
greeting, Elizabeth should sweep forward, take the young girls by
the hand, present them graciously to all her court, and lead them
back to their mother before she went to take her place beside the
Landgrave on the daïs.

---

1. Edith Livermore's translation misleadingly renders 'Bühnenregisseur' and
'Menschendarsteller' as 'manager' and 'character actor' respectively.

In the Minnesingers' contest where Tannhäuser's usual proceeding had been to advance to Wolfram, and, flourishing his fist
in the latter's face, to sing, 'O Wolfram, der du also sangest!'
Wagner forbade this crude gesture entirely. In the closing scene, as
he showed Tannhäuser his position at the cry, 'Weh mir, Unglück-
sel'gen!' his acting was a triumph of art. Then turning abruptly,
he took the part of Elizabeth, and mounting the steps of the throne
with an expression of lofty exaltation, he stood till the fall of the
curtain, his hands clasped and eyes raised in fervid appeal –
carrying us along with him and inspiring us all with an indescribable awe for the scene.

But he reached his greatest heights in Tannhäuser's account of
his pilgrimage. His first words to Wolfram, 'Hör an, Wolfram, hör
an!' began with touching eagerness, but he rose to heart-rending
intensity where he describes the curse, 'Hast du so böse Lust
geteilt,' etc. In each one of these scenes it was a great dramatic
genius who stood before us.

Neumann 1909: 9–11

HUGO WOLF (1860–1903)

Hugo Wolf was a student at the Vienna Conservatory
when Wagner visited the city in November and December 1875. He wrote to tell his parents of his first sighting
of the great man.

Richard Wagner has been in Vienna since 5 November and is
staying at the Imperial Hotel. He occupies seven rooms there with
his wife. Although he has already been in Vienna for so long, I did
not have the good fortune and pleasure of seeing him until around
a quarter to eleven on 17 November, when I spotted him outside
the stage door at the Court Opera, and from there went on stage
and listened to the rehearsals that he was attending.

It was with truly religious awe that I gazed upon this great
master of music, for, according to current opinion, he is now the
world's leading opera composer. I took a few steps towards him
and greeted him very respectfully, whereupon he thanked me in
a friendly manner. From that moment onwards I conceived an

insuperable desire to get to know Richard Wagner better, even though I had as yet absolutely no inkling of his music.

Wolf 1912: 8–9

> The performance of *Tannhäuser* on 22 November proved a revelation and from now on Wolf redoubled his efforts to see Wagner, taking up his position outside the Imperial Hotel and no doubt cutting a distinctly curious figure with his provincial plaid cloak. On 11 December his efforts were finally rewarded.

You'll never guess who I've been with!!! With the Master, with Richard Wagner. I'll tell you how it happened. These are the very words that I wrote in my diary:[1]

On Saturday 11 December at half past ten I saw Richard Wagner for the second time, at the Imperial Hotel, where I stood on the stairway for half an hour, waiting for him to arrive. (I knew that on this day he would hold the final rehearsal for *Lohengrin*.) Finally the Master came down from the second floor, and I greeted him very respectfully while he was still some distance away. He thanked me most amiably. Then, as he reached the door, I leapt after him and opened it for him, whereupon he stared at me for a few seconds, before driving off to the rehearsal at the opera house. I ran on ahead as fast as I could and arrived at the opera house before he got there in his cab. I greeted him again there and tried to open the door for him, but as I couldn't get it open, the driver jumped down and opened it himself. He then said something to the driver, I think it was about me. I then followed him on stage, but this time I wasn't allowed in. (I had already been on stage at the *Tannhäuser* rehearsal, when Wagner had been present.) As I had often waited for the Master at the Imperial Hotel, I had got to know the hotel manager, and he promised to put in a good word for me. Who was more pleased than I when he told me to come back the next day, Saturday 11 December, during the afternoon, when he would introduce me to Frau Cosima's chambermaid (Frau Cosima is Richard Wagner's wife, the daughter of the great Liszt) and to Richard Wagner's valet. I arrived at the appointed

1. As Frank Walker points out in his edition of Wolf's Viennese diary (1947: 14), Wolf took the opportunity to polish his style when transcribing this entry.

hour and had a brief meeting with the chambermaid. I was told to return the next day, Sunday 12 December, at two o'clock. I turned up at the time agreed, but found the chambermaid, valet de chambre and manager still at table, so I drank a cappucino with them. Then I went with the maid to the Master's apartments, where I waited for about a quarter of an hour before the Master arrived. Finally Wagner appeared, accompanied by Cosima, Goldmark etc.[1] (He had just come from a Philharmonic concert.) I greeted Cosima most respectfully, but she did not consider it worth her while to bestow so much as a single glance on me; indeed, she is known to the whole world as an extremely arrogant and self-important person. Wagner went into his room without noticing me, but the chambermaid called after him in a pleading tone of voice: 'Ah, Herr Wagner, there's a young artist here who has waited for you so often and who would like to speak to you.' He came out, looked at me and said: 'I've seen you once before, I think you are – – – – – – – – – – (presumably he was about to say, 'You are a fool'). He then went in and opened the door to the reception room for me, where the dominant impression was one of right royal splendour. In the middle stood a couch, all velvet and silk. Wagner himself was swathed in a long velvet coat with fur trimmings. As I went in, he asked me what I wanted. When I was alone with him, I said: 'Revered Master! For a long time I have longed to hear someone pass judgement on my compositions, and I would . . .' At this point the Master cut me off and said: 'My dear child, I cannot judge your compositions and have far too little time at present and cannot even write any letters. I understand absolutely nothing about music.' When I asked the Master to tell me whether I had any talent for music and whether I would ever come to anything, he said: 'When I was as young as you are now, no one could say from my compositions whether I would go far in music. You would at least have to play me your compositions on the piano, but I have no time just now. When you are older and have written larger pieces and I am in Vienna again, you can show me your compositions. It's no use; I can't give you my opinion.' When I told the Master that I took the classical composers as my models,

1. The composer Karl Goldmark (1830–1915), who had met Wagner in the 1860s and who was instrumental in setting up the Vienna Wagner Society in 1872.

he said: 'Well yes, that's right, you can't be original straightaway.' (With that he laughed.) Finally he said: 'My dear friend, I wish you lots of luck in your career. Continue to work hard, and when I return to Vienna, you can show me your compositions.' With that I left the Master, deeply moved and touched.

Wolf 1912: 10–14; see also Decsey 1903: 44–5

LUDWIG STRECKER (1853–1943)

Ludwig Strecker fell heir to the publishing house of B. Schott's Söhne on Franz Schott's death in 1874. In January 1876 he paid his first visit to Wahnfried and recorded his impressions in a diary.

17 January 1876. I set out armed with a scrap of paper filled with a hundred or more subjects for discussion and firmly resolved not to yield to any attempts to extort money from me, a determination inculcated by the firm's former managing directors, who still recalled Wagner's first personal contacts with Franz Schott.

The door was opened by a frock-coated servant who asked me politely what I wanted. Master and Mistress were working, I was told, and were not receiving visitors, but a message had been left at my hotel. And so I retraced my steps and found in my room a visiting card from Wagner, announcing that I would be welcome at five o'clock. When I passed through the grille for a second time at five o'clock, I found the Master preoccupied with two large Newfoundland dogs and a cigar, taking his constitutional in the garden. We said hello and eyed each other up. From the business circular that I had sent him and the fact that correspondence had been conducted not by me but by my company secretary, Adam Mazière, Wagner had concluded that I was only a stock-holding partner, with the result that, as he later told me, he had imagined me as a grumpy old lawyer.

For my own part I found in him a not very tall old man,[1] with a friendly face from which two very clear blue eyes peered out from behind a pair of spectacles; when he removed his hat, I saw

1. Strecker's own note reads: '1.60 m (like Beethoven)' = 5 feet 3 inches.

the well-known brow and a full head of grey hair. His voice was deep and euphonious. He was dressed like other mortals. [. . .]

We sat down and began to discuss business matters, by which I mean that, having sorted out various general points, I asked for Wagner's opinion on a number of them. He now started to speak and launched into a long narrative, passing from one point to a thousand others, so that from now on all I had to do was listen in silence. He began by praising Schott's generosity and liberality and soon touched on a subject that exercises him greatly: the court case in which he is engaged with Fürstner over the performing rights to the new scenes in *Tannhäuser*.[1] He then started to tell me the whole story of his first three operas, which he himself published in Dresden – through Meser – with money scraped together from friends. On these operas, which, following the death of Meser's successor, Fürstner bought for 26,000 marks in 1872, he – Wagner – still owes several of his friends 5,000 thalers, to say nothing of the interest. 'Yes, I'll have to reach a ripe old age if I want to pay off even a part of my debts.' At the word 'debts', I smiled and looked first at him and then at the precious objects displayed in the room; he understood what I meant, laughed out loud and said: 'You like my house? God, if only you knew! The 20,000 florins from Schott's aren't my only debt;[2] apart from the 25,000 marks[3] which my young master – whose latest portrait I received today – has given me for my house, nothing is paid for.' It was with some bitterness that he went on: 'No, he didn't keep his word, he left me in the lurch and instead of supporting my undertaking, as he should have done, he follows his own whims. Well, I can manage without him; I've just received an invitation from America to write a march to celebrate their centenary; I wrote back to say that they should first do something for me and send me money for my theatre, perhaps I'd then get some ideas!'

Money in general is a favourite subject with him. On another

1. Adolph Fürstner (1833–1908) took over the firm of C. F. Meser in 1872 and thus acquired the rights to *Rienzi, Der fliegende Holländer* and the original Dresden version of *Tannhäuser*. Now he claimed a share in the royalties from performances of the Paris version of this last-named work, even though the score had been published by Flaxland.
2. The advance on *Parsifal*.
3. *Recte* 75,000 marks.

occasion he said: 'It's a crying shame that in the whole of Germany there isn't a wealthy individual to say: "Here's credit for you, do what you think best, I'm entirely at your disposal" – what difference would this make to a Rothschild or a Bleichröder? And so my friends and I – but mainly my female friends – have to scrape the money together, and if there weren't a few loyal people to help me, my entire life's work would never have been realized.'

He went on like this for over an hour, then finally dismissed me and asked me to return at eight o'clock, saying that he would invite Rubinstein, too,[1] to come round for the evening – 'You'll then get to know my wife.'

When I returned, I found not only Rubinstein but also Frau Cosima, who was wearing a large green eyeshade to protect her eyes, but she then removed it – partly from vanity, I think, as her eyes are very beautiful. An interesting, narrow face, large nose, equally large mouth with splendid teeth, blond hair simply knotted, very beautiful, aristocratic hands and a very slim figure. When she becomes animated, her voice is agreeably deep, but normally the tone is somewhat blasé. At all events, she is a clever, interesting woman who can be utterly charming, as she proved in the course of the evening and following day.

She often mentioned her 'father', apparently with great affection, but spoke of her mother only once. She worships the Master to distraction, following his every movement and hanging on his every word – he rewards her with exceptional and, as it appears, sincere gallantry and attentiveness. On this occasion he was wearing his well-known Renaissance costume, which does nothing to improve his appearance, but at least it does not look out of place on him and must certainly be comfortable to wear: a black, loose-fitting cloth jacket, black knee-breeches, black stockings and cloth shoes. The beret familiar from pictures of him he carried in his hand and placed beside him on a chair. At table I was struck by the fact that from time to time he would impale morsels of food on his fork and dip them in a salt cellar placed there for that purpose.

Strecker 1951: 277–80

---

1. Joseph Rubinstein (1847–84) was Wagner's pianist in residence.

HERMANN RITTER (1849–1926)

Another visitor to Wahnfried during the winter of
1875/6 was Hermann Ritter, who was studying art and
history at Heidelberg University. He was also interested
in the history of musical instruments and had recently
built a large viola for which he claimed improved reson-
ance and a more brilliant tone. The instrument – which
he called a *viola alta* – came to Wagner's attention and,
in response to the latter's invitation, Ritter turned up
at Wahnfried on 9 February 1876 to demonstrate his
invention.

I entered the Villa Wahnfried in Bayreuth with the awe that one
normally feels on entering a place of worship. At that time, my
viola alta still had no case to show for itself and was wrapped only
in a large paper bag. After my arrival had been announced, I and
my *viola alta* and its paper bag were ushered through the vestibule
into the famous rotunda which, lit from above, is lined with Wagnerian characters by Zumbusch, all of them placed on large plinths.
I did not have to wait long before the man who has delighted and
exalted millions with his mighty art came striding towards me. He
was dressed in a brown jacket and light grey trousers. His head,
with its powerfully domed forehead, lively eyes and a nose that
revealed the greatest energy and initiative, towered above his body,
which was of medium height. 'I'm glad you've come,' said the
Master, shaking my hand. 'So you're studying philosophy and are
bent on improving the viola?' he went on and, with a smile, exam-
ined my paper bag. 'So that's the new viola? – Well, unpack it and
let's see it and, above all, hear it.' I'd barely struck a handful of
notes when I saw from the Master's expression that all doubts
about its intonation had vanished. 'It sounds wonderful! Go on!
Let me hear the whole range of the instrument!' I did so, adding
the well-known church aria falsely ascribed to Stradella.[1] When I
had finished, Wagner said: 'Listen, this is an excellent invention,'
and took the *viola alta* in order to play a few notes of the C
major scale on the C string. 'But there's one thing I must tell you
straightaway: you'll encounter great resistance to your instrument
on the part of viola players, who will object to its size.' 'Master,'

1. The *aria di chiesa*, 'Pietà, Signore', 11:27; see Stradella 1991.

I replied, 'it's natural that when you've been used to riding a
donkey, you find it less easy to control a thoroughbred.' Wagner
laughed heartily at this comparison and said: 'But I see that you
play the instrument very easily, so others should be able to do so,
too. They should learn to do so.' With that he called to his wife
Cosima and briefly explained to her why I had come and what I
hoped to achieve by improving the tone of the viola, a point that
I was again required to demonstrate by playing a number of pieces.
'Right, young man, put the instrument down and come and have
a bite to eat with us,' and with that the Master invited me to
have breakfast with them. I now had to explain the whole business
all over again and he even asked me to deliver a proper lecture on
the evolution of string instruments. I told the Master that the faulty
intonation of most violas in use today justified the rebirth of the
alto viola and how that great authority on instrumentation Berlioz
had lamented the inadequacies of the existing alto viola in his
treatise on instrumentation: 'Most alto violas in use today are the
wrong size. They are generally large violins strung with viola strings
and have neither the size nor tone of genuine alto violas – they are
bastard instruments.' 'Yes, Berlioz,' Wagner smiled, 'he treated
instruments like puppets on a string. I'm grateful to you, that was
most interesting. Cosima, you can add Herr Ritter's name to the
list of viola players in the Nibelung orchestra.' And so I suddenly
found myself a participant in that summer's forthcoming festival,
the first great performance of *Der Ring des Nibelungen*.[1] [. . .]

The following evening a small party had been arranged at Wahnfried, and I was invited to attend and bring my *viola alta*. Apart
from the Master and Frau Cosima, the others present were
Wagner's disciples who were then working in the so-called Chancellery: Franz Fischer[2] and Felix Mottl[3] (both now famous as

1. Ritter returned to play in the orchestra in the summer of 1876. By 1889 five
of his pupils were in the Bayreuth orchestra playing the *viola alta*, but, as Strauss
points out in his revised version of Berlioz's *Traité d'instrumentation*, the
instrument's size and unwieldiness militated against its wider acceptance; Strauss
1905: 81.
2. Franz Fischer (1849–1918) was Court Kapellmeister in Mannheim (1877–9)
and Munich (1879–1912). Between 1882 and 1884 he shared conducting duties
at Bayreuth with Hermann Levi, returning in 1899.
3. Felix Mottl (1856–1911) joined the Chancellery in 1876. He first conducted
at Bayreuth in 1886 and returned frequently between then and 1906.

conductors in their own right), the leader from Meiningen, Fried-
hold Fleischhauer, and a few friends of the Wagners.

I myself arrived at Wahnfried somewhat earlier than the others,
and this was the occasion for some curious exchanges with Wagner.
The large salon at Wahnfried looks out over the garden and houses
Wagner's library. I inspected its contents and, prompted by my
high opinion of Ludwig Nohl, asked the Master whether he had
Nohl's writings among his collection of books.[1] 'Nohl?' he said
curtly. 'Listen, I find him a strange person.' 'Why?' I asked. 'Because
he writes so much about my work. He should stop. Far too much
is written and said about it. People should just come and see it
and hear it. A single bowstroke is worth more than all this useless
twaddle. Listen, you're not one of those people who'll publish an
article in tomorrow's newspapers, "Breakfast with Richard
Wagner", or the like?' I assured the Master that this was not my
way of going about things and he was satisfied. I considered it
my duty to defend my teacher, Professor Nohl, and responded to
Wagner's outburst by saying that Nohl was one of his chief
admirers and supporters and that he championed his artistic ideals
even in the lecture theatre at the university. Wagner exploded in
anger: 'That's just what I don't want,' he cried, 'it does me more
harm than good. I need an audience that understands none of all
this and that doesn't adopt a critical response. The people I like
best are those who don't even know that we write music on five
lines. You want to take a doctorate? Didn't you say so earlier?'
'Certainly, Master, that's my intention,' I answered. 'What's the
point? What do you hope to achieve?' As someone who assiduously
attended university lectures, I found this question curious, even
frightening, not least when Wagner began to take a whimsical line,
reminding me of Mephistopheles in the scene with the student in
Faust. When I observed that it was the usual practice and a part
of university life to take a doctorate on completion of one's studies,
he broke into mocking laughter interrupted only by the words
'coffee doctor', 'tea doctor' and 'visiting doctor'. He then started
to fulminate in the most terrible fashion against universities and

1. Wagner owned copies of Nohl's *Richard Wagner, Gluck und Wagner* and
Beethoven. The first two he held in low regard (see CT, 29 September 1869
and 20 February 1870) but seems to have thought more highly of the third, a
collection of eyewitness accounts of Beethoven (CT, 17–25 January 1877).

conservatories, ending with the words: 'Remarkable! The things you can learn!' He had only just finished this dressing-down when my eye was caught by a picture standing on an easel. 'Is that your father, Master?' By now Wagner could control himself no longer and was literally screaming with laughter: 'Ja, ja – studying for a doctorate and you don't even know who that is!' It was a half-length portrait in oils of Schopenhauer. Until then I had never seen a portrait of this philosopher, who at that time was barely tolerated at Heidelberg University. When I apologized for my ignorance, the Master consoled me and said: 'Make sure you study Schopenhauer; he'll do you far more good than all your quackery! Do you know Nietzsche? There's a man for you!' 'Only the name,' I replied, 'though I know something of him thanks to Nohl.' 'What, for example?' *The Birth of Tragedy from the Spirit of Music.*' 'Well, that's something; but you can't use that at university. It's really utter nonsense for those learned gentlemen. Don't you agree?' An ironic smile played around Wagner's lips.

Ritter 1901: 496–8

FELIX MOTTL (1856–1911)

Felix Mottl had made Wagner's acquaintance in May 1872, but it was not until March 1875 that he was invited to help with the musical preparations for the 1876 *Ring*. He arrived in Bayreuth on 22 May 1876 and kept a diary of his impressions.

25 May 1876. To the Master. He talks a lot about Mendelssohn, whose sense of form he mentions approvingly. He also speaks appreciatively about Mendelssohn's concert overtures. Especially 'Hebrides'.

I speak the word 'Sieglinde' with the accent on the second syllable. He is furious with me, complains that the Austrians aren't German (they're half Slav & half Italian!), but then, as soon as he notices my dismay, immediately comes over all kind & friendly and says: 'There, my child! I didn't mean to be so cross! Let's be friends again!' Begging letters arrive for him. One from a ladies' quartet, another from a poor watchmaker, who demands a pair of his trousers. Wagner gives them all to his wife to answer, saying: 'She takes charge of the trouserless watchmakers!'[1]

1 June 1876. Piano rehearsal for Act One of Siegfried. Is very pleased with us young people. Says we're capable and devoted. Levi[2] has arrived from Munich. Try out swimming machines. Master very affable. Invites us to restaurant. Richter and Levi, Christian and Jew! Very stark contrast!

2 June 1876. Rehearsal with Hill & Schlosser.[3] Tells Schlosser: 'Everything strictly in time! No recitative, there's none of that here. Nothing but "arias"!' Tells us how, after a gathering of German princes, King Ludwig had told him that he couldn't abide the company of his fatuous princely colleagues. Tells stories about Berlioz and Meyerbeer. Calls Virginia cigars 'rats' tails'.

3 June 1876. More rehearsals. Wagner in high spirits. He says it would be no bad thing if a few stout lads were to give Herr Hanslick a sound thrashing here in Bayreuth.

9 June 1876. Dinner at Wagner's. Asparagus soup. Fish. Roast beef. Charlotte russe. Dessert. Malaga. Rosé. Hock. Champagne. Wagner very affable. He says the Slavs have the greatest future ahead of them and will take over civilization when all things Germanic have died out. 'For me, a "cosmopolitan" or a "member of the international community" is the same as a "knave".'

20 June 1876. [...] Spend most evenings with Wagner at the restaurant, where he drinks grog. Annoyance with Levi over the altered passage in the 'Eroica'.[4] Levi bursts into tears & carries on in a thoroughly childish manner. [...]

1. Fricke (1906: 54) and Gautier (1910: 51–2) report similar anecdotes.
2. Hermann Levi (1839–1900) was Court Kapellmeister in Munich from 1872 to 1896.
3. Karl Hill (1831–93) sang Alberich at Bayreuth in 1876 and Klingsor in 1882. He died insane. Max Schlosser (1835–1916) created David in *Die Meistersinger* (1868) and Mime in *Das Rheingold* (1869) and *Siegfried* (1876). Other roles in his repertory included Max, Almaviva (*Il barbiere di Siviglia*), Tonio (*La fille du régiment*) and, towards the end of his career, Beckmesser.
4. In the first movement, where the first horn enters with the main theme in E flat major, while the violins play a tremolando on B flat and A flat just before the recapitulation. When he conducted the piece in Vienna on 12 May 1872, Wagner changed the second violins' A flat to G.

28 June 1876. Levi gives us conducting lessons. Upbeat, *alla breve* etc. Wagner praises *Kater Murr*![1] 'Together with Bismarck, I am the only living German who is worth a rap.' Wilhelmj recently held a party for the orchestra at the restaurant. In the afternoon, when it was very hot. He had some excellent wine sent from Wiesbaden, and we all had such a high old time that several musicians had to be brought back in carts, like the wounded after a battle. The trumpeter Kühnert was found in the forest above the Bürgerreuth the next morning, sleeping off his hangover.[2]

11 July 1876. After one of the final piano rehearsals, Wagner tries to thank Joseph Rubinstein for the work he has done. He starts off very amiably and then says something along the lines of: 'If we never really drew any closer on a human level, the fault is not mine but yours. You are a member of a foreign race with which we have no sympathy.' (Jewish). By the end he gets quite worked up, so that his planned speech of thanks turns into an expression of anger and ill-feeling.

Mottl 1943: 196–202

RICHARD FRICKE (1818–1903)

Richard Fricke was choreographer to the Ducal Court at Dessau from 1853 to 1893. His work came to the Wagners' attention in December 1872 when they attended a performance of Gluck's *Orfeo ed Euridice* and were sufficiently impressed to engage Fricke as movement director for the first Bayreuth Festival. His diary of the 1876 rehearsals provides an invaluable insight into the chaotic behind-the-scenes preparations.

15 May 1876. We fell to talking about the production and I noted that, in the case of a work like this, unique as it was, there was the need to provide posterity with a written account of the production. I said that, as it would now take too long to draw up a

---

1. By E. T. A. Hoffmann.
2. For further accounts of this riotous event on 18 June, see Fricke 1906: 104–6 and Wilhelmj 1928: 41, who adds that Levi's ritual humiliation continued, when he was left tied to a tree.

production outline of four such works by 1 June, I would follow his instructions to the letter and then prepare a production book, a suggestion with which he was in full agreement.[1]

Wagner was in a bad mood because, although he had vowed not to set foot in the theatre before 1 June,[2] he had been there this morning with the delegates following his meeting with them. There is still scaffolding in the princes' box, although it would be possible to continue working there unimpeded. There is still a great deal to be done, but when you ask them why no work is being done, they always shift the blame on to someone else.

Before we parted, I could not resist drawing Wagner's attention to the difficulty of the Norns' scene with the throwing of the rope. I said: 'When you read a scene of such seriousness and essential sombreness, your imagination is fully engaged; but as soon as something like this is presented visually, when all our other senses are alert, the image created in our imagination risks being absurdly diminished. In the case of this particular scene, which we have to present both to the eye and to the senses in order for us to stage it, I see a very real problem! The rope must be long, golden and light but, at the same time, heavy enough to be thrown, and I am afraid that the three ladies will not be able to master it.' 'Then they must practise until they do,' he interjected. 'And if they don't learn how to do it? I've been thinking about this scene all winter: here's what I suggest! How would it be if we operated the rope mechanically, by means of wires invisible to the audience, and if that doesn't work, I suggest not having a rope at all but expressing it all by mime.' He stopped in his tracks. 'No, never – not by mime – well, we'll see.' 'Yes,' I retorted, 'if all my performers were like Frau Jachmann-Wagner (she is playing the First Norn), we'd get by not just with my suggestion for operating the rope mechanically, we'd also be able to arrange for the rope to be thrown in the way that you yourself imagined it.' I was on the point of drawing his attention to other difficulties, some of them almost harder to solve, things which our imagination transforms into the most beautiful images but which, as noted, are in fact going to call the whole

1. In fact, Wagner was so keen to establish a tradition for producing the *Ring* that he had already written to Heinrich Porges on 6 November 1872, inviting him to keep notes; see Porges 1983.
2. Wagner was depressed at the lack of progress on the building.

staging into question: we realize how impossible it is to stage them, and the curse of absurdity destroys the illusion. But I was satisfied for the present that I had succeeded in saying this one thing to him, volatile as he is. Also, we were distracted by his two big Leonberg dogs, one of which almost knocked him over with its slobbering affection. [. . .]

3 June 1876. Today was an absolute nightmare. I felt unwell and everything conspired to make me clumsy, listless and out of sorts. During the morning I gave the children their lessons as usual.[1] Wagner had gone to the orchestral rehearsal, and so I was free till three o'clock, at which time a swimming rehearsal was arranged. The sisters Lilli and Marie Lehmann had arrived, together with Fräulein Lammert.[2] We were introduced. They took one look at the machines and at the gymnasts who were swimming in them: 'No,' said Lilli, 'you can't expect me to agree to that, I'll not do it at any price. I've only just got over a serious illness, quite apart from the fact that I suffer from vertigo.' The other two were silent. 'Fräulein Marie,' I said, 'where's your courage? Give it a try and I bet your fears will pass and that pleasure in swimming will gain the upper hand.' The ladder was placed in position and Brandt and I helped her in. Amid many 'Ohs' and 'Ahs' and squeaks and squeals we buckle her in and the ride begins, very slowly. The look of terror disappears from her face and she starts to laugh, saying that it is going quite nicely. Lilli, too, now decides to try it for herself and, lo and behold, within seconds she is the more fearless of the two. Fräulein Lammert now follows and all three of them swim to the sound of merry laughter. Wagner appears and the whole scene is played right through. And, on top of everything, the three ladies sing their parts quite ravishingly. They move well. The feeling that came over me was indescribable, tears came into my eyes at the fact that it worked, something which all of us (with

1. Fricke was giving Wagner's children dancing lessons.
2. Minna Lammert (1852–1921) sang Floßhilde and Roßweiße at the 1876 Festival. Each of the three Rhinepersons had her own swimming machine, a harness mounted at the top of a seven-metre pole and attached at its lower end to a trolley on wheels, which was trundled around the stage by a stagehand under instructions from a member of the music staff. For a detailed description of these swimming machines, see Baumann 1980: 188–91; for Lilli Lehmann's account, see Lehmann 1914: 221–2.

the exception of Wagner) had doubted. Indeed, we'd assumed that the girls would never agree to it. The scene in itself is so strangely beautiful that it is quite possible to be completely carried away by it. Until now we've had only small, young gymnasts in the machines, who moved in a rather ungainly way, but to see their pretty figures now was wonderful. After the ladies had got out of the machines, Wagner thanked them with tears of joy in his eyes, petting them and smothering them with kisses – and I suddenly realized that I was feeling much better!

8 June 1876. Rehearsal this morning at eleven o'clock for all the singers – male and female – involved in Scene Two of *Das Rheingold*. Wagner wanted to see them to work out positions, gestures, etc., but the same thing happened as with Unger:[1] they are getting discouraged since he wants it one way today and another way tomorrow. It's completely impossible to agree on the scene with all these changes. He keeps interrupting and making altogether comical demands which the performers (who are not, after all, completely untried on stage) find thoroughly confusing. For example, he demands that when the two giants enter over the mountains, they should adopt a particular way of walking. He showed them how to do it, but it was so absurdly comical that I intervened and said to him (in confidence), 'Master, it won't work like that, it's unnatural, let me show you how I imagined it' (lumbering gait in time with the motif). 'Very good, very good,' said Wagner, 'my way of walking was useless.' In much the same way he demanded wholly unnatural gestures from Eilers (Fasolt), which I had to correct.

6–8.30 stage rehearsal of Scenes Two and Three of *Das Rheingold* with orchestra and sets but still no props. Still the same interruptions, the same tendency to jump in and alter the staging. It really is enough to drive one to distraction. The entrance and exit of the gymnasts[2] is greeted with acclaim on each occasion, and yet the whole scene is so straightforward. The scene changes work well with the help of steam, but Alberich's transformations and disappearance using a steam curtain and trapdoors still leave a lot to be desired. Dear old Hill has a lot to put up with. The

1. Georg Unger (1837–87) created the role of Siegfried.
2. Gymnasts were recruited to play the part of the Nibelung dwarfs.

musicians are complaining that the steam is coming through the connecting wall behind one of the raised sections in the orchestra pit, so that the harps won't stay in tune. They also complain about a draught, which they say is intolerable. Wagner sends someone to have a look, then goes himself and, on his way back, calls down into the orchestra, 'I've written the opera, and now you expect me to shut the windows as well.' [. . .]

17 June 1876. The horse, Grane, is involved in today's rehearsal. Brünnhilde led it slowly over the rocky terrain, as it has to be. In the third scene, in which Brünnhilde has to tell Siegmund that Hunding will slay him in battle, Wagner felt that the horse would distract attention from this extremely important and, be it added, magnificent scene. I agreed with him, saying that, although the grouping of the scene was very fine and it was a matter for regret that the tableau was not supplemented by Grane, the scene was far too important and too highly dramatic not to raise considerable doubts. It is by no means out of the question that some incalculable accident might make the animal restive, which would ruin the scene entirely. And so Grane will be left out and Brünnhilde will enter alone. The end of Act Two will be good. The fight between Siegmund and Hunding takes place high on the mountain peaks, shrouded in clouds and lit by occasional flashes of lightning. Wotan enters at the critical moment, the sword shatters and Siegmund falls. Brünnhilde makes good her escape in order to rescue Sieglinde, who has remained below. Grane appears with Brünnhilde. Everything disappears in cloud and steam. It was extremely interesting, and also rather comical, when Fräulein Scheffsky [sic][1] failed to throw herself at Siegmund with sufficient ardour at the words, 'Wehre dem Kuß des verworf'nen Weibes nicht!' (Do not resist this accursed woman's kiss!). Wagner showed her how to do it, the diminutive composer suddenly hanging from the neck of the much taller Niemann, so that the latter could hardly keep his balance, while Wagner's toes barely touched the ground. At the same time he sang the relevant passage, dragging Siegmund round,

1. Josephine Schefsky (1843–1912) created the part of Sieglinde and proved something of a disappointment (see Lehmann 1914: 215–17 for a particularly spiteful assessment), but the problem may have been the role's tessitura, since Schefsky's normal repertory was Fidès, Azucena, Maddalena (*Rigoletto*) and Magdalene, in which she made her British début in 1882.

saying, 'This is where the two of you change places'. Wagner released Niemann and, passing where I was sitting, said, 'Women don't like doing that, they think it will put men off.' This is also the moment at which Hunding has to enter with the words 'Wehwalt, Wehwalt, steh' mir zum Streit' (Wehwalt, Wehwalt, stand there and fight!). 'Heavens, what a mouth!' said Wagner. It was downright alarming to see him directing the fight on the mountain summit. Niemann turned away: 'Merciful heavens, if only he'd come down; if he falls, we're done for.' But he didn't fall; he leapt down into the valley like a young goat, his face still swollen and bandaged in cottonwool and a thick towel. Wagner is, and remains, one of the most remarkable people I've ever met. [. . .]

13 August 1876. Rehearsal in the Wagner Theatre at six o'clock. The dragon[1] has arrived. As soon as I saw it, I whispered to Döpler,[2] 'Hide the thing away where no one will find it! Get rid of it! This dragon will be the death of us!' [. . .]

In the evening, first performance of *Das Rheingold*. Many of the scene changes went wrong and I can truthfully say that none of these mistakes had been made at any of the rehearsals. For half an hour or more at the end, the audience went on calling for Wagner to come out on stage – but he didn't. He sat in his room, beside himself with fury, hurling abuse at all the performers with the exception of Hill and me, who were both with him. There was no consoling him.

Fricke 1906: 58–138

BERTHOLD KELLERMANN (1853–1926)

The first cycle of the *Ring* was sold out when the pianist Berthold Kellermann arrived in Bayreuth, but Liszt, with whom he was studying, was able to procure tickets

1. The dragon and other *Ring* fauna were supplied by Richard Keene of Milton Road, Wandsworth; see Forman 1930.
2. Carl Emil Doepler (1823–1905) designed the costumes. Cosima notoriously thought him a 'hack': 'The costumes are reminiscent throughout of Red Indian chiefs and still bear, along with their ethnographic absurdity, all the marks of provincial tastelessness' (CT, 28 July 1876); for Doepler's own version of events, see Doepler 1900.

for *Siegfried* and *Götterdämmerung*. Here, in a letter to
his parents of 20 August 1876, he reports on the final
performance and subsequent celebrations.

Götterdämmerung began at four in the afternoon. Wonderful. All
who are not moved by it must be blind and deaf, for this music
and staging must move even the most uneducated person and fill
him with at least an inkling of awestruck presentiment at the
heights that Wagner has scaled. The cheering seemed to go on for
ever. Finally Wagner came out and expressed his thanks, saying:
'You've seen now what I want to achieve in art, you've also seen
what my artists, what we can achieve. If you, too, want the same,
we shall have an art.'

I saw Liszt early on Friday morning. He invited me to join him
at the great festival supper that was to begin at eight that evening.
All manner of distinguished people were there, around 500 in all.
Before the meal, Wagner spoke warmly and with profound
emotion, thanking first his artists and then his patrons and all his
guests, saying that he had heard that his words yesterday had been
misunderstood in some quarters and that people thought he had
meant that only because of him did we have an art. He now made
it clear what he meant. He explained that until now there had been
no national opera in Germany, in other words, the sort of art that
speaks in pure and authentic German to the German heart and
springs from our innermost being. 'France and Italy have a national
art, but ours has been mixed with French and Italian elements until
now. To purge it of these elements, I have worked for twenty years
and with the help of my friends I have managed to achieve my
goal, in spite of the infinite number of attacks that I've suffered
(I've been called a company promoter and a fraud), and it is for
this reason that I said that we have shown what we can do. It is
now up to you and us to take advantage of this. You must now
will it so! And if you will it so, we shall have an art, a national
art. I am being honest with you and with art. Trust in my leader-
ship. Let me end with these words from Goethe's *Faust*:

All that shall pass away
Is but reflection.
All insufficiency

Here finds perfection.
All that's mysterious
Here finds the day.
Woman in all of us
Shows us the way.[1]

(The idea that raises us up through itself and to itself.)

A certain Count Apponyi from Hungary spoke next.[2] He spoke in the form of a parable, taking his text from Wagner's Nibelungs: 'Brünnhilde (the new national art) lay asleep upon a rock surrounded by a great fire. The god Wotan had lit this fire, and only the victorious and finest hero, a hero who did not know fear, was to win her as his bride. Around the rock were mountains of ash and clinker (the miscegenation of our own music with non-German elements). Along came a hero, the like of whom had never been seen before, Richard Wagner, who forged a weapon from the shards of the sword of his fathers (the classical German masters), and with this he penetrated the fire and with his kiss awoke the sleeping Brünnhilde. "Hail to you, victorious light!", and with her we join our voices: "Three cheers to our Master, Richard Wagner! One! Two! Three!" '[3] Wagner was deeply moved and held him in a lengthy embrace. He – Wagner – was then presented with a silver laurel wreath, and with this he passed along the rows of guests. At each table he was greeted with a rousing cheer. When he came to me (from time to time he took off the wreath), he put it down and said, 'There, I expect you want to see me as well!' and offered me his hand in a gesture of friendship.

Wagner then spoke again: 'Everything that I am and that I have achieved I owe to one man, without whom not a single note of my music would be known, a dear friend who, when I was exiled from Germany, drew me back into the light with incomparable devotion and self-denial and who was the first to recognize me. It

1. *Faust* II, ll.12,104–11, tr. Robert David Macdonald.
2. In fact, Wagner's speech was followed by one from the Reichstag deputy, Max von Forckenbeck (1821–92), that cast such a dismal spell on the company that Apponyi was persuaded to improvise a speech to dispel the mood of gloom; see Apponyi 1935: 94–8.
3. This speech was well received at Wahnfried; see CT, 18 August 1876. It echoes nationalist sentiments in Wagner's letters to Ludwig of 23 September 1865 and 25 April 1867: SL 665 and 717.

is this dear friend to whom the greatest honour is due. It is my august friend and master, Franz Liszt!!'

Both men fell into each other's arms, weeping. Total silence filled the vast hall and everyone was held in thrall by the solemnity of this moment, as our two greatest composers stood clasped in each other's arms.

But finally endless cheering broke out. I almost felt like falling to my knees, so great and hallowed was the moment. We all felt that Wagner's human failings had now been forgotten, and the cheers turned to howls of delight when Liszt spoke a few words. Pale with emotion, he said: 'Thank you for your words of appreciation, which have made me very happy. I remain devoted to my friend in deepest reverence – your most obedient servant.'

Kellermann 1932: 193–5

COUNT ALBERT APPONYI (1846–1933)

A friend of Liszt, Apponyi had entered the Hungarian Diet in 1872. In 1899 he joined the Liberal Government party and from 1906 to 1910 was Minister of Culture. Here he recalls an evening at Wahnfried on 1 September 1876, after the artists had left.

A few of us were together at Wahnfried after dinner. Wagner, being tired, had left the company, and Ferencz Liszt took the lead in a conversation which turned on Beethoven's last sonatas. Liszt was very interesting on the subject. He spoke especially of the famous *Hammerklavier*, and more particularly of the fine adagio in F Sharp minor which it contains. In the midst of a sentence he stood up and exclaimed: – 'I will prove it to you!' – We retired to the music-room, which at Wahnfried reached from ground level, past the first floor and up to the glass roof. On the first floor there is an open gallery, on which the bedroom doors open, and from which a spiral staircase leads down to the ground floor. In the middle of the hall stood the huge piano, at which Liszt sat down, and filled our souls with the mysticism of Beethoven's last works. The atmosphere in which we listened was essentially that of the rehearsal in Budapest,[1] but the absence of any accompaniment, or of any visible *mise en scène*, and the thought that we were in Richard Wagner's house, gave it a character of its own. As on that other occasion, Liszt seemed once more to have surpassed himself, to have established an inexplicable, direct contact with the dead genius whose interpretation for him was a religious task. When the last bars of the mysterious work had died away, we stood silent and motionless. Suddenly, from the gallery on the first floor, there came a tremendous uproar, and Richard Wagner in his nightshirt came thundering, rather than running, down the stairs. He flung his arms around Liszt's neck and, sobbing with emotion, thanked him in broken phrases for the wonderful gift he had received.

Apponyi 1935: 100–101

> The deficit on the first Bayreuth Festival turned out to be 148,000 marks, with the result that plans to revive the *Ring* in 1877 ('Next year we'll do it all differently'; Fricke 1906: 143)[2] had to be aborted. Wagner reluctantly agreed to Wilhelmj's suggestion that he conduct a series of concerts in London in May 1877 as a way of paying off the deficit, but the profits of £700 proved disappointing.[3] The Wagners arrived in London on 1 May and stayed with Edward and Chariclea Dannreuther at 12 Orme Square, Bayswater. The circumstances of their visit are recalled by the English writer on music Hermann Klein.

HERMANN KLEIN (1856–1934)

Wilhelmj, delighted at having secured the master's promise, at once set about finding a responsible manager who would undertake the arrangements and advance the necessary capital for the preliminary outlay. Herein lay the initial mistake. Instead of employing some

1. For the concert on 10 March 1875, when Liszt played Beethoven's E flat major Piano Concerto.
2. Wagner expressed similar views to Apponyi (Apponyi 1935: 93), Fritz Brandt (CT, 29 September 1878) and Reinhard von Seydlitz (Seydlitz 1931).
3. The deficit was finally paid off by Wagner's heirs in 1906.

well-known concert agent, the violinist placed the whole business in the hands of a very respectable but inexperienced firm,[1] whose place of business was at the Hengler Circus building in Argyll Street. I will not deny that this firm worked hard and did their best. But unfortunately both they and Herr Wilhelmj were far too lavish in their expenditure. They engaged Materna and the pick of the Bayreuth artists at big prices.[2] The orchestra, with Wilhelmj as leader, was nearly two hundred strong.[3] The disbursements for advertising, printing, programmes, etc., were enormous, and everything was done in the costliest fashion. All this might have been justified had the attendance at the festival reached the expected level. But unluckily the prices charged for seats were prohibitive,[4] and the public refused to come in anything like the necessary numbers.

On the night after Wagner's arrival in London a dinner was given in his honor by his managers at their show-rooms in Argyll Street. Only recognized friends of the 'cause' were invited, and I had the honor of being among the number. Toasts were given and responded to, and Wagner made one of the characteristic little speeches for which he was famous. Late in the evening I was introduced to him. He asked me to sit beside him a few minutes, and began by demanding in German my age.

'Nearly twenty-one,' I replied.

'Why, you were not born when I was last here. I suppose you know, though, that your critics did not display any great affection for me then. Do you think they are better inclined toward me now?'

1. Hodge and Essex; for further details of the arrangements, see Kapp 1927: 90–96 and Newman iv.555–6.
2. The singers were Amalie Materna (1844–1918), who had sung Brünnhilde at Bayreuth, Friederike Sadler-Grün (1836–1917), who sang Fricka and the Third Norn in 1876 (but whose normal repertory encompassed Elisabeth, Norma, Valentine and Agathe), Babette Waibel and Elisabeth Exter, neither of whom had been involved in the 1876 *Ring*, Joseph Chandon (1838–1903), Karl Hill, Max Schlosser and Georg Unger. According to Newman (iv.556), their fees were: Materna £600, Hill £500, Unger £100, Sadler-Grün £200, Schlosser £150, Chandon £100 and Waibel and Exter £50 each. Richter received £100.
3. The programme names 169 players: 24 first violins, 24 second violins, 15 violas, 20 cellos, 22 double basses, 6 flutes, 7 oboes, 8 clarinets, 7 bassoons, 8 horns, 5 trumpets, 5 trombones, 5 tubas, 6 percussionists and 7 harpists.
4. Prices ranged from five guineas for a private box to 2s. 6d. for the gallery.

I answered that I fancied he would perceive an improved attitude all round.

'I hope so,' said Wagner. 'I know that some of my best and truest friends live in London, and, sooner or later, their influence must begin to tell.'

I ventured to remark that I thought his music in the long run would suffice to accomplish the desired conversion. He turned his keen glance toward me for a moment, and paused, as though wishing to read me through. The inspection appeared to be satisfactory; for a smile suffused his features as he replied:

'Yes; but here they still call it "music of the future," and in this land of oratorio who knows how long they will take to get rid of their prejudices, unless the agitators keep stirring them up?[1] Well, we shall see what happens next week.'

Then he turned to speak to Wilhelmj, and the brief chat was at an end. I sat still, however, a minute or two longer, and watched with intense interest the play of facial expression, the eloquent curves of the mouth, the humorous light in the eyes, the quiet, subtle laugh, while he addressed in turn the various friends gathered around him. That evening Wagner was thoroughly happy. He felt himself in a congenial atmosphere, content with the present, and hopeful – nay, sanguine – of the morrow. I was glad to have seen him in that beatific mood, and not a little proud to have spoken with him. What a pity that he was not to bid a final farewell to England in an equally satisfied frame of mind!

The final rehearsal for the opening concert of the festival took place at the Albert Hall on May 5. Wagner had himself chosen the programmes. He was to conduct each first part, consisting of selections from all his operas, from 'Rienzi' to 'Tristan'; while Hans Richter, who now made his first appearance in England, was to direct the excerpts from 'Der Ring des Nibelungen' that formed each second part. Most of the preliminary work had been done under Mr. Dannreuther, in whom Wagner reposed great confidence. All that remained was to give the finishing touches and for the composer-conductor to accustom himself to the vast auditorium

1. *L'Olandese dannato* had been staged at the Theatre Royal on 23 July 1870, *Lohengrin* at the Royal Opera on 8 May 1875 and *Tannhäuser* on 6 May 1876. With the exception of *Parsifal*, Wagner's mature music dramas reached London in 1882.

and the huge crescent-shaped phalanx of orchestral players spread
before him.

From the outset, as it seemed to me, he failed to place himself
en rapport with either. The abnormal conditions appeared completely to upset him. In a word, he succumbed there and then to a
severe attack of Albert Hall stage fright – an illness familiar to
nearly every artist on stepping for the first time upon the platform
of that gigantic amphitheatre. However, after a glance of astonishment round the empty hall, and a few whispered words to
Wilhelmj, and yet a few more to Hans Richter (who was posted
beside the conductor's desk), the great man raised his baton and
gave the signal for the start. The inaugural piece was the 'Kaisermarsch,' and it was well chosen for the purpose. Its pompous and
sonorous strains, proceeding with stately rhythmical movement
throughout, were perfectly calculated to show off the imposing
volume of the big orchestra in such a building as that. It gave no
trouble, and the effect was superb. But, unluckily, instead of
imbuing Wagner with a little confidence, this preludial essay left
him more palpably nervous than before.

The second piece on the list was the overture to the 'Fliegende
Holländer.' Here, I confess, I looked for something exceptional. I
had always understood that Wagner was a fine conductor, at least
of works with which he was in true sympathy, and I expected his
reading of the 'Dutchman' overture to be in the nature of a revelation. Imagine, then, my disappointment and sorrow when it
resulted in a complete breakdown! Twice – nay, thrice – did he
make a fresh start, while Mr. Dannreuther and Mr. Deichmann (the
faithful leader of the second violins) took it by turns to translate his
complaints and instructions to the orchestra. But it was of no avail.
He utterly failed either to indicate or to obtain what he wanted,
and at last, in sheer despair, he threw down his stick and requested
Richter to do the work for him. Well do I remember the sharp
round of applause with which the band greeted the Viennese conductor as he mounted the rostrum. It was thoughtless – unkind, if
you will; for it must have smote with unpleasant sound upon the
ears of the sensitive composer. But the overture went without a
hitch. It was played as I had never heard it played before.

After this Wagner decided that he would conduct only one or
two pieces at each concert, leaving all the rest to Richter. But

would the public be satisfied? They were paying to see Wagner as
well as to hear his music. The matter was discussed, and it was
suggested, as a compromise, that when he was not conducting he
should sit upon the platform in an arm-chair facing the audience.
This course was actually adopted. At each of the six concerts[1]
comprising the festival scheme, after he had conducted the opening
piece and acknowledged a magnificent reception, he sat down in
his arm-chair and gazed at the assemblage before him with a
sphinx-like expression of countenance that I shall never forget. He
must have felt as though he were being exhibited, like some strange,
interesting animal, for all the world to stare at; and his reflections
doubtless were as unenviable as his situation.

Klein 1903: 70–77

EDWARD DANNREUTHER (1844–1905)

> Dannreuther founded the London Wagner Society in
> 1872 and did much to champion Wagner's cause in
> England, conducting his music and translating a number
> of his prose works. Here he recalls Wagner's residency
> at 12 Orme Square.

He felt at home with us, and we found him delightfully kind and
fatherly. He spoke German with my wife and often, in a playful
sort of way, tried a little Greek. He usually sat up with me for an
hour or two in the music-room over a glass of grog, talking at his
ease. Callers were not admitted, except by appointment. Professor
Herkomer had two morning sittings for the powerful portrait

---

1. On 7, 9, 12, 14, 16 and 19 May. Two extra concerts were subsequently given
on 28 and 29 May. Reports on Wagner's conducting at these Albert Hall concerts
vary. Hubert Parry, then a piano student of Dannreuther's, claimed that his
conducting was 'quite marvellous; he seems to transform all he touches, he
knows precisely what he wants, and does it to a certainty. The *Kaisermarsch*
became quite new under his influence, and supremely magnificent' (Fifield 1993:
124), but Richter's diary (Fifield 1993: 125), Bernard Shaw (Shaw 1981: i.208)
and one of the second violinists, William Michael Quirke (Quirke 1914: 11–13),
all confirm Hueffer's view that 'as a conductor he scarcely did himself justice on
this occasion' (Hueffer 1889: 72).

which is now in the German Athenæum Club.[1] George Eliot and
G. H. Lewes came to dinner. A party at Sir John Millais' were
disappointed, as Wagner at the last moment felt indisposed and
unable to leave his room.[2] He went to the Lyceum and warmly
praised Irving's 'Richard the Third.'[3] Jefferson's 'Rip van Winkle'
charmed him – 'perfect in its way,' he said.[4] 'Tannhäuser' at Covent
Garden was *not* exactly perfect. We got there just as the orchestra
began the Introduction to the second act. 'First rate strings,' he
said, 'tone magnificent.' Then came *Elisabeth's* greeting to the Hall
of Song (or rather to the audience and the prompter's box), and
the duet with *Tannhäuser*: 'Oh! the puppets' – he grew restless; at
last, when the knights and ladies filed in, quadrille fashion, he fled!
'Let us march too,' he said, and we trotted down Drury Lane to
the Strand, where he had discovered a German restaurant. The
opera seemed to be entirely forgotten; as if to make up for it, he
poured out dozens of comic anecdotes. I had to remind him that
the ladies were waiting. 'Very well then, let us get them out of
purgatory' – and so we went back and listened to the end
of *Tannhäuser's* pilgrimage.[5]

He delighted in telling stories. The more grotesque the better.
Once after a rehearsal at the Albert Hall, Madame Wagner went
to Burne-Jones's studio to sit for her portrait – which unfortunately

1. According to Wagner's letter to Ludwig of 11 September 1878, the German
Athenæum Club in London commissioned a portrait of him from the Bavarian
artist Hubert Herkomer (1849–1914). The original gouache, which Wagner
describes as 'not bad' (*Königsbriefe* iii.136), was lost in 1945. Herkomer himself
produced an etching of it, a copy of which was sent to Ludwig in 1878. Wagner
complained that it made him look 'furiously angry'; see Weber 1993: i.110.
2. Cosima went on her own on 20 May.
3. Cosima reports: 'The company not good, but some things in it gripping and
well done, such as the scene in the tent and the scene with the aldermen' (CT,
10 May 1877).
4. At the Princess's Theatre on 8 May; see also Bauer 1998: 148.
5. The performance took place on 25 May with a cast including Emma Albani
(1847–1930) as Elisabeth, Carlo Carpi (1842–1930) as Tannhäuser and Victor
Maurel (1848–1923) as Wolfram. The conductor was Auguste Vianesi
(1837–1908). The manager, Frederick Gye (1809–78), noted in his diary: 'First
night this season of Tannhauser [*sic*] – Carpi & Maurel in bad voice. M^ade Wagner
was there & I went to her box. She said the Italians did not understand the
music – After the 1st act Wagner himself came in & I told him the singers were
ill, – I saw he left after the 2nd act – Only £225 in the house!!' (Royal Opera
House Archives).

came to nothing[1] – and I took Wagner to the grill room at the South Kensington Museum. There, over a chop and a pint of Bass's ale, he began to pour out story after story – *Judengeschichten* this time – stories about German Jews, told in their peculiar jargon. A young foreigner, a painter apparently, had taken his seat at a table opposite, and was quietly watching and listening. Soon, his face began to twitch – I could see that he was making efforts to look serene. But the twitches increased – and, when one of the stories came to the final point, the man fairly choked. He snatched up his hat and vanished. The great event at Orme Square was the reading of 'Parsifal.' During the intervals between the rehearsals and concerts Wagner had been making a fair copy of the poem intended for the King of Bavaria. When the copy was finished, a small circle of friends, consisting of about twenty people, 'who belong,' as they say in the navy, gathered together in the music room at 8.30 on May 17, 1877. The reading was a wonderful feat. The great actor-poet at his best – an improvisation perfectly balanced – every part stood forth as that of an individual – voice, enunciation, moderation, exquisite – particularly in the second act (*Blumenmädchen, Amfortas*). One heard the words, and one heard the latent music. Bayreuth in miniature.[2]

Dannreuther 1898: 651–2

HANS VON WOLZOGEN (1848–1938)

Wolzogen was introduced to Wagner in 1875 and two years later became editor of the *Bayreuther Blätter*, a position he held for sixty years, superintending its trans-formation from an in-house journal designed to acquaint Bayreuth's patrons with the ideological back-ground to *Parsifal* to an openly nationalistic organ. The following reminiscences were written in the immediate aftermath of Wagner's death.

1. Cosima had three sittings for Edward Burne-Jones (1833–98) on 29, 30 and 31 May; see Skelton 1982: 235–41.
2. George Henry Lewes (1817–78) noted in his diary on 17 May: 'Dined at the Dannreuters with the Wagners – no one else present, until the evening when a small party assembled to hear Wagner read his "Parzival" which he did with great spirit & like a fine actor' (Eliot vi.373).

It was music that was the most effective way of reforming the world of the emotions along artistic lines, and it was for this reason that the reformer had to be German. For what could fill us Germans with a greater sense of pride than the observation that the purest language of the ideal world, the language of music as a highly stylized art, is *German*. Music has achieved its supreme artistic development in the German spirit, and the German spirit has found its purest and freest expression in music. No one has felt this more deeply or taken greater advantage of it than Wagner.

I still recall a conversation with him: 'It was highly significant that I begged two groschen from my mother to buy the manuscript paper to write out Weber's *Lützows wilde verwegene Jagd* in order to have my own copy.[1] That Germany "owned" Weber's music was its good fortune. Here the poor German without a fatherland found that fatherland. When I heard my teachers at school telling me about Saxony's history in all its pitifulness and I was forced to tell myself that this was where I was supposed to belong and, deeply depressed, I sought something outside and discovered the existence of Weber's music – then I knew where my home was and felt that I was German. This feeling has never left me.' [...]

But if there is one thing that may serve to shed light on the character of the great man, it is the realization that all his works and all that moves us so deeply in his works (springing, as it does, from the depths of his own human nature) is an expression of his true personality and could not have been created by any other 'self'. 'The poem of my life, all that I am and feel,' he once described the *Ring*. An artist from whom the human being could be separated could never have written such works, he said. He would have created artificial works, not works of art that are always the works of man, in the highest sense of the word.

Wolzogen 1891: 21–2, 38–9

---

[1]. The second of Weber's settings of Theodor Körner's *Leyer und Schwert* for male-voice chorus; see CT, 3 January 1878.

FRIEDRICH VON SCHOEN (1850–1941)

> Friedrich von Schoen was a factory owner from Worms
> who entered the Wagners' circle in 1879. He later
> contributed 10,000 marks to the establishment of the
> Bayreuth Festival Scholarship Fund to allow young
> people without means to attend the Festival. Here he
> recalls a visit to Wahnfried which, according to Cosima
> Wagner's diary, took place on 10 January 1881.

In the early eighties I was a guest at Wahnfried when, following
the evening meal, the admirable Feustel[1] arrived and a conversation
began, sparked off by his remark that he had read in today's
newspaper something that he felt sure would interest the Master,
namely, that in Berlin there were now more Jews than in the
whole of France; if my memory serves, there were then 80,000 (the
number of Jews in Berlin is now said to be several times that
figure). Wagner seized on the topic with relish and stressed the
perniciousness and danger that the activities and the very nature
of the Jews presented to the German nation. Feustel was reluctant
to follow him quite so far down this road; he was a National
Liberal member of the Reichstag, and this was a time when,
according to the *Frankfurter Zeitung*, there was no such thing as
a 'Jewish question' for a 'liberal'. The princes, too, shared the view
that it was safe to pay no heed to the warnings of the genuinely
anxious Court Chaplain, Adolf Stöcker, a view, moreover, that
persuaded Bismarck to ignore the petition signed by 250,000 indi-
viduals protesting at the rampancy of the Jews.

After so many years, I can unfortunately no longer recall all the
details of this relatively lengthy conversation; but I do clearly
remember that Feustel, who was an extremely intelligent man,
approached the question more from the standpoint of practical
civilization, whereas the Master observed it from the vantage point
of culture and that the conversation also touched on other, social
questions. One of the points that Feustel made was that a farmer
who had a cow for sale previously had to take it to market himself
and sell it, thereby wasting a good deal of time that he now had
free for other useful activities, now that the Jew came to his farm

---

1. Friedrich Feustel (1824–91) was chairman of the Bayreuth town council.

and made everything so much simpler for him. At this point Wagner interrupted him with some warmth. I remember his words very clearly: 'Yes, in order to fleece him!' And so the conversation proceeded, with arguments and objections on either side constantly trumped by others. I still clearly recall that when Feustel said that farmers and workers now lived much better than before and that one shouldn't just look on the black side but should take a look at their homes, where there were nice curtains that you didn't find before and that the workers now had secure jobs and, indeed, carefree incomes – the Master flew into a rage, saying: 'Yes, and they stand there all day in their factories and see and hear nothing but bare halls and the noise and pounding of the machines – is that an existence fit for human beings?!' Feustel was unwilling to concede this point, but sought, rather, to support his views with new and compelling arguments, whereupon Wagner flared up in a fit of the most profound and painful emotion, summing up all that he had to say on the subject in a single exclamation: 'Children, children, do you not recall Jesus Christ?!!'

He uttered these words with so indescribable an expression in his eyes and voice, with so shatteringly powerful a sense of fellow feeling at the darker aspects of our social lives and with such moving reverence for the divinity of the name that he had just spoken that we were all moved to the depths of our being. All of us, including Feustel, felt that the last word had been spoken, a word, moreover, that brooked no further contradiction. The effect was as if the Master had placed the figure of the Redeemer before our innermost eye: 'I saw Him – then His gaze fell upon me!'[1]

Not another word was spoken. We rose and took our leave, our hearts profoundly stirred.

Schoen 1924: 230–32

LUDWIG SCHEMANN (1852–1938)

Ludwig Schemann studied philology and history and for a time worked as a librarian at the University in Göttingen, before ill health forced him to retire and

---

1. A quotation from Act Two of *Parsifal*.

devote himself to private tutoring. In spite of his affin-
ities with the writings of the self-styled Comte Joseph-
Arthur de Gobineau, whose four-volume *Essai sur l'in-
égalité des races humaines* of 1853–5 he translated into
German, he had no time for National Socialism, whose
rise he lived long enough to observe at first hand. He
paid his first visit to the Wagners in December 1877.

At the end of 1880 Wagner returned to Germany from Italy, and
I was fortunate enough to spend some days in his company both
at Easter and Whitsuntide of the following year. I was not alone
in observing the change that had overcome him and finding that
he had outgrown himself, if that were possible. The Master's
tremendous final writings, 'Religion and Art' and the various essays
intended to explain it, the last of which was currently exercising
him,[1] will afford everyone who knows them the clearest indication
of what I mean by this. Although one often hears it said that all
that mattered for Wagner was art and his own art in particular,
this is true least of all for the final years of his life, and this may
explain the change in his personality that was overwhelmingly
apparent to his intimates at this time.

There is no doubt that humanity's sufferings had always gnawed
at his heart, but as an artist he had regularly used the artist's
divine prerogative to turn suffering into joy to break free from this
concern and to allow thousands of other to do the same. Now his
final work of art had been created, and the thinker in Wagner
(always the equal of the artist in him, whatever others may say)
had once again come into his own; the future of humanity lay
heavy on his heart and the question how he could avert its terrible
decline – a decline that two French thinkers had attributed to
the corruption of the blood, one[2] approaching the issue from the
standpoint of diet, the other[3] from an ethnological standpoint –
now caused all other considerations, including for a time even his
art, to pale into insignificance. It was as a sublime seer concerned

1. The virulently anti-Semitic 'Know Yourself' was completed in February 1881,
'Heroism and Christianity' on 4 September 1881.
2. The French philosopher Jean-Antoine Gleizes (1773–1843), whose two-volume
Thalysie, ou La nouvelle existence of 1840–42 was translated into German by
Robert Springer in 1872.
3. Joseph-Arthur Gobineau (1816–82).

for the spiritual welfare of the greater part of humanity that Wagner now appeared before us, and I may say that only those who got to know him in this supremely hallowed state ever really knew him. For me, at least, he never appeared greater than he did that year. [. . .]

Perhaps I may be allowed to mention Wagner's attitude to the most powerful man of our age, Bismarck. The extent of Wagner's admiration for the founder of the German Reich is clear from his recently published letter to him.[1] That this admiration waned with the passage of time and that doubts gained the upper hand with the Master, indeed, that he was finally profoundly alienated by the former we must tacitly accept as an expression of the world spirit. It is perfectly understandable for more than one reason, even though it may no longer be possible to explain and demonstrate it in detail.[2] In December 1877 I myself was once party to one of Wagner's most embittered attacks on Bismarck, when he complained that he had, to say the least, done nothing to prevent Jews from breeding within the body of the German nation, a complaint that welled up within him with elemental force. His complaints at the unspeakable misery that the Jews had brought down on our nation culminated in his description of the fate of the German peasant who would soon no longer possess a single clod of earth on which to eat his breakfast. 'And all this happens under the eyes of that Teuton Bismarck!' [. . .]

That Gobineau's racist thinking had the same sort of revolutionary impact on his view of history as Schopenhauer's concept of the Will had earlier had on his view of philosophy emerges from his final writings, and it was a pleasure to hear him hold forth on individual themes and historical phenomena as he now saw them: on one occasion, for example, he spoke with the greatest enthusiasm of Brahmanism as the highest of all existing social systems, while on another he spoke of feudalism and loyalty, honour and the *point d'honneur* that lends the Aryan race its true distinction, which is why poor Rubinstein, for example, of whom he had recently spoken, was simply incapable of understanding these terms.

Schemann 1902: 25–6, 46–8

1. The letter, dated 24 June 1873, was first published in the *Bayreuther Blätter*, xxiv (1901), 220–21; see SL 818–19.
2. But see Large 1978.

AUGUSTE RENOIR (1841–1919)

One of the leading French Impressionists, Renoir had already produced a sketch of Wagner in 1867 before paying an extended visit to Italy in the winter of 1881/2. Hearing that the composer was staying in Palermo, he wrote to ask whether he could paint his portrait. Here he describes his experiences in a letter to an unnamed correspondent.

After having resisted my brother for a long time, he eventually sends me a letter of introduction to Naples from M. de Brayer.[1] I don't read the letter; not even the signature, and there I am on the boat with the prospect of being seasick for at least fourteen hours. It then occurs to me to look for it in my pocket. No letter! I probably left it at the hotel. I go through everything: no sign of it. You can see what a fix I was in by the time I got to Palermo. I find the city rather depressing, and wonder whether I shouldn't perhaps take the boat back in the evening. Then I go to the Post Office to try and find out where Wagner is staying. Nobody speaks French; nobody has ever heard of Wagner. But at the hotel where I am staying there are some Germans, and they tell me he is staying at the Hôtel des Palmes. I take a carriage and visit Monreale, where there are some fine mosaics, and on the way I indulge in a lot of melancholy thoughts. Before leaving I send a telegram to Naples, without any hope or optimism, however, and sit around waiting. Nothing happens so I decide I should introduce myself on my own, so there I am writing a note, in which I ask permission to pay my respects to the Master, and end it by saying that I shall be glad to take news of him back to M. Lascoux[2] and Mme Mendès in Paris. I wasn't able to add the name of M. de Brayer, because I hadn't looked at the signature on the original letter of introduction. So here I am at the Hôtel des Palmes. A servant takes my letter, goes away, comes back and says 'Non salue il Maestro' and vanishes. Next day my original letter turns up from Naples. I take it round again; the same servant takes it, with obvious contempt. I wait

---

1. For a full biography of Jules de Brayer (1837–1917), see Schuh 1959: 46–7.
2. An intimate of Chabrier and his circle, Antoine Lascoux (?–1906) figures in Fantin-Latour's *Autour du piano*.

under the carriage entrance, anxious not to be seen, and not in the mood to meet anyone, since I only screwed myself up to this second attempt in order to prove that I hadn't just come to beg 40 sous.

Finally along comes a fair-haired young man, whom I take to be English. In fact he's a Russian, and his name is Joukovski.[1] He says he knows my work very well, that Mme Wagner regrets not being able to receive me now, and asks if I could stay in Palermo for one more day as Wagner is putting the final touches to *Parsifal*, and is unwell and in a state of nerves, has lost his appetite and so on and so forth.

I beg him to give my apologies to Mme Wagner, and ask to be excused. We spend some minutes talking, and when I tell him the purpose of my visit, I can see by the smile on his face that he thinks it will be a failure. He confesses to me that he himself is a painter, that he too would like to do a portrait of the Master, and to achieve this has been following him everywhere for two years, in vain. But he advises me to stay, saying that what he had denied him, he may grant to me, and that anyway I can't go away without actually seeing Wagner. This Russian is charming; he ends up by consoling me, and we make an appointment for the next day at two o'clock. Next day I meet him at the post office. He tells me that yesterday, 13 February,[2] Wagner finished his opera, that he is very tired, and that he can't see me till five o'clock, but that he will be there, so I won't feel uneasy. I accept enthusiastically, and go away happy. I'm there at five o'clock sharp, and again meet the same servant who greets me with a deep bow, asks me to follow him, takes me through a small greenhouse and into an adjoining sitting room, asks me to sit down in a huge armchair, and with a gracious smile asks me to wait a moment. I see Mlle Wagner, and a youth who must be a little Wagner, but no Russian. Mlle Wagner tells me that her mother is out, but that her father is coming, and then she disappears. I hear the sound of footsteps muffled by thick

1. The son of the leading Russian poet and translator Vasily Zhukovsky (1783–1852), Paul von Joukowsky (1845–1912) spent much of his adult life in Germany (hence the Germanicized form of his name). He was introduced to Wagner on 18 January 1880 and he and his male lover were soon admitted to the inner sanctum. He designed the sets and costumes for *Parsifal* in close consultation with Wagner.
2. An error for January: the full score of Act Three of *Parsifal* was completed on 13 January 1882.

carpet. It's the Master, in his velvet dressing gown, the wide sleeves lined with satin. He is very handsome, very courteous. He shakes my hand and begs me to sit down, and then the most extraordinary conversation takes place, half German, half French – with guttural endings.

'I am very content. You are coming from Paris.' 'No,' I say, 'from Naples.' I tell him about losing my letter, which makes him laugh a lot. We talk a great deal, though when I say we, all I did was to keep repeating 'Yes, dear Master,' 'Of course, dear Master.' I would get up to leave, and he would take my hand and keep pushing me back into the chair. 'Wait a little more. My wife will be coming soon. And that good Lascoux, how is he?' I tell him that as I have been in Italy for some time I don't know, and he doesn't even know I'm here. We talk about *Tannhäuser* at the Opera, in short we keep at it for more than three quarters of an hour, whilst I keep looking anxiously for the arrival of the Russian. Finally he comes in with Mme Wagner, who asks me if I know M. de Breyer well. Not understanding her accent, I reply, 'Not at all, is he a musician?' 'So,' she replies, 'he is not the one who gave you the letter?' 'Oh, M. de Brayé, yes of course I know him. We do not pronounce the word the same way.' I apologize, blushing furiously. But I make up for my gaffe with Lascoux, whose voice I mimic. She then told me to give their regards to their friends when I get back to Paris, especially to Lascoux, insisting on it, and repeating it before I left. We talked about the Impressionists of music. What a lot of nonsense I must have talked! I ended up all hot and bothered, in a state of utter confusion and red as a rooster. I was a typical example of the shy man who plunges in too far, and yet I think he was very pleased with me. I don't know why. He detests the German Jews, among others the art critic Albert Wolff.[1] He asked me whether we still liked *Les diamants de la couronne* in France.[2] I attacked Meyerbeer. In the long run I was given the chance to utter all the nonsense I felt like.

1. After working as secretary to Alexandre Dumas *père*, Albert Wolff (1835–1891) became music (and, later, drama) critic of *Le Figaro*. His review of the 1876 *Ring* appeared on 25 August 1876 under the provocative title 'Le crépuscule de M. Wagner'.
2. Auber's opera had been unveiled at the Opéra-Comique on 6 March 1841 and is discussed in one of Wagner's reports from Paris: SS xii.74–86; PW viii.118–31.

Then, all of a sudden, he said to M. Joukovski, 'If I'm feeling all right at midday I'll give a sitting until lunch. You know you'll have to be understanding, but I will do what I can. If it doesn't last long, it won't be my fault. M. Renoir, please ask M. Joukovski if it's all right if you do me too, that is if it doesn't bother him.'

M. Joukovski replies, 'But, dear Master, I was just about to ask you, etc., etc.'

'How would you like to do it?' I say, 'Full-face.'

He says, 'That's fine,' because he wants to paint the back, whilst I do the front.

Then Wagner says to him, 'You're going to paint me turning my back on France, and M. Renoir will do me from the other side. Oh dear!'

Next day I was there at noon; you know the rest. He was very cheerful, but I felt very nervous, and regretted that I wasn't Ingres. In short I think that my time – 35 minutes, which was not much – was well spent. If I had stopped sooner it would in fact have been better, because my model started to lose some of his cheerfulness, and he was starting to get constrained. I recorded these changes a bit too closely. Anyway, you'll see.

At the end Wagner asked if he could have a look, and said 'Ach! I look like a Protestant minister' – which was true enough. Anyway I was glad not to have made a botch-up of it; I now have a little souvenir of that splendid head.[1]

I'm not re-reading my letter; if I did I would tear it up again, and that would be my fifteenth try. If there are things I've forgotten I'll tell you. He repeated several times that the French read art critics too much, this with a roar of laughter. 'Ach! Those German Jews! But, M. Renoir, I know there are a lot of fine French people,

1. Renoir worked up the sketch into the portrait now in the Musée d'Orsay. Cosima records the sitting as follows: 'At 12 o'clock a sitting for the French painter Renouard, whom R. jokingly claims to have mistaken for Victor Noir [a French journalist shot dead by Prince Pierre Napoléon Bonaparte in January 1870]. This artist, belonging to the Impressionists, who paint everything bright and in full sunlight, amuses R. with his excitement and his many grimaces as he works, so much so that R. tells him he is the painter from the *Fl. Blätter* [a humorous periodical published in Munich]. Of the very curious blue-and-pink result R. says that it makes him look like the embryo of an angel, an oyster swallowed by an epicure' (CT, 15 January 1882).

whom I do not confuse with them.' Unfortunately I cannot recreate
the openness and gaiety of this conversation with the Master.

Renoir 1987: 131–4

ENGELBERT HUMPERDINCK (1854–1921)

Engelbert Humperdinck made Wagner's acquaintance
in Naples on 9 March 1880. He was soon charmed into
joining the team of musical assistants needed to prepare
Parsifal and arrived in Bayreuth on 8 January 1881.
Rehearsals began in June 1882.

There now began a period of intensive rehearsals with chorus and
soloists, who gradually arrived in increasing numbers. The chorus
of Flowermaidens was the particular responsibility of the loyal
Heinrich Porges, whom Wagner jokingly called his 'Flower Father'.
Since the Munich Court Orchestra was playing at the performances, it was their conductor, Hermann Levi, who was placed in
charge of the orchestra. It had not been easy for him to overcome
the Master's initial resistance, since Wagner would have preferred
an Aryan conductor for his *Parsifal*, but Levi was able to win the
Master's trust as a result of his untiring devotion and reliability in
the service of the Grail, soon making himself indispensable.

I shall never forget the days when Wagner first led his group of
soloists on to the stage in order to work on their roles in detail.
Anyone who has ever attended a performance of *Parsifal* can
imagine how much work was involved in getting the complex
apparatus to work and keeping it in working order. That there
were bound to be unforeseen difficulties goes without saying. The
following incident may serve as an example of what I mean.

One particular day we had a music call at which soloists, chorus,
bells, on-stage band *e tutti quanti* were to be put through their
paces. The stage was completely bare, so we could see right up
into the top of the building, where the temperature resembled that
of a furnace (in those days gas was still used throughout the
theatre),[1] with every inch of space filled with people singing and
playing. The effect was magnificent, the Master was totally satisfied

1. Electric lighting was not installed in the Festspielhaus until 1888.

and could not have asked for anything better. Alas, his delight was short-lived. When the rehearsals with scenery and props began shortly afterwards, everything suddenly sounded different, nothing worked any longer and the acoustics seemed to have changed beyond recognition; in short, it was enough to drive us all to despair, with the result that we had to start all over again. Even worse, the diorama¹ started to misbehave. Even at the piano it transpired that it was too long. The only thing for it was to add more music, the machinist, Herr Brand from Darmstadt,² calmly announced, watch in hand: he needed so many minutes to unroll the sets. 'What! You now expect me to compose by the metre?' the Master exclaimed in his horror. Well, there was no way round it, Brand replied, the machine couldn't operate any quicker and the sets couldn't be altered – it would cost a king's ransom and, in any case, there wasn't time. Wagner was beside himself and, swearing that he would have nothing more to do with the rehearsals and performances, stormed out in high dudgeon.

Dismayed, we watched him go. What was to be done? It was simply not possible to risk the whole production, with all its attendant difficulties, merely because of a stupid miscalculation. And it wasn't as bad as all that, Levi thought; just as cuts could be made, so it was possible to repeat the odd phrase. I thought the matter over. To expect the already overburdened Master to undertake such a thorough revision at the eleventh hour was out of the question. I preferred to try my own solution. I ran home, quickly sketched out a few transitional bars, orchestrated them and incorporated them into the original score. Then, filled with trepidation, I took the original to the Master. He looked through

---

1. The *Wandeldekoration* or diorama was a series of four painted cloths set a few metres apart across the whole depth of the stage. Four were used to create a sense of perspective. They were wound on rollers situated in the wings and represented the gradually changing scene as Gurnemanz leads Parsifal (and, in the case of Act Three, Kundry) to the Grail hall in Acts One and Three. Although the principle had been in use since the age of Baroque opera, it had not previously been used on such a massive scale. The *Parsifal* diorama covered an area of more than 2,500 square metres, weighed some 700 kilograms and cost 17,694 marks. For a full description, see Baumann 1980: 154–65.
2. Friedrich ('Fritz') Brandt (1854–95) worked closely with his father on the technical aspects of the first *Ring* and was invited to assume overall responsibility for the techical arrangements for *Parsifal* on his father's sudden death in 1881.

it, nodding affably, then said: 'Well, why not? It should work! Be off with you to the Chancellery and copy out the parts, so that we can get on.' No sooner said than done. The sets and music were now in glorious accord, and no one in the audience had the least suspicion at any of the performances that the score had been patched together by a backstreet cobbler plying his modest trade. Of course, the sets were altered in time for the following year's performances; the interpolated passage, dignified by Levi with the conscientious note, 'H. ipse fecit', was removed and the original music restored.[1]

Humperdinck 1927: 222–4; see also Gay 1979: 189–230

EMIL HECKEL

Heckel reports on the last of the sixteen performances on 29 August 1882.

At the end Wagner gave us a grand surprise, an experience I shall never forget. Before the last performance he unexpectedly resolved to conduct the last act of his Bühnenweihfestspiel himself, from the changing scene onwards. His intention was made known to few. Levi and Fischer, the regular conductors of *Parsifal*, remained in the orchestra, so that the executants might not miss their accustomed cues at certain passages. The master was therefore able to devote himself exclusively to a thoroughly adequate rendering of rhythm and expression. It was marvellous, the profound feeling and mighty breadth conferred on the drawn-out phrases. The puissance of the great scene for Amfortas exceeded anything I have ever witnessed; Reichmann,[2] its exponent, told me after the performance: 'A thing like that, one can only go through once. To such an expenditure of breath, such a tax on one's strength of voice in general, only the master himself can pin one.' The wind-players in the orchestra said much the same. Every executant had

1. In the event, the second transformation was abandoned at the 1882 performances.
2. Theodor Reichmann (1849–1903) sang Amfortas at every performance in 1882, returning to Bayreuth regularly until 1902.

willingly put forth his utmost power. What that hour revealed to us, never came back.

Heckel 1899: 131–2

SIEGFRIED WAGNER (1869–1930)

Wagner's only son recalls his childhood and the intellectual environment in which he was brought up.

Happy the man who has a carefree childhood. No frost or tempest in later life can dispel the warmth that the sunbeams of a happy infancy bring to a human soul. Such a childhood was enjoyed by myself and my sisters, and for that we are eternally grateful to our parents. Their aim was to bring us up as happy, true human beings. Sullen faces were not allowed. If my sisters had to slave over written homework and the sun tempted them outside, I was soon sent to my parents: 'Papa,' I would call, 'I'm all on my own and have no one to play with. Can't my sisters come into the garden?' And within moments all five of us were romping in the garden. In this way, the educational principles of my mother, who had been brought up entirely according to the rules of the *ancien régime*, were often thwarted by those of my father; but, genial by nature, she finally acquiesced in these disruptions to her plans. Even after-noon visits to the cake shop – our greatest pleasure was to go to Lavena's famous coffee shop in Venice – even these she agreed to when she saw what pleasure it gave my father to treat us with sweets. As a result we were not unduly troubled by lessons. Our beautiful garden at Wahnfried was our school, our school friends dogs, hens, canaries and also, I think, salamanders and frogs which, hidden in cupboards, were supposed to feel at home, though they would no doubt have felt even more at home in water. I have only a vague recollection of the first important event of my childhood, the laying of the foundation stone at the Festspielhaus in 1872. My family told me that I had been exceptionally well behaved. When I was asked what I had understood of the festival address, I answered: 'German men, good men!' We learnt languages from a very early age. English governesses ensured that we mastered their idiom, but my mother had difficulty reconciling us to French, as the artificial nature of this language tended, rather, to repel us children. Italian was the easiest for us to learn, since we heard it spoken on our frequent visits to Italy. [. . .]

Of decisive influence on my whole development were our repeated trips to Italy. Tired of the everlasting grey skies of Germany – I remember my father shaking his clenched fists at the clouds and shouting: 'Those damned potato sacks!' – he crossed the Alps with his whole family and with the generous support of King Ludwig II, in order to forget his cares and troubles, even if only for a time, and to enjoy the sun, the visual arts and the carefree life of the Italians. Our first such journey was made possible not only by the king's help but also by the fee for his Festival March which had just arrived and which was very generous by the standards of the time.[1] Following the first Festival, which, although a brilliant artistic success, proved a financial disaster, our journey took us via Verona, Venice and Bologna to Rome and Naples. It was there that my passion for architecture was born. I ran like a man possessed from church to church, from palace to palace, and although my initial attempts to reproduce these impressions with paper and pencil were extremely awkward, they gradually became quite acceptable, so that, their indulgent smiles notwithstanding, my parents were genuinely pleased to watch this talent develop – much to everyone's surprise.

My father was in the best of moods throughout this journey. Only in Rome did his mood remain depressed. He was pestered by tactless people, and the sight of so many priests irritated him; and on top of everything there was also bad news from Bayreuth concerning the Festival deficit. A ray of light was provided by our first meeting with Count Gobineau. [. . .]

The unhappy Joseph Rubinstein, busy preparing the vocal score of *Parsifal*, was not one of the more attractive characters among our circle of friends. He made it clear to my mother and to us children that he was there only because of our father and that the family was really an unnecessary and tiresome adjunct. My mother bore this calmly, since she recognized his good points, but for us children he became so unsympathetic that our mother had to

1. 5,000 dollars.

remind us not to show our disappoval quite so openly. I said that
he was 'unhappy'. And so he was. He often confessed to my father
that he suffered from his Jewishness: he was a Kundry figure,
yearning for redemption. He thought he would find this redemption
through my father and his art. [. . .]

But my happiest memory of this period[1] was the performance of
my father's early symphony to mark my mother's birthday. It was
the third time I had seen him conduct. A few years previously,
also on my mother's birthday,[2] it had been Beethoven's A major
Symphony and movements from the F major, which he conducted
at Wahnfried with the Meiningen Orchestra. His manner of conducting, which pupils such as Hans von Bülow, Klindworth,
Richter and later, indirectly, Mottl, Muck and Nikisch[3] strove with
some success to emulate, was notable for its economy of gesture
and great clarity. [. . .] My father achieved his results through his
eyes above all else and, indeed, he himself repeatedly described
them as the most important means of conveying a conductor's
wishes. As a result, his passion was more restrained in its outward
manifestations and was evident only to those who, at the end of
the performance, observed him at close quarters and saw how
much he had perspired. For the spectator, the impression was
always aesthetically pleasing, with none of the exaggerated gestures
that are so popular nowadays and that lead one to think that the
ultimate aim of the music is the conductor and that the work being
performed is secondary. It was his eyes that electrified his players.
[. . .]

I still clearly recall one particular incident on the day that my
father died. It concerns my mother. Although she was an excellent

1. The winter of 1882/3, which the Wagners spent at the Palazzo Vendramin in
Venice. On 24 December Wagner conducted his early C major Symphony at the
Teatro La Fenice.
2. On the evening of 25 December 1878 (Cosima's official birthday), when
Wagner paid for the Meiningen Court Orchestra to travel to Bayreuth to perform
the Prelude to *Parsifal*, the *Siegfried Idyll* and the Beethoven movements
mentioned here.
3. Carl Muck (1859–1940) learned the Wagner repertory in Prague at Angelo
Neumann's Deutsches Landestheater. He conducted *Parsifal* at every Bayreuth
Festival from 1901 to 1930. Arthur Nikisch (1855–1922) played the violin in the
performance of the Ninth Symphony conducted by Wagner on 22 May 1872
and also performed under him in Vienna. He never conducted at Bayreuth.

pianist – her music teacher Séghers[1] had said of the two sisters: 'Blandine sera une excellente musicienne, Cosima une grande artiste' – I had never heard her play; she was always so busy ministering to my father's manifold needs that she had been obliged to neglect the instrument. But on that 13 February I was sitting in the salon and practising the piano when my mother came in. She went over to the grand piano and began to play. When I asked her what she was playing, she replied, with a completely rapt expression, 'Schubert's *Lob der Tränen'*. A few minutes later the chambermaid brought the news that my father had been taken ill. I shall never forget the sight of my mother rushing out through the door. It expressed the force of the most passionate anguish; and she ran into the half-open door so hard that it almost broke. I was often reminded of that moment in Venice when I watched her at Festival rehearsals in later years, showing her singers how to perform roles such as Kundry, Isolde, Sieglinde and Brünnhilde. There was an antique grandeur to her performances of a kind that I have seen on stage on only one other occasion: in the portrayal of Othello by the then seventy-seven-year-old Salvini.[2]

Wagner 1923: 5–36

HUGH REGINALD HAWEIS (1838–1901)

The English preacher and writer H. R. Haweis studied at Trinity College, Cambridge, served under Garibaldi in 1860 and, on his return to England, was ordained, attracting crowded congregations to St James's, Marylebone, with what one writer has called his 'dwarfish figure and lively manner'. He travelled widely and met Wagner on a number of occasions. Although he was not present at Wagner's death (only Cosima was in attendance, and she has left no account of the day's

1. The violinist and conductor François Séghers (1801–81) was one of the co-founders of the Paris Conservatoire concerts. In 1848 he founded the Société Sainte-Cécile and on 24 November 1850 introduced Paris audiences to the *Tannhäuser* Overture.
2. Tommaso Salvini (1829–1915) was noted for his Shakespearean roles, which he performed all over the world.

events), his version of Wagner's last hours appears to
be based on reliable reports and has the additional
merit of rounding off Wagner's life in an appropriately
effective manner.

February 13th came black with clouds. The rain poured in torrents.
WAGNER rose as usual, and announced his wish not to be disturbed
till dinner-time, two o'clock. He had much to do – much to finish
– overmuch indeed, and the time was short.[1]

The master did not feel quite well, and COSIMA, his wife, bade
BETTY, the servant, take her work and not leave the ante-room in
case her master should call or ring.

The faithful creature seemed to have some presentiment that all
was not right. She listened hour after hour – heard the master
striding up and down as was his wont.

Wife COSIMA came in from time to time. 'The master works
ever,' said BETTY, 'and has not called for anything – now he walks
to and fro.'

At one o'clock WAGNER rang his bell and asked: 'Is the gondola
ordered at four o'clock? Good; then I will take a plate of soup up
here, for I don't feel very well.'

There was nothing unusual about this, for when absorbed in
work he would often thus have his light luncheon alone.

The servant brought in a plate of soup and retired. All seemed
quiet for some time. Then suddenly a hurried pacing up and down
the room was heard. The footsteps ceased – a sharp cough,
checked. BETTY threw down her work, walked on tip-toe to the
door, and listened with all her ears. She heard one deep groan; she
stood for a moment divided between a resolve to call COSIMA or
break through her master's orders and go into his room at once.
The suspense was soon over. 'BETTY!' It was WAGNER's voice, very
faint. BETTY rushed in. WAGNER was leaning back on his sofa, his
fur coat was half off, his foot rested on a foot-stool. His face was
fearfully changed – his features cadaverous and drawn down with
pain evidently; with the utmost difficulty he contrived to murmur,

1. At the time of his death, Wagner was working on an essay, 'On the Feminine
in the Human'.

but almost inaudibly, 'Call my wife and the doctor.' He never spoke again.[1]

The terrified BETTY rushed off to tell wife COSIMA. The instant she saw him she cried, 'To the doctor, Betty!' DR. KEPPLER was sent for three times; at last he was found just finishing an operation. Meanwhile MADAME WAGNER had sat down by her husband. He immediately laid his head on her shoulder, groaning, but speechless; and she placed her arms about him, and with one hand rubbed his heart, an act which had sometimes eased him when in pain. His breathing grew softer and lighter, and presently he seemed to subside into a quiet, motionless sleep. She thought it a good sign.

About half an hour afterwards the doctor came. One glance was enough. He found MADAME WAGNER still holding her husband in both her arms, with his head resting on her shoulder. 'He sleeps,' she said – and the good doctor, suppressing his emotion with a great effort, did not tell her that it was the sleep of death, and that now for a long time she had been embracing a corpse.

DR. KEPPLER, after feeling for the pulse that was never to beat again, gently took the body of Wagner in both his arms and carried it to the bed. It could not be called his death-bed, for Wagner died as he had lived, working – the table before him was strewn with books and MSS., with the ink scarcely dry upon the last page.

DR. KEPPLER then turned to COSIMA and said, with irrepressible emotion, 'He is dead!' The poor wife, who had been so absolutely one in body, soul, and mind with her husband, fell prostrate with a great cry upon his lifeless body, nor for some time could any persuasion induce her to leave the corpse which she continued to embrace.

Haweis 1908: 455–8

---

1. There has been much recent speculation on the events that may have precipitated Wagner's final heart attack, ranging from his appalled perusal of Nietzsche's *The Gay Science* (see Vogel 1984) to an altercation with Cosima over a visit by Carrie Pringle, a Flowermaiden at the 1882 Festival (see Westernhagen 1979 and Gregor-Dellin 1983: 521–2). Given the state of Wagner's health (see Thiery and Seidel 1995), it is perfectly possible to account for Wagner's rupture of the heart without recourse to sensation.

LIST OF SOURCES

Abbate 1984 — Carolyn Abbate, *The 'Parisian' Tannhäuser* (diss., Princeton University 1984)

Abert 1916 — Hermann Abert, *Johann Joseph Abert (1832–1915): Sein Leben und seine Werke* (Breitkopf & Härtel: Leipzig 1916)

Alexander 1850 — J. H. Alexander, *Universal Dictionary of Weights and Measures Ancient and Modern* (Wm. Minifie and Co.: Baltimore 1850)

Apponyi 1935 — *The Memoirs of Count Apponyi* (William Heinemann Ltd: London 1935)

AS — 'Wagner's Autobiographical Sketch', *Wagner: A Documentary Study*, ed. Heinrich Barth, Dietrich Mack and Egon Voss (Thames and Hudson: London 1975), 11–16

Avenarius 1883 — Ferdinand Avenarius, 'Richard Wagner als Kind', *Allgemeine Zeitung*, lxxiii (14 March 1883), 1066–8 and lxxiv (15 March 1883), 1082–4

Bartlett 1995 — Rosamund Bartlett, *Wagner and Russia* (Cambridge University Press: Cambridge 1995)

Bauer 1998 — Oswald Georg Bauer, *Richard Wagner Goes to the Theatre*, tr. Stewart Spencer (Bayreuth Festival: Bayreuth 1998)

Baumann 1980 — Carl-Friedrich Baumann, *Bühnentechnik im Festspielhaus Bayreuth* (Prestel-Verlag: Munich 1980)

BB — Richard Wagner, *Das Braune Buch: Tagebuchaufzeichnungen 1865 bis 1882*, ed. Joachim Bergfeld (Atlantis Verlag: Zurich and Freiburg 1975)

Bloom 1987 — Peter Bloom, 'The fortunes of the Flying

Dutchman in France', *Wagner*, viii (1987), 42–66

Boetticher 1979   *Briefe und Gedichte aus dem Album Robert und Clara Schumanns*, ed. Wolfgang Boetticher (VEB Deutscher Verlag für Musik: Leipzig 1979)

Burrell 1953   Richard Wagner, *Briefe: Die Sammlung Burrell*, ed. John N. Burk (S. Fischer Verlag: Frankfurt am Main 1953)

Carr 1975   E[dward] H. Carr, *Michael Bakunin* (The Macmillan Press Ltd: London 1975)

Chamberlain 1894   Richard Wagner, *Echte Briefe an Ferdinand Praeger: Kritik der Praeger'schen Veröffentlichungen* von Houston Stewart Chamberlain (Im Commissions-Verlag der Grau'schen Buchhandlung: Bayreuth 1894)

Chamberlain 1897   Houston Stewart Chamberlain, *Richard Wagner*, tr. G. Ainslie Hight (Verlagsanstalt F. Bruckmann: Munich 1897)

Comini 1997   Alessandra Comini, 'The Visual Wagner: Environments, Icons, and Images', *The Threat to the Cosmic Order*, ed. Peter Oswald and Leonard S. Zegans (International Universities Press, Inc.: Madison 1997), 25–56

Cormon 1895   H[ippolyte] Fiérens-Gevaert, 'Tannhaeuser: Souvenirs des contemporains de la première représentation à Paris', *Journal des débats* (27 April 1895), 3

CT   *Cosima Wagner's Diaries*, ed. Martin Gregor-Dellin and Dietrich Mack, tr. Geoffrey Skelton, 2 vols. (Collins: London 1978–80)

Dannreuther 1898   'Edward Dannreuther', *The Musical Times*, xxxix (1898), 645–54

Deas 1940   Stewart Deas, *In Defence of Hanslick* (Williams & Norgate Ltd: London 1940)

Decsey 1903   Ernst Decsey, *Hugo Wolf. Erster Band: Hugo Wolfs Leben* (Schuster & Loeffler: Leipzig and Berlin 1903)

Devrient 1964   Eduard Devrient, *Aus seinen Tagebüchern*, ed. Rolf Kabel, 2 vols. (Hermann Böhlaus Nachfolger: Weimar 1964)

Dierauer 1917   Johannes Dierauer, *Geschichte der*

Schweizerischen Eidgenossenschaft.
Fünfter Band: Bis 1848 (Friedrich Andreas
Perthes: Gotha 1917)

Doepler 1900 — Carl Emil Doepler, *75 Jahre Leben,*
Schaffen, Streben (Schuster & Loeffler:
Berlin 1900)

Dorn 1870 — Heinrich Dorn, *Aus meinem Leben:*
Musikalische Skizzen (B. Behr's
Buchhandlung: Berlin 1870)

Eger 1975 — Manfred Eger, 'Richard Wagner an Dr.
Eduard Liszt: Ein bisher unveröffentlichter
Brief', *Die Programmhefte der Bayreuther*
Festspiele 1975, iii (*Die Meistersinger von*
Nürnberg), 14–17, 70–71

Eger 1992 — Manfred Eger, 'The Patronage of King
Ludwig II', *Wagner Handbook*, ed. Ulrich
Müller, Peter Wapnewski and John
Deathridge (Harvard University Press:
Cambridge, Mass., 1992), 317–26

Eliot — *The George Eliot Letters*, ed. Gordon S.
Haight, 7 vols. (Oxford University Press:
London 1954 and Yale University Press:
New Haven 1955)

Ellis — William Ashton Ellis, *Life of Richard*
Wagner, 6 vols. (Kegan Paul, Trench,
Trübner & Co., Ltd: London 1900–8)

Evers 1986 — Hans Gerhard Evers, *Ludwig II. von*
Bayern: Theaterfürst – König – Bauherr
(Hirmer Verlag: Munich 1986)

Family Letters — *Family Letters of Richard Wagner*, tr.
William Ashton Ellis. Enlarged edition with
introduction and notes by John Deathridge
(Macmillan: London 1991)

Fay 1893 — Amy Fay, *Music-Study in Germany*
(Macmillan and Co.: London 1893)

Fehr — Max Fehr, *Richard Wagners Schweizer Zeit*,
vol. i (H. R. Sauerländer & Co., Aarau and
Leipzig [1934]), vol. ii (H. R. Sauerländer &
Co., Aarau and Frankfurt am Main [1954])

Fiérens-Gevaert 1895 — H[ippolyte] Fiérens-Gevaert, 'Tannhaeuser:
Souvenirs des contemporains de la
première représentation à Paris', *Journal des*
débats (3 May 1895), 2–3

Fifield 1993 — Christopher Fifield, *True Artist and True*

	Friend: A Biography of Hans Richter (Clarendon Press: Oxford 1993)
Finck	Henry T. Finck, *Wagner and His Works*, 2 vols. (Charles Scribner's Sons: New York 1893)
Floud and others 1990	Roderick Floud and others, *Height, Health and History: Nutritional Status in the United Kingdom* (Cambridge University Press: Cambridge 1990)
Forman 1930	W. Courthope Forman, 'Stage Fauna for "The Ring" ', *The Daily Telegraph* (12 July 1930), 16
Fricke 1906	Richard Fricke, *Bayreuth vor dreissig Jahren: Erinnerungen an Wahnfried und aus dem Festspielhause* (Richard Bertling: Dresden 1906)
Gasperini 1866	A[uguste] de Gasperini, *Richard Wagner* (Heugel et Cie: Paris 1866)
Gautier 1910	Judith Gautier, *Wagner at Home*, tr. Effie Dunreith Massie (Mills & Boon, Limited: London 1910)
Gay 1979	Peter Gay, *Freud, Jews and Other Germans: Masters and Victims in Modernist Culture* (Oxford University Press: Oxford 1979)
Glasenapp	Carl Friedrich Glasenapp, *Das Leben Richard Wagners*, 6 vols. (Breitkopf & Härtel: Leipzig 1908–23)
Gregor-Dellin 1983	Martin Gregor-Dellin, *Richard Wagner: His Life, His Work, His Century*, tr. J. Maxwell Brownjohn (Collins: London 1983)
Grey 1992	Thomas S. Grey, 'Wagner's working routine', *The Wagner Compendium*, ed. Barry Millington (Thames and Hudson: London 1992), 102, 113–14
Gruber 1991	Gernot Gruber, *Mozart and Posterity*, tr. R. S. Furness (Quartet Books: London 1991)
GS	Richard Wagner, *Gesammelte Schriften und Dichtungen*, 10 vols., 4th edn (C. F. W. Siegel's Musikalienhandlung: Leipzig 1907)
Gutzkow 1875	Karl Gutzkow, *Rückblicke auf mein Leben* (A. Hofmann & Co.: Berlin 1875)
Hall 1992	Michael Hall, 'Wagner's impact on the visual arts', *The Wagner Compendium*, ed.

Barry Millington (Thames and Hudson: London 1992), 398–401

Hallé 1896 — *Life and Letters of Sir Charles Hallé*, ed. C. E. Hallé and Marie Hallé (Smith, Elder, & Co.: London 1896)

Hallock and Wade 1906 — William Hallock and Herbert T. Wade, *Outlines of the Evolution of Weights and Measures and the Metric System* (The Macmillan Company: New York and London 1906)

Hanslick 1894 — Eduard Hanslick, *Aus meinem Leben*, 2 vols. (Allgemeiner Verein für Deutsche Litteratur: Berlin 1894)

Haweis 1908 — H[ugh] R[eginald] Haweis, *My Musical Life* (Longmans, Green, and Co.: London 1908)

Heckel 1899 — *Letters of Richard Wagner to Emil Heckel. With a Brief History of the Bayreuth Festivals*, tr. William Ashton Ellis (H. Grevel & Co.: London 1899)

Hohenlohe 1938 — Marie Fürstin zu Hohenlohe, *Erinnerungen an Richard Wagner* (Herm. Böhlaus Nachf.: Weimar 1938)

Hohenlohe-Schillingsfürst — *Memoirs of Prince Chlodwig of Hohenlohe Schillingsfürst*, ed. Friedrich Curtius, tr. George W. Chrystal, 2 vols. (William Heinemann: London 1906)

Hollinrake 1970 — Roger Hollinrake, 'The Title-Page of Wagner's "Mein Leben" ', *Music and Letters*, li (1970), 415–22

Hollinrake 1982 — Roger Hollinrake, *Nietzsche, Wagner, and the Philosophy of Pessimism* (George Allen and Unwin Ltd: London 1982)

Hopkinson 1973 — Cecil Hopkinson, *Tannhäuser: A Study of 36 Editions* (Hans Schneider: Tutzing 1973)

Hornstein 1908 — Robert von Hornstein, *Memoiren* (Süddeutsche Monatshefte: Munich 1908)

Hornstein 1911 — Ferdinand Freiherr von Hornstein, *Zwei unveröffentlichte Briefe Richard Wagners an Robert von Hornstein* (E. W. Bonsels & Co.: Munich 1911)

Horowitz 1994 — Joseph Horowitz, *Wagner Nights: An American History* (University of California Press: Berkeley 1994)

Hueffer 1889   Francis Hueffer, *Half a Century of Music in England 1837–1887* (Chapman and Hall, Limited: London 1889)

Humperdinck 1927   Engelbert Humperdinck, ' "Parsifal"-Skizzen', *Bayreuther Festspielführer 1927* (Verlag der Hofbuchhandlung Georg Niehrenheim: Bayreuth 1927), 215–29

Janz 1978   Curt Paul Janz, *Friedrich Nietzsche: Biographie*. 3 vols. (Carl Hanser Verlag: Munich 1978)

Joncières 1898   Victorin de Joncières, 'Notes sans portée', *Revue internationale de musique*, i (1 March 1898), 9–14

Kapp 1927   Julius Kapp and Hans Jachmann, *Richard Wagner und seine erste 'Elisabeth' Johanna Jachmann-Wagner* (Dom-Verlag: Berlin 1927)

Karpath 1907   Ludwig Karpath, *Zu den Briefen Richard Wagners an eine Putzmacherin: Unterredungen mit der Putzmacherin Bertha. Ein Beitrag zur Lebensgeschichte Richard Wagners* ('Harmonie' Verlagsgesellschaft für Literatur und Kunst: Berlin [1907])

Kashkin 1913   Nikolay Dmitrievich Kashkin, 'Vagner v Moskve (po lichnym vospominaniyam)', *Muzïka*, cxxxi (1913), 372–8

Katz 1986   Jacob Katz, *The Darker Side of Genius: Richard Wagner's Anti-Semitism*, tr. Allan Arkush (University Press of New England: Hanover and London 1986)

Kellermann 1932   Berthold Kellermann, *Erinnerungen* (Eugen Rentsch Verlag: Erlenbach and Leipzig 1932)

Kersten 1926   Kurt Kersten, *Michael Bakunins Beichte aus der Peter-Pauls-Festung an Zar Nikolaus I* (Deutsche Verlagsgesellschaft für Politik und Geschichte: Berlin 1926)

Kesting 1988   *Franz Liszt – Richard Wagner: Briefwechsel*, ed. Hanjo Kesting (Insel Verlag: Frankfurt am Main 1988)

Kietz 1907   Gustav Adolph Kietz, *Richard Wagner in den Jahren 1842–1849 und 1873–1875*, 2nd edn (Carl Reißner: Dresden 1907)

Kirchmeyer 1993   Helmut Kirchmeyer, 'The 1852 Ballenstedt Music Festival', *Die Programmhefte der Bayreuther Festspiele 1993*, ii (*Tannhäuser*), 62–74

Kitzler 1904   Otto Kitzler, *Musikalische Erinnerungen mit Briefen von Wagner, Brahms, Bruckner und Rich. Pohl* (Carl Winiker: Brünn 1904)

Klein 1903   Hermann Klein, *Thirty Years of Musical Life in London 1870–1900* (William Heinemann: London 1903)

Klindworth 1898   'Karl Klindworth', *The Musical Times*, xxxix (1898), 513–19

Königsbriefe   *König Ludwig II. und Richard Wagner: Briefwechsel*, ed. Otto Strobel, 5 vols. (G. Braun: Karlsruhe 1936–9)

Konrad 1987   Ulrich Konrad, 'Robert Schumann und Richard Wagner: Studien und Dokumente', *Augsburger Jahrbuch für Musikwissenschaft 1987*, ed. Franz Krautwurst (Hans Schneider: Tutzing 1987), 211–320

Koury 1986   Daniel J. Koury, *Orchestral Performance Practices in the Nineteenth Century: Size, Proportions, and Seating* (UMI Research Press: Ann Arbor 1986)

Kramer 1999   Bernd Kramer, *'Laßt uns die Schwerter ziehen, damit die Kette bricht...'* Michael Bakunin, Richard Wagner und andere während der Dresdner Mai-Revolution 1849 (Karin Kramer Verlag: Berlin 1999)

Large 1978   David C. Large, 'The Political Background of the Foundation of the Bayreuth Festival', *Central European History*, xi (1978), 162–72

Laube   *Heinrich Laubes ausgewählte Werke in zehn Bänden*, ed. Heinrich Hubert Houben (Max Hesses Verlag: Leipzig n.d.)

Lehmann 1914   Lilli Lehmann, *My Path through Life*, tr. Alice Benedict Seligman (G. P. Putnam's Sons: New York and London 1914)

Leroy 1884   Léon Leroy, 'Une après-midi à Villiers-sur-Marne', *Bayreuther Festblätter* (Bayreuth 1884), 41

Leverett 1990   Adelyn Peck Leverett, 'Liszt, Wagner and

Heinrich Dorn's *Die Nibelungen*',
Cambridge Opera Journal, ii (1990),
121–44

Lippert 1930   Woldemar Lippert, *Wagner in Exile*
1849–62 (George G. Harrap & Co. Ltd:
London 1930)

Love 1963   Frederick Rutan Love, *Young Nietzsche and*
the Wagnerian Experience (University of
North Carolina Press: Chapel Hill 1963)

Mann 1985   Thomas Mann, *Pro and contra Wagner*, tr.
Allan Blunden (Faber and Faber: London
1985)

Mason 1901   William Mason, *Memories of a Musical Life*
(The Century Co.: New York 1901)

Massenet 1961   Karl Lahm, 'Pariser Wagneriana: Franzosen
die ihn erlebten', *Opernwelt*, i (July 1961),
4–5

Meißner 1884   Alfred Meißner, *Geschichte meines Lebens*,
2 vols. (Verlag der k.k. Hofbuchhandlung
Karl Prochaska: Vienna and Teschen 1884)

Mendès 1892   Catulle Mendès, *Richard Wagner*
(Bibliothèque-Charpentier: Paris 1892)

Metternich 1921   Princess Pauline Metternich, *The Days That*
Are No More: Some Reminiscences
(Eveleigh Nash & Grayson, Ltd.: London
1921)

Meyerbeer   Giacomo Meyerbeer, *Briefwechsel und*
Tagebücher, ed. Heinz and Gudrun Becker
and Sabine Henze-Döhring, 5 vols. (Walter
de Gruyter & Co: Berlin 1960–99)

Meysenbug 1937   Malwida von Meysenbug, *Rebel in a*
Crinoline, tr. Elisa von Meysenbug Lyons
(George Allen & Unwin, Ltd: London 1937)

Millington 1986   Barry Millington, ' "The Flying Dutchman",
"Le vaisseau fantôme" and other Nautical
Yarns', *The Musical Times*, cxxvii (1986),
131–5

ML   Richard Wagner, *My Life*, tr. Andrew Gray,
ed. Mary Whittall (Da Capo: New York
1992)

Mottl 1943   Willy Krienitz, 'Felix Mottls
Tagebuchaufzeichnungen aus den Jahren
1873–1876', *Neue Wagner-Forschungen*,

	ed. Otto Strobel (G. Braun: Karlsruhe 1943), 167–234
NA	Nationalarchiv der Richard-Wagner-Stiftung, Bayreuth
Neumann 1909	Angelo Neumann, *Personal Recollections of Wagner*, tr. Edith Livermore (Archibald Constable & Co. Ltd.: London 1909)
Newman	Ernest Newman, *The Life of Richard Wagner*, 4 vols. (Cambridge University Press: Cambridge 1976)
Nietzsche 1983	Friedrich Nietzsche, *Untimely Meditations*, tr. R. J. Hollingdale (Cambridge University Press: Cambridge 1983)
Nietzsche 1986	Friedrich Nietzsche, *Sämtliche Briefe: Kritische Studienausgabe in 8 Bänden*, ed. Giorgio Colli and Mazzino Montinari (Deutscher Taschenbuch Verlag: Munich 1986)
Nohl 1869	Ludwig Nohl, *Neues Skizzenbuch: Zur Kenntnis der deutschen, namentlich der Münchener Musik- und Opernzustände der Gegenwart* (Carl Merhoffs Verlag: Munich 1869)
Nordmann 1886	Johannes Nordmann, 'Eine Begegnung mit Richard Wagner in Dresden (1847)', *Richard Wagner-Jahrbuch*, ed. Joseph Kürschner (Im Selbstverlag des Herausgebers: Stuttgart 1886), 73–8
Oberzaucher-Schüller 1998	Gunild Oberzaucher-Schüller, Marion Linhardt and Thomas Steiert, *Meyerbeer – Wagner: Eine Begegnung* (Böhlau Verlag: Vienna 1998)
Ollivier 1961	Émile Ollivier, *Journal 1846–1869*, ed. Theodore Zeldin and Anne Troisier de Diaz, 2 vols. (René Julliard: Paris 1961)
Otto 1990	Werner Otto, *Richard Wagner: Ein Lebens- und Charakterbild in Dokumenten und zeitgenössischen Darstellungen* (Buchverlag Der Morgen: Berlin 1990)
Pecht 1894	Friedrich Pecht, *Aus meiner Zeit* (Verlagsanstalt für Kunst und Wissenschaft: Munich 1894)
Petipa 1895	H[ippolyte] Fiérens-Gevaert, 'Tannhaeuser: Souvenirs des contemporains de la

première représentation à Paris', *Journal des débats* (21 April 1895), 3

Petzet 1970 — Detta and Michael Petzet, *Die Richard Wagner-Bühne Ludwigs II.* (Prestel-Verlag: Munich 1970)

Porges 1983 — Heinrich Porges, *Wagner Rehearsing the 'Ring'*, tr. Robert L. Jacobs (Cambridge University Press: Cambridge 1983)

Praeger 1892 — Ferdinand Praeger, *Wagner As I Knew Him* (Longmans, Green, and Co.: London 1892)

PW — *Richard Wagner's Prose Works*, tr. William Ashton Ellis, 8 vols. (Kegan Paul, Trench, Trübner & Co.: London 1892–9, 1993–5 (repr.))

Quirke 1914 — William Michael Quirke, *Recollections of a Violinist* (Wm. Dawson and Sons, Limited: London 1914)

Renoir 1987 — Bernard Denvir, *The Impressionists at First Hand* (Thames and Hudson: London 1987)

Ritter 1901 — Hermann Ritter, 'Eine Erinnerung an Richard Wagner', *Allgemeine Musik-Zeitung*, xxviii (1901), 496–9

Roche 1863 — Edmond Roche, *Poésies posthumes*. Avec une notice par M. Victorien Sardou (Michel Lévy Frères: Paris 1863)

Röckl — Sebastian Röckl, *Ludwig II. und Richard Wagner*, 2 vols. (C. H. Beck'sche Verlagsbuchhandlung: Munich 1913–20)

Rose 1992 — Paul Lawrence Rose, *Wagner: Race and Revolution* (Faber and Faber: London 1992)

Sagan 1895 — H[ippolyte] Fiérens-Gevaert, 'Tannhaeuser: Souvenirs des contemporains de la première représentation à Paris', *Journal des débats* (2 May 1895), 3

Sasse 1895 — H[ippolyte] Fiérens-Gevaert, 'Tannhaeuser: Souvenirs des contemporains de la première représentation à Paris', *Journal des débats* (27 April 1895), 3

Sasse 1902 — Marie Sasse, *Souvenirs d'une artiste* (Librairie Molière: Paris 1902)

SB — Richard Wagner, *Sämtliche Briefe*, ed. Gertrud Strobel, Werner Wolf, Hans-

Joachim Bauer and Johannes Forner, 8 vols. (VEB Deutscher Verlag für Musik: Leipzig 1967–93)

Schack 1888   Adolf Friedrich Graf von Schack, *Ein halbes Jahrhundert: Erinnerungen und Aufzeichnungen*, 3 vols. (Deutsche Verlags-Anstalt: Stuttgart and Leipzig 1888)

Schemann 1902   Ludwig Schemann, *Meine Erinnerungen an Richard Wagner* (Fr. Frommanns Verlag: Stuttgart 1902)

Schmidt and Hartmann 1909   *Richard Wagner in Bayreuth: Erinnerungen*, ed. Heinrich Schmidt and Ulrich Hartmann (Carl Klinner: Leipzig 1909)

Schoen 1924   Friedrich von Schoen, 'Eine Erinnerung an Richard Wagner', *Offizieller Bayreuther Festspielführer 1924* (Verlag Georg Niehrenheim: Bayreuth 1924), 230–32

Schönaich 1897   Gustav Schönaich, 'Johannes Brahms', *Die Reichswehr* (4 April 1897)

Schuh 1959   Willi Schuh, *Renoir und Wagner* (Eugen Rentsch Verlag: Erlenbach and Stuttgart 1959)

Schumann   Robert Schumann, *Tagebücher*, ed. Georg Eismann and Gerd Nauhaus, 4 vols. (Stroemfeld/Roter Stern: Basel and Frankfurt am Main n.d.)

Schumann 1913   Clara Schumann, *An Artist's Life* based on material found in diaries and letters by Berthold Litzmann, tr. Grace E. Hadow, 2 vols. (Macmillan & Co., Ltd and Breitkopf & Härtel: London and Leipzig 1913)

Schuré 1933   Édouard Schuré, *Richard Wagner: Son œuvre et son idée* (Librairie Académique Perrin: Paris 1933)

Seidl 1887   Anton Seidl, 'Wagner's Traits and Work', *New-York Daily Tribune* (27 February 1887), 10

Serova 1891   Valentina Serova, 'Rikhard Vagner: Otryvok iz moikh vospominanii (pervaya poezdka zagranitsu v 1864 g.)', *Artist*, xii (1891), 64–72

Servières 1895   Georges Servières, *Tannhæuser à l'Opéra en 1861* (Librairie Fischbacher: Paris 1895)

Seydlitz 1931	Reinhard von Seydlitz, 'Erinnerungen an Richard Wagner' *Völkischer Beobachter* (13/14, 16, 17, 18, 19 and 20/21 December 1931)
Shaw 1898	Bernard Shaw, *The Perfect Wagnerite: A Commentary on the Ring of the Niblungs* (Grant Richards: London 1898)
Shaw 1981	*Shaw's Music*, ed. Dan H. Laurence, 3 vols. (The Bodley Head: London 1981)
Skelton 1982	Geoffrey Skelton, *Richard and Cosima Wagner: Biography of a Marriage* (Victor Gollancz Ltd: London 1982)
SL	*Selected Letters of Richard Wagner*, tr. and ed. Stewart Spencer and Barry Millington (J. M. Dent & Sons Ltd: London 1987)
Spencer 1981	Stewart Spencer, 'Zieh hin! Ich kann dich nicht halten!', *Wagner*, ii (1981), 98–120
Spencer 1982	Stewart Spencer, 'Wagner in London (1)', *Wagner*, iii (1982), 98–123
Spencer 1992	Stewart Spencer, 'Wagner's Nuremberg', *Wagner*, xiv (1993), 3–29
Spencer 1994	Stewart Spencer, ' "Judaism in Music": An unpublished letter', *Wagner*, xv (1994), 99–104
Spencer 1998	Stewart Spencer, 'Wagner behind bars?', *Wagner*, xix (1998), 95–102
SS	Richard Wagner, *Sämtliche Schriften und Dichtungen: Volks-Ausgabe*, 16 vols. (Breitkopf & Härtel and C. F. W. Siegel: Leipzig [1911–14])
Stradella 1991	*Alessandro Stradella (1639–1682): A Thematic Catalogue of His Compositions* compiled by Carolyn Gianturco and Eleanor McCrickard (Pendragon Press: Stuyvesant 1991)
Strauss 1905	*Instrumentationslehre von Hector Berlioz*, rev. Richard Strauss (C. F. Peters: Leipzig 1905)
Strecker 1951	Ludwig Strecker, *Richard Wagner als Verlagsgefährte* (B. Schott's Söhne: Mainz 1951)
Suneson 1985	Carl Suneson, *Richard Wagner och den indiska tankevärlden* (Almqvist & Wiksell: Stockholm 1985)

Swafford 1998 — Jan Swafford, *Johannes Brahms: A Biography* (Macmillan: London 1998)

Thiery and Seidel 1995 — Joachim Thiery and Dietrich Seidel, ' "I feel only discontent": Wagner and his doctors', *Wagner*, xvi (1995), 3–22

Tiersot 1935 — Julien Tiersot, *Lettres françaises de Richard Wagner* (Éditions Bernard Grasset: Paris 1935)

Uhl 1908 — Friedrich Uhl, *Aus meinem Leben* (J. G. Cotta'sche Buchhandlung Nachfolger: Stuttgart and Berlin 1908)

Vetter 1992 — Isolde Vetter, 'Wagner in the History of Psychology', *Wagner Handbook*, ed. Ulrich Müller, Peter Wapnewski and John Deathridge (Harvard University Press: Cambridge, Mass., 1992)

Villiers 1887 — Jean-Marie-Mathias-Philippe-Auguste, comte de Villiers de l'Isle-Adam, 'Souvenir', *Écrits pour l'art* (7 June 1887)

Vogel 1984 — Martin Vogel, *Nietzsche und Wagner: Ein deutsches Lesebuch* (Verlag für systematische Musikwissenschaft: Bonn 1984)

Wagner 1923 — Siegfried Wagner, *Erinnerungen* (J. Engelhorns Nachf.: Stuttgart 1923)

Walker — Alan Walker, *Franz Liszt*, 3 vols. (Faber and Faber: London 1983–97)

Walker 1947 — Frank Walker, 'Hugo Wolf's Vienna Diary, 1875–76', *Music and Letters*, xxviii (1947), 12–24

Weber 1993 — Solveig Weber, *Das Bild Richard Wagners: Ikonographische Bestandsaufnahme eines Künstlerkults*, 2 vols. (B. Schott's Söhne: Mainz 1993)

Weißheimer 1898 — W[endelin] Weißheimer, *Erlebnisse mit Richard Wagner, Franz Liszt und vielen anderen Zeitgenossen nebst deren Briefen* (Deutsche Verlags-Anstalt: Stuttgart and Leipzig 1898)

Wesendonck 1896 — Mathilde Wesendonck, 'Erinnerungen', *Allgemeine Deutsche Musik-Zeitung*, xxiii/7 (14 February 1896), 91–4

Westernhagen 1979 — Curt von Westernhagen, 'Wagner's Last

Day', *The Musical Times*, cxx (1979),
395–7

Wilhelmj 1928   Ernst Wagner, *Der Geigerkönig August
Wilhelmj* (Verlag Taunusbote-
Buchdruckerei GmbH: Bad Homburg 1928)

Wille 1908   *Richard Wagner an Eliza Wille: Fünfzehn
Briefe des Meisters nebst Erinnerungen und
Erläuterungen von Eliza Wille* (Schuster &
Loeffler: Berlin and Leipzig 1908)

Wolf 1912   *Hugo Wolf: Eine Persönlichkeit in Briefen.
Familienbriefe*, ed. Edmund von Hellmer
(Breitkopf & Härtel: Leipzig 1912)

Wolzogen 1891   Hans von Wolzogen, *Erinnerungen an
Richard Wagner*, 2nd edn (Philipp Reclam
jun.: Leipzig [1891])

WWV   *Wagner Werk-Verzeichnis (WWV):
Verzeichnis der musikalischen Werke
Richard Wagners und ihrer Quellen*, ed.
John Deathridge, Martin Geck and Egon
Voss (B. Schott's Söhne: Mainz 1986)

INDEX